Building Bots with Microsoft Bot Framework

Creating intelligent conversational interfaces

Kishore Gaddam

BIRMINGHAM - MUMBAI

Building Bots with Microsoft Bot Framework

Copyright © 2017 Packt Publishing

All rights reserved. No part of this book may be reproduced, stored in a retrieval system, or transmitted in any form or by any means, without the prior written permission of the publisher, except in the case of brief quotations embedded in critical articles or reviews.

Every effort has been made in the preparation of this book to ensure the accuracy of the information presented. However, the information contained in this book is sold without warranty, either express or implied. Neither the author, nor Packt Publishing, and its dealers and distributors will be held liable for any damages caused or alleged to be caused directly or indirectly by this book.

Packt Publishing has endeavored to provide trademark information about all of the companies and products mentioned in this book by the appropriate use of capitals. However, Packt Publishing cannot guarantee the accuracy of this information.

First published: May 2017

Production reference: 1310517

Published by Packt Publishing Ltd.
Livery Place
35 Livery Street
Birmingham
B3 2PB, UK.
ISBN 978-1-78646-310-4

www.packtpub.com

Credits

Author
Kishore Gaddam

Reviewer
Allen ONeill

Commissioning Editor
Ashwin Nair

Acquisition Editor
Shweta Pant

Content Development Editor
Onkar Wani

Technical Editor
Shweta Jadhav

Copy Editor
Dhanya Baburaj

Project Coordinator
Ulhas Kambali

Proofreader
Safis Editing

Indexer
Mariammal Chettiyar

Graphics
Abhinash Sahu

Production Coordinator
Shraddha Falebhai

About the Author

Kishore Gaddam is the CEO and a co-founder of Astrani Technologies and is recognized as an industry expert in mobile, cloud, and bot software development. He is a forward-thinking technology leader with 17+ years of international experience in building technology organizations, strategic planning, rolling out multiple platforms/products, IT program and project management, strategy and transformation (businesses, people, processes, and technologies), and growing business units across IoT, smart cities, NLP, AI, bots, cloud, robotics, mobile, healthcare, industrial automation, financial systems, retail, procurement (EPC), travel & leisure, logistics, manufacturing, and automotive domains.

He is a champion of the technical pre-sales, architecture, and software development of enterprise Azure IoT/bot/web applications using cognitive services, microservices, Service Fabric, Azure IoT Hub, Stream Analytics, Cortana Intelligence Suit, Logic Apps, Notification Hubs, Big Data, Azure Web Apps, Azure App service, Azure API Apps, Application Insights, API Management, Machine Learning, Azure SQL databases, Cosmos DB, Data Factory, Data Lake, HD Insight, Redis Cache, Key Vault, and Azure Service Bus, and a champion of implementing DevOps using Azure, PowerShell scripts, ARM templates, and VSTS. He has huge experience in startup leadership, including building teams, and developing a Minimum Viable Product (MVP) with little to no supervision. Kishore is comfortable at all layers of the startup people stack, from individual contributor (software development, product management) to CxO.

Kishore graduated in Technology Entrepreneurship from Stanford University, CA, and is a speaker at various conferences in the USA. Kishore is the author of the popular Microsoft Technologies blog. He has a love for mentoring and a passion for sharing new tools, programming languages, and technology trends at national conferences, regional code camps, local user groups, meetups, and hackathons.

> *I would like to thank my family and friends, who helped me make this book a reality. First, I want to thank my wife, Prathima. Her encouragement and support was invaluable. I would like to thank all my family members for their immense support in everything that I do, and my friends, who motivate me to move forward.*

About the Reviewer

Allen ONeill is a chartered engineer with a background in enterprise systems. He is a fellow of the Brisith Computing Society, a Microsoft MVP (most valued professional) and writes for CodeProject, C-Sharp Corner and DZone. His core technology interests are Big Data engineering and machine learning, in particular using Data Science to create intelligent bots/agents for the web. He is also a ball throwing slave to his family dogs.

www.PacktPub.com

For support files and downloads related to your book, please visit `www.PacktPub.com`.

Did you know that Packt offers eBook versions of every book published, with PDF and ePub files available? You can upgrade to the eBook version at `www.PacktPub.com` and as a print book customer, you are entitled to a discount on the eBook copy. Get in touch with us at `service@packtpub.com` for more details.

At `www.PacktPub.com`, you can also read a collection of free technical articles, sign up for a range of free newsletters and receive exclusive discounts and offers on Packt books and eBooks.

`https://www.packtpub.com/mapt`

Get the most in-demand software skills with Mapt. Mapt gives you full access to all Packt books and video courses, as well as industry-leading tools to help you plan your personal development and advance your career.

Why subscribe?

- Fully searchable across every book published by Packt
- Copy and paste, print, and bookmark content
- On demand and accessible via a web browser

Customer Feedback

Thanks for purchasing this Packt book. At Packt, quality is at the heart of our editorial process. To help us improve, please leave us an honest review on this book's Amazon page at http://www.amazon.in/dp/1786463105.

If you'd like to join our team of regular reviewers, you can e-mail us at customerreviews@packtpub.com. We award our regular reviewers with free eBooks and videos in exchange for their valuable feedback. Help us be relentless in improving our products!

Table of Contents

Preface   1
Chapter 1: Setting up Microsoft Bot Framework Dev Environment   9
    Conversation as a Service (CaaS)   10
    Your bot   13
    The Bot Connector   13
    The Bot Directory   14
    Setting up the development environment   14
        Prerequisites   14
        Setting up the Bot Framework Connector SDK .NET   15
    Messages   17
        Basic format   17
        Rich text   18
        Skype emoticons   19
        Welcome messages   19
        Pictures and videos   19
    Cards and buttons   20
        Hero card   20
        Thumbnail card   22
        Carousel   23
            Images   24
            Buttons   24
            Actions   24
        Sign in   24
        Receipt   25
    Groups   27
    Calling   28
    Summary   29
Chapter 2: Developing Your First Bot Using the Connector and Builder SDK   31
    Bots are evolving   32
    Bots use cases   32
    Developing your first bot   33
    Creating our first bot   34
        Building a bot using the C# SDK   35

AssemblyInfo.cs	37
References	39
Microsoft Bot Builder	39
Microsoft Bot Connector	40
WebApiConfig.cs	40
MessageController.cs	42
Default.htm	44
Global.asax	45
Packages.config	45
Web.config	45
Post method	46
BotID	49
Microsoft App ID	49
MicrosoftAppPassword	49
How to deploy and run the bot application in the Bot Framework emulator locally	49
How to use dialogs in bot applications	53
How to use FormFlow in the bot application	58
Summary	64
Chapter 3: Developing WeatherBot Using Dialogs and LUIS	**65**
Language Understanding Intelligent Service (LUIS)	66
Intents and Entities	73
Training your bot using utterances	78
Testing your LUIS app	80
Development of WeatherBot code	81
Calling LUIS from the bot	89
Calling the Weather API	91
Using cards	93
Natural speech and Intent processing bot using Microsoft Cognitive Services	95
Identifying the name of a person, place, and company using LUIS	110
Training your app	113
Calling LUIS from the bot	116
Summary	123
Chapter 4: Natural Speech and Intent Processing Bot Using Microsoft Cognitive Services	**125**
Microsoft Cognitive Services	126
Signing up for Microsoft Cognitive Services	126

Building a bot application using Cognitive Services APIs	129
Analyzer's results	139
Identifying the name of a person, place, and company using LUIS	**144**
Training your app using utterances	**148**
Calling LUIS from the bot	**153**
Summary	**155**

Chapter 5: Developing Bots Using LUIS Prompt Dialogs with State and Nearby Bot Using Custom APIs — 157

Employee Enroll bot using LUIS prompt dialogs	**157**
Training the service	165
Training and publishing	169
Creating the C# class for LUIS response	**171**
Creating the bot application	173
Bot state service	**184**
Creating a state client	185
Get/SetProperty methods	185
Updating your Post method	187
Updating your QueryLUIS method	190
Developing a Nearby Bot using custom APIs	**191**
Summary	**207**

Chapter 6: Developing an IVR Bot for a Bank Using Advanced Microsoft Bot Framework Technologies — 209

High-level architectural diagram	**210**
Let's start coding	**211**
Creating an account with the bot	212
Storing the bot conversation (new account info) data in an Azure SQL database	**223**
Checking your savings account balance using the bot	**227**
Checking your current account balance using the bot	**232**
Paying your credit card bill using the bot	**236**
Deleting an account using the bot	**238**
Summary	**242**

Chapter 7: Intelligent Bots with Microsoft Bot Framework and Service Fabric — 243

Getting started using stateless microservices	**245**
Setting up your development environment for Service Fabric	245
Prerequisites	245
Installing the SDK and tools	246

[iii]

Enabling PowerShell script execution	246
Creating a stateless Service Fabric web API	246
Publishing a Service Fabric project in Azure	**261**
Create Key Vault	262
Adding certificates to the Key Vault	262
Creating a cluster in the Azure portal	264
Summary	**278**

Chapter 8: Developing Intelligent Facial Expression Identification Bot for IoT Using Azure and Power BI — 279

Before getting started	**280**
Configuring Raspberry Pi and sensors	**280**
Prerequisites	281
Hardware	281
Software	281
Setting up sensors	282
Schematic diagram	292
Device identity and registry with IoT Hub	**293**
Using Device Explorer	293
Face API	**297**
Emotion API	**298**
Sign Up Microsoft Cognitive Services	**298**
Development of facial expressions identification bot	300
Let's code to know the emotions	306
Registering your Bot in Bot Framework	**308**
Publish and test your bot	311
Configure Direct Line Channel	**314**
Develop an UWP app for Raspberry Pi device	**316**
Create an UWP App project	317
How to detect the motion of the object using PIR Sensor and How to define the LED states	319
Initializing camera on detection of motion	323
How to send picture file to Facial Expression Bot and receive reply from it	325
Send Picture to Bot	327
Deploy Code in to Raspberry Pi	**328**
Show facial analytics data in Power BI	**332**
Set up Azure Stream Analytics to send IoT Hub data to Power BI	332
Set up Power BI	339
Summary	**347**

Chapter 9: Publishing a Bot to Skype, Slack, Facebook, and the GroupMe Channel — 349
- **Publishing bots to various channels** — 350
  - Publishing your bot application to Microsoft Azure web app — 351
- **Registering your bot with Microsoft Bot Framework** — 357
  - Configuration — 359
  - Testing the connection to your bot — 363
- **Configuring channels** — 364
  - Configuring your bot with Slack — 366
  - Configuring your bot with Skype — 378
  - Configuring your bot with Facebook Messenger — 382
  - Configuring your bot with GroupMe — 398
- **Summary** — 404

Index — 405

Preface

This is a book for those who want to build fully functional and scalable Natural Language Processing Bots using Microsoft Bot Framework. Its learn-while-doing approach delivers the practical knowledge and experience a reader needs to design and build real-world bots. We explain concepts when needed to develop a bot, so that programming knowledge and experience grow together.

This book will take you from software installation to developing a fully-functional bot that is deployed and run in Azure. This book leads the reader through the essential programming tools and techniques for developing bots for various conversation platforms, such as Skype, Slack, web chat, and so on. In each chapter, the reader will learn Microsoft Bot Framework programming concepts and apply them immediately, as you build a bot or enhance one from a previous chapter.

These bots have been designed and developed to teach the associated concepts and to provide practice working with the standard development tools, such as Visual Studio, the bot emulator, and Azure. Many of the discussions in the book will be clarified to make some of the more complex topics easier to understand. All of the projects have been built from scratch using Microsoft Bot Framework.

What this book covers

Chapter 1, *Setting up the Microsoft Bot Framework Dev Environment,* introduces the reader to what Microsoft Bot Framework is and how it helps in the development of bots. It walks the reader through on how to set up development environment, emulator, and the tools needed for programming. Reader gets to set up their development environment and install all the software required for getting started with programming a bot. The reader is also introduced to all the programming concepts involved in the development of bots.

Chapter 2, *Developing Your First Bot Using the Connector and Builder SDK,* this chapter introduces the reader to bot programming by building and locally deploying a simple Hello World bot application. The readers will get their feet wet with Visual Studio, C# .NET, Bot Framework, and the related technologies, along with all the steps required to create projects. This chapter includes a discussion of Bot Emulator and how it relates to bot development.

Chapter 3, *Developing a WeatherBot Using Dialogs and LUIS*, guides the reader through developing a fully functional weather bot. This bot communicates the current weather in a given city. Readers will interact with this bot on Skype or any other channel to find out the current weather at a given location.

Chapter 4, *Natural Speech and Intent Processing Bot using Microsoft Cognitive Services*, introduces the reader to the RichText Message technology, as well as Cortana Intelligence Services, by developing a fully functional bot. This bot identifies the concepts and actions in the text that is sent to the bot with part-of-speech tagging, finds phrases and concepts using natural language parsers, and returns all the identified intents that are created and trained in a custom LUIS app. If you say "Hi John, I am going to New York tonight," the bot will return part-of-speech tagging, as well as parsing data for natural speech and intent processing to find out the name, location, and so on.

Name: John

Place: New York

Whether you're mining customer feedback, interpreting user commands, or consuming web text, understanding the structure of the text is a critical first step and this chapter teaches that.

Chapter 5, *Developing Bots Using LUIS Prompt Dialogs with State and Nearby Bot Using Custom APIs*, is about how we can integrate APIs into bot development. Currently, every enterprise has web and mobile applications built on top of their APIs, which contain business functionality. Now, it would be natural to extend those APIs so that they can be used for bots as well. This chapter introduces readers to how to use Microsoft Bot Framework to develop a Nearby bot using APIs. This Nearby bot will provide the reader with all the available places near their location, with details for each and every one of them. This bot helps you to easily find nearby banks, clubs, restaurants, hotels, museums, pharmacies, hospitals, or any other place you want to search for.

Chapter 6, *Developing an IVR Bot for a Bank using Advanced Microsoft Bot Framework Technologies*, includes a real-world project that we will build from the ground up, so that readers can learn the concept as well as relate it to real-world scenarios. The following topics are explained in this chapter:

- Building **Interactive Voice Response (IVR)** solutions
- Learning how to build bots using dialogs, third-party authentication, Rich Text Format, and Bot State Service.
- Learning how to use Form Builder while developing bots
- Learning how to program using prompt dialogs

- Learning how to implement Buttons in buttons
- Third-party authentication
- Bot State Service

Chapter 7, *Intelligent Bots with Microsoft Bot Framework and Service Fabric*, introduces the reader to the concept of microservices and how microservices can be used in bot development. They get to learn about and work on microservices development, as well as learn to program a bot using microservices, and will get to learn how to use this microservice-based bot and publish it to various channels.

Chapter 8, *Developing an Intelligent Facial Expression Identification Bot for IoT using Azure and Power BI*, introduces the reader to IoT and how bots can help in IoT development. Here, the reader will develop an IoT project and connect it to a bot for automation. Power BI is used to show report from bots. The reader will learn to develop, deploy, and connect an IoT project to a bot. They will get to learn how IoT, bots, Azure, and Power BI fit together in an enterprise application development scenario.

Chapter 9, *Publishing a Bot to Skype, Slack, Facebook, and the GroupMe Channel*, guides the reader on how to publish the Hello World bot we developed in a previous chapter to the Slack, Skype, and Facebook Messenger platforms. In this chapter readers will learn the following:

- **Registering bot**: Once registered, the reader uses the dashboard to test their bot to ensure that it is talking to the connector service. They can also use the web chat control, an auto-configured channel, to experience what their users will experience when conversing with the bot.
- **Connecting to channels**: Connect your bot to conversation channels such as Skype, Slack, and Facebook Messenger using the channel configuration page.
- **Testing the bot**: The reader gets to test their bot's connection to the Bot Framework and try it out using web chat controls.
- **Publishing the bot**: The reader gets to publish the bot.
- **Analyzing the bot**: The reader gets to learn how to link their bot to Azure Application Insights analytics directly from the bot dashboard of the Bot Framework website.
- **Managing a bot**: Once registered and connected to channels, you can manage your bot via your bot's dashboard in the Bot Framework Developer Portal.

What you need for this book

- Visual Studio 2015 or higher
- Internet access
- Microsoft Azure trial subscription

Who this book is for

This book is for developers who are keen on building powerful services with a great interactive bot interface. Experience with C# is needed.

Conventions

In this book, you will find a number of text styles that distinguish between different kinds of information. Here are some examples of these styles and an explanation of their meaning.

Code words in text, database table names, folder names, filenames, file extensions, pathnames, dummy URLs, user input, and Twitter handles are shown as follows: "We can include other contexts through the use of the `include` directive."

A block of code is set as follows:

```
public async Task MessageReceivedAsync(IDialogContext context,
IAwaitable<IMessageActivity> argument)
    {
        var message = await argument;
        await context.PostAsync("Hello World: " + message.Text);
        context.Wait(MessageReceivedAsync);
    }
```

Any command-line input or output is written as follows:

```
Set-ExecutionPolicy -ExecutionPolicy Unrestricted -Force -Scope CurrentUser
```

New terms and **important words** are shown in bold. Words that you see on the screen, for example, in menus or dialog boxes, appear in the text like this: "Update all VS extensions to their latest versions by navigating to **Tools | Extensions and Updates | Updates**."

Warnings or important notes appear in a box like this.

 Tips and tricks appear like this.

Reader feedback

Feedback from our readers is always welcome. Let us know what you think about this book-what you liked or disliked. Reader feedback is important for us as it helps us develop titles that you will really get the most out of.

To send us general feedback, simply e-mail feedback@packtpub.com, and mention the book's title in the subject of your message.

If there is a topic that you have expertise in and you are interested in either writing or contributing to a book, see our author guide at www.packtpub.com/authors.

Customer support

Now that you are the proud owner of a Packt book, we have a number of things to help you to get the most from your purchase.

Downloading the example code

You can download the example code files for this book from your account at http://www.packtpub.com. If you purchased this book elsewhere, you can visit http://www.packtpub.com/support and register to have the files e-mailed directly to you.

You can download the code files by following these steps:

1. Log in or register to our website using your e-mail address and password.
2. Hover the mouse pointer on the **SUPPORT** tab at the top.
3. Click on **Code Downloads & Errata**.
4. Enter the name of the book in the **Search** box.
5. Select the book for which you're looking to download the code files.

6. Choose from the drop-down menu where you purchased this book from.
7. Click on **Code Download**.

Once the file is downloaded, please make sure that you unzip or extract the folder using the latest version of:

- WinRAR / 7-Zip for Windows
- Zipeg / iZip / UnRarX for Mac
- 7-Zip / PeaZip for Linux

The code bundle for the book is also hosted on GitHub at `https://github.com/PacktPublishing/Building-Bots-with-Microsoft-Bot-Framework`. We also have other code bundles from our rich catalog of books and videos available at `https://github.com/PacktPublishing/`. Check them out!

Downloading the color images of this book

We also provide you with a PDF file that has color images of the screenshots/diagrams used in this book. The color images will help you better understand the changes in the output. You can download this file from `https://www.packtpub.com/sites/default/files/downloads/BuildingBotswithMicrosoftBotFramework_ColorImages.pdf`.

Errata

Although we have taken every care to ensure the accuracy of our content, mistakes do happen. If you find a mistake in one of our books-maybe a mistake in the text or the code-we would be grateful if you could report this to us. By doing so, you can save other readers from frustration and help us improve subsequent versions of this book. If you find any errata, please report them by visiting `http://www.packtpub.com/submit-errata`, selecting your book, clicking on the **Errata Submission Form** link, and entering the details of your errata. Once your errata are verified, your submission will be accepted and the errata will be uploaded to our website or added to any list of existing errata under the Errata section of that title.

To view the previously submitted errata, go to `https://www.packtpub.com/books/content/support` and enter the name of the book in the search field. The required information will appear under the **Errata** section.

Piracy

Piracy of copyrighted material on the Internet is an ongoing problem across all media. At Packt, we take the protection of our copyright and licenses very seriously. If you come across any illegal copies of our works in any form on the Internet, please provide us with the location address or website name immediately so that we can pursue a remedy.

Please contact us at `copyright@packtpub.com` with a link to the suspected pirated material.

We appreciate your help in protecting our authors and our ability to bring you valuable content.

Questions

If you have a problem with any aspect of this book, you can contact us at `questions@packtpub.com`, and we will do our best to address the problem.

1
Setting up Microsoft Bot Framework Dev Environment

In the past several decades, the corporate, government, and business world has experienced several waves of IT architecture foundations, moving from mainframes, to minicomputers, to distributed PCs, to the Internet, to social media / mobile, and now to the **Cloud / Internet of Things** (**IoT**) stack. We call this the *sixth wave* of corporate IT, and like its predecessors, cloud and IoT technologies are causing significant disruption and displacement, even while they drive new levels of productivity. Each architecture focuses on key business processes and supports **killer technology** applications to drive new levels of value. Very soon we will be looking at an enormous networked interconnection of everyday machines to one another, as well as to humans.

Lets have a look at the fifth wave of corporate IT:

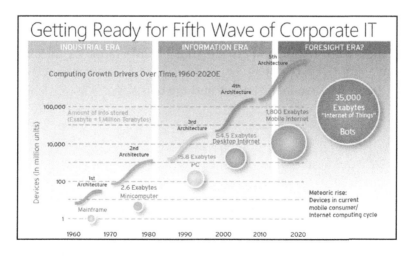

The machine-to-machine-to-human connectivity will have a profound impact on the consumer and corporate IT experience. As these machines become social and talk to us, we have an enormous opportunity to greatly enhance their value proposition through improved product quality, customer experience, and lowered cost of operations. A heightened consumer expectation for more personal and real-time interactions is driving business to holistically embrace the next wave of technology innovation such as cloud, IoT, and bots to boost business performance. In this age of billions of connected devices, there is a need for such a technology where our apps, such as bots, could talk back. Bots that have specific purposes and talk to any device or any app or to anyone, live in the cloud, we can talk to via any communication channel such as e-mail, text, voice, chat, and many others, can go where no apps have gone before when it comes to the machine-to-machine-to-human connectivity. In order to make this happen, we will need a whole new platform, a platform for conversations.

Conversation as a Service (CaaS)

Messaging apps in general are becoming a second home screen for many people, acting as their entry point to the Internet; where the "youngins" are, the brands will follow. Companies are coming up with messaging apps as bots and apps that offer everything from customer service to online shopping and banking.

Conversations are shaping up to be the next major human-computer interface. Thanks to advances in natural language processing and machine learning, the technology is finally getting faster and accurate enough to be viable. Imagine a platform where language is the new UI layer. When we talk about conversation as a platform, there are three parts:

- There are people talking to people. The Skype translator is an example where people can communicate across languages.
- Then, there is the opportunity to enhance a conversation by the ability to be present and interact remotely.
- Then, there are personal assistants and the bots.

The following screenshot shows the **Conversation as a Service**:

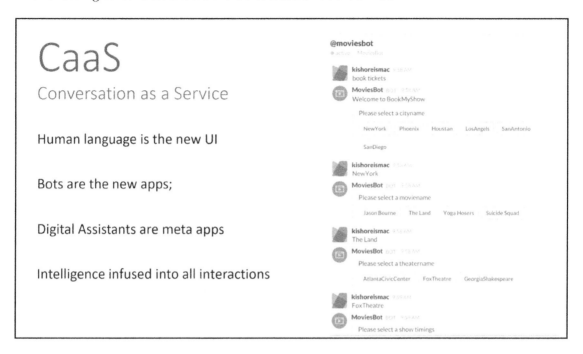

Think of bots as the new mechanism that you can converse with. Instead of looking through multiple mobile apps or pages of websites, you can call on any application as a bot within the conversational canvas. Bots are the new apps, and digital assistants are the meta-apps. This way, intelligence is infused into all our interactions.

Setting up Microsoft Bot Framework Dev Environment

This leads us to the **Microsoft Bot Framework**, which is a comprehensive offering from Microsoft to build and deploy high quality bots for your users to interact using **Conversation as a Platform** (**CaaP**). This is a framework that lets you build and connect intelligent bots. The idea is that they interact naturally wherever your users are talking, such as Skype, Slack, Facebook Messenger, text/SMS, and others. Basically, with any kind of channel that you use today as a human being to talk to other people, you will be able to use them to talk to bots, all using natural language:

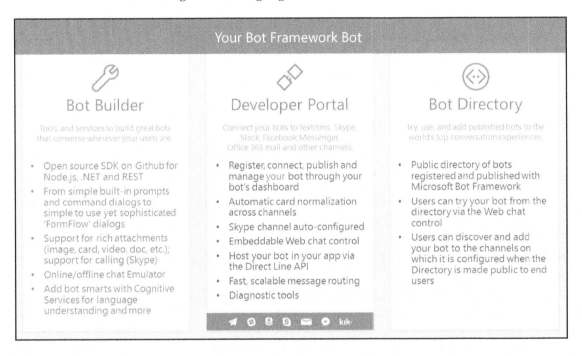

The Microsoft Bot Framework is a Microsoft operated CaaP service and an open source SDK. The Microsoft Bot Framework is one of the many tools that Microsoft is offering for building a complete bot. Other tools include **Language Understanding Intelligent Service** (**LUIS**), Speech APIs, Microsoft Azure, Cortana Intelligence Suit, and many more.

Your bot

The **Microsoft Bot Builder SDK** is one of three main components of the Microsoft Bot Framework. First, you have to build your bot. Your bot lives in the cloud and you host it yourself. You write it just like a web service component using Node.js or C#, like the **ASP.NET Web API** component. The Microsoft Bot Builder SDK is open source, so it will support more languages and web stacks over time. Your bot will have its own logic, but you also need a conversation logic using dialogs to model a conversation. The Bot Builder SDK gives you facilities for this, and there are many types of dialogs that are included, from simple yes or no questions, to full LUIS, which is one of the APIs provided by **Microsoft Cognitive Services**. This is what the architecture of bot looks like:

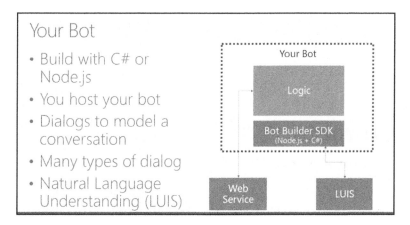

The Bot Connector

The **Bot Connector** is hosted and operated by Microsoft. Think of it as a central router between your bots and many channels to communicate with your bots. Apart from routing messages, it manages state within the conversation. The Bot Connector is an easy way to create a single backend and then publish it to a bunch of different platforms called **channels**.

The following screenshot illustrates the Bot Connector:

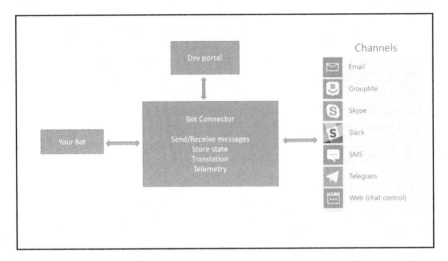

The Bot Directory

The **Bot Directory** is where the user will be able to find bots. It's like an App Store for mobile apps. The Bot Directory is a public directory of all the reviewed bots registered through the developer portal. Users will be able to discover, try, and add bots to their favorite conversation experiences from the Bot Directory. Anyone can access it and can submit bots to the directory.

As you begin your development with the Microsoft Bot Framework, you might be wondering how best to get started. Bots can be built in C#; however, Microsoft's Bot Framework can also be used to build bots using Node.js. For developing any bots, we need to first set up the development environment and have the right tools installed for successfully developing and deploying a bot. Let's see how we can set up a development environment using Visual Studio.

Setting up the development environment

In this section, we will see how to set up the development environment but, before that, let's check out the prerequisites needed for setting it up.

Prerequisites

To use the Microsoft Bot Framework Connector, you must have the following:

- A Microsoft account (Hotmail, Live, or Outlook) to log into the Bot Framework developer portal, which you will use to register your bot.
- An Azure subscription (free trial at https://azure.microsoft.com/en-us/). This Azure subscription is essential for having an Azure-accessible REST endpoint exposing a callback for the Connector service.
- Developer accounts on one or more communication service (such as Skype, Slack, or Facebook) where your bot will communicate.

In addition, you may wish to have an Azure Application Insights account so that you can capture telemetry from your bot. There are additionally different ways to go about building a bot: from scratch, coded directly to the Bot Connector REST API, the Bot Builder SDK's for Node.js and .NET, and the Bot Connector .NET template, which is what this quick start guide demonstrates.

Setting up the Bot Framework Connector SDK .NET

This is a step-by-step guide to setting up the development environment to develop a bot in C# using the Bot Framework Connector SDK .NET template:

1. Install the prerequisite software:
    1. You can download the community version of Visual Studio 2015 (latest update) for free at www.visualstudio.com.
    2. Update all VS extensions to their latest versions by navigating to **Tools | Extensions and Updates | Updates**.
2. Download and install the **Bot Application** template:
    1. Download the file from the direct download link, http://aka.ms/bf-bc-vstemplate.
    2. Save the ZIP file to your Visual Studio 2015 templates directory, which is traditionally in %USERPROFILE%DocumentsVisual Studio 2015TemplatesProjectTemplatesVisual C#.
3. Open Visual Studio.

Setting up Microsoft Bot Framework Dev Environment

4. Create a new C# project using the new **Bot Application** template:

5. The template is a fully functional Echo Bot that takes the user's text utterance as input and returns it as output. In order to run, however, the following has to take place:
   1. The bot has to be registered with the Bot Connector.
   2. The AppId and AppPassword from the Bot Framework registration page have to be recorded in the project's `web.config`.
   3. The project needs to be published to the web.
   4. Use the Bot Framework emulator to test your bot application.

The Bot Framework provides a channel emulator that lets you test calls to your bot as if they were being called by the Bot Framework cloud service. To install the Bot Framework emulator, download it from `https://emulator.botframework.com/`.

Once installed, you're ready to test, by starting your bot in Visual Studio using a browser as the application host:

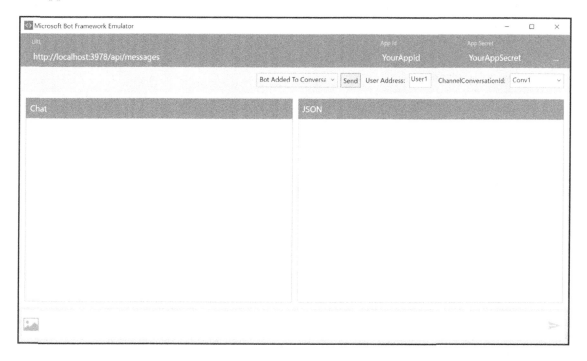

Messages

Your bot can send rich text, emoticons, pictures, and cards to a user or group. Users can send rich text and pictures to your bot. You can specify the type of content your bot can handle in the Skype settings page for your bot:

Content	From user to bot	From bot to user	Description
Rich text	✓	✓	**Including emoticons :)**
Pictures	✓	✓	PNG, JPEG, or GIF up to 20 Mb
Video	Coming soon	✓	MP4, AAC+h264 up to 15 Mb (approx. 1 minute), plus JPEG thumbnail
Cards	✓	✓	

Basic format

Each Skype user is assigned a unique ID for your bot, which is sent along with the display name with every message:

```
{
  "text": "Hello (wave)",
  "id": "1466182688092",
  "type": "message/text",
  "timestamp": "2016-06-17T16:58:08.74Z",
  "channelId": "skype",
  "serviceUrl": "https://apis.skype.com",
  "from": {
    "id": "29:2hJJkjmGn4ljB2X7YYEju-sgFwgvnISvE6G3abGde8ts",
    "name": "Display Name"
  },
  "conversation": {
    "id": "29:2hJJkjmGn4ljB2X7YYEju-sgFwgvnISvE6G3abGde8ts"
  },
  "recipient": {
    "id": "28:29415286-5a43-4a00-9dc5-bcbc2ce1f59e",
    "name": "Trivia Master"
  }
}
```

The `from` field contains the unique user ID (prefixed by `29`) and user `Display Name`. The `recipient` field contains the app ID (prefixed by `28`, which indicates a bot in Skype) and the bot's display name. In Skype, your bot is addressed using the Bot Framework App ID (a GUID).

> You cannot currently use slash (/) commands as part of conversations with your bot. This is a reserved character in Skype.

Rich text

Users can communicate with the bot using rich text format as well. Users can make the chat text as bold if needed or a bot can communicate with the user and make certain words as bold. Most of the channels support all the text properties supported by the Microsoft Bot Framework.

Skype emoticons

Skype emoticons can be sent by using the emoticon keyword in parentheses:

```
{
  "text": "(heart)"
}
```

The output of the preceding code is as follows:

 If a user sends your bot an emoticon, it may include `<ss>` tags around the emoticon, which can be ignored; for example, `<ss type="skype">(wave)</ss>`. Sending Skype Mojis (short, expressive video clips) is not currently supported.

Welcome messages

To send a welcome message to a user, listen for the `contactRelationUpdate` activity. To send a welcome message to a group, listen for the `conversationUpdate` activity.

Pictures and videos

Let's check out, how pictures and videos are sent:

- Pictures and videos are sent by adding attachments to a message
- Pictures can be PNG, JPEG, or GIF up to 20 Mb
- Videos can be MP4 or AAC+h264 up to 15 Mb (approx. 1 minute), plus JPEG thumbnails

Cards and buttons

Skype supports the following cards, which may have several properties and attachments. You can find information on how to use cards in the .NET SDK and Node.js SDK docs:

- Hero card
- Thumbnail card
- Carousel card (with hero or thumbnail images)
- Sign in card
- Receipt card

Images sent to Skype cards need to be stored on an HTTPS endpoint. Skype cards do not currently support `postBack` actions.

Hero card

The hero card renders a title, subtitle, text, large image, and buttons:

The hero card provides a very flexible layout; for example, it might contain the following:

- Image, title, subtitle, text, and three buttons
- Title, subtitle, text, and five buttons
- Title and six buttons
- Image and six buttons

The following table illustrates the flexible layout of hero card:

Property	Type	Description
`title`	Rich text	Title of the card, maximum two lines.
`subtitle`	Rich text	Subtitle appears just below the title, maximum two lines.
`text`	Rich text	Text appears just below the subtitle; two, four, or six lines depending on whether the title and subtitle are specified.
`images:[]`	Array of images	Image displayed at top of the card; aspect ratio is 16:9.
`buttons:[]`	Array of action objects	Set of actions applicable to the current card: three buttons, up to a maximum of six (+two if no is image is shown, +one if the title or subtitle are not included, +two if the text is not included.)
`tap`	Action object	This action will be activated when the user taps on the card itself.

Thumbnail card

The thumbnail card renders a title, subtitle, text, small thumbnail image, and buttons:

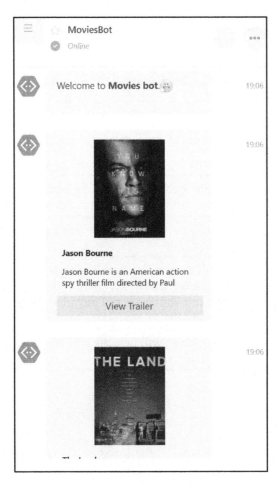

The following table explains the properties of a thumbnail card:

Property	Type	Description
title	Rich text	Title of the card, maximum two lines.
subtitle	Rich text	Subtitle appears just below the title, maximum two lines.
text	Rich text	Text appears just below the subtitle: two, four, or six lines depending on whether the title and subtitle are specified.

`images:[]`	Array of images	Image displayed at top of the card; the image aspect ratio in a thumbnail card is 1:1.
`buttons:[]`	Array of action objects	Set of actions applicable to the current card; maximum three buttons.
`tap`	Action object	This action will be activated when the user taps on the card itself.

Carousel

The carousel card can be used to show a carousel of images and text, with associated action buttons:

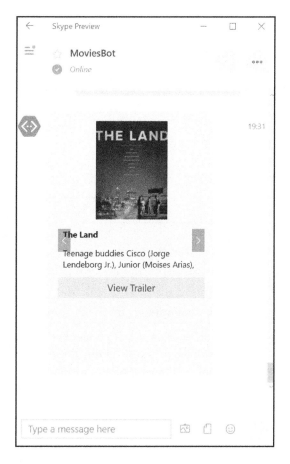

Properties are the same as for the hero or thumbnail card.

Images

Images are scaled up or down in size while maintaining the aspect ratio to cover the image area, and then cropped from the center to achieve the image aspect ratio for the card.

Images should be stored on an HTTPS endpoint, up to 1024x1024, up to 1 MB in size, and in PNG or JPEG. The properties are explained in the following table:

Property	Type	Description
url	URL	URL to the image; *Must be HTTPS*.
alt	String	Accessible description of the image.
value	String	Action assigned to the image.

Buttons

Buttons are shown at the bottom of the card--in a single row if they fit, or stacked. Button text is always on a single line and will be trimmed if it is too long. If more buttons than can be supported by the card are included, they will not be shown.

Actions

The following table consists of properties, types and descriptions for actions:

Property	Type	Description
type	String	Required field. One of openURL (opens the given URL), imBack (posts a message in the chat to the bot that sent the card), call (Skype or phone number), showImage (for images only, displays the image), or signin (sign in card only).
title	String	Text description that appears on the button.
tap	Action object	Value depending on the type of action. For openURL it is a URL, for signin it is the URL to the authentication flow, for imBack it is a user defined string (which may contain hidden metadata for the bot for, example, <meta roomid='10'/>, for call it can be skype:skypeid or tel:telephone, and for showImage it is not required.

Sign in

The sign in card can be used to initiate an authentication flow with predefined images and title:

The following table illustrates the properties, types and descriptions of sign in:

Property	Type	Description
text	Rich text	Text appears just below the subtitle: two lines maximum.
buttons:[]	Array of action objects	Single button of type signin.

Receipt

The receipt card can be used to send a receipt. If the height of the card is too large, it is partially folded and a **Show all** action is shown to expand it:

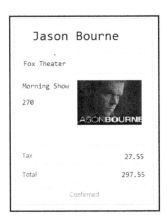

The following table explains the properties, types and descriptions of receipt card:

Property	Type	Description
`title`	Rich text	Title of the card. Maximum two lines.
`facts:[]`	Array of fact key-value pairs	Fact key is left aligned, value is right aligned.
`items:[]`	Array of purchased objects	Properties: title (maximum two lines), subtitle (one line), text (up to six lines depending if the title, subtitle, and price are present), price, image (1:1 aspect ratio), tap.
`total`	Rich text	Title of the card. Maximum two lines.
`tax`	Rich text	Title of the card. Maximum two lines.
`vat`	Rich text	Title of the card. Maximum two lines.
`items:[]`	Rich text	Title of the card. Maximum two lines.
`images:[]`	Array of images	Image displayed at top of the card. Aspect ratio 16:9.
`buttons:[]`	Array of action objects	Set of actions applicable to the current card.

Chapter 1

Property	Type	Description
`tap`	Action object	This action will be activated when the user taps on the card itself.

Groups

A bot can be enabled for groups in the Skype settings for the bot. It can be added to a group chat in the same way as adding a participant to a chat. In a group, the bot will only receive messages directly addressed to it--for example, `@YourBot This is the message`. It will not receive other messages sent by group participants or notifications of users joining or leaving the group:

[27]

To enable a bot to be added to a group chat, you need to add this capability in **Settings**. Go to your bot **Dashboard** and edit the Skype channel:

Calling

You can build Skype bots that can receive and handle voice calls using the .NET SDK, Node.js SDK, or the Skype API.

Each time a Skype user places a call to your bot, the Skype bot platform will notify the bot using the calling **WebHook** you specify in **Settings**. In response, the bot can provide a set of basic actions called a workflow.

These are the supported actions:

- Answer
- Play prompt
- Record audio
- Speech to text
- DTMF tones
- Hang up

The Skype bot platform will execute the actions on the bot's behalf according to the workflow.

If the workflow is successful, Skype will post a result of the last action to your calling WebHook. For example, if the last action was to record an audio message, the result will be audio content.

During a voice call, your bot can decide, after each result, how to continue interaction with the Skype user.

 Skype bots with calling enabled are for preview only and cannot currently be published. To publish a bot in Skype, you will need to disable calling in the Skype settings for your bot and then set **Published** to **enable** in the bot dashboard. Bots can handle one-to-one calls, but not group calls.

Summary

In this chapter, we introduced the Microsoft Bot Framework and explained how it helps in the development of bots. Also, we have seen how to set up the development environment, emulator, and the tools needed for programming. This chapter is based on the thought that programming knowledge and experience grow best when they grow together. In the next chapter, we will introduce bot programming by building and locally deploying a simple Hello World bot application. You will get to know Visual Studio, C# .NET, the Bot Framework, and the related technologies along with all the steps for creating projects.

2
Developing Your First Bot Using the Connector and Builder SDK

In this chapter, we will use the Microsoft Bot Connector, part of the Microsoft Bot Framework, as a way to create a single backend and then publish it to a bunch of different platforms called channels as quickly as possible. The goal is to have the user input natural language and your bot to perfectly understand and execute the action your user wants.

As we saw in Chapter 1, *Setting up the Microsoft Bot Framework Dev Environment*, two decades ago, we saw a major shift in the technology industry and consumers as well, where they moved from desktop client applications to Internet web applications. We are on the edge of a similar shift with mobile devices, with even bigger consequences--given the fact that no one can live without their mobile devices. **Conversation as a Platform** (**CaaP**) has become the new platform, incorporating the role played by the mobile apps. Just as Internet websites replaced desktop client applications in the 1990s, messaging bots will replace mobile apps now. Bots are the new apps, and the bot store is the new app store. Also, as we move into the **Internet of Things** (**IoT**), bots are the default applications for monitoring these massive IoT devices. Just as mobile apps decluttered our websites, bots will declutter our mobile experience. One of the salient features of bots is that they reside in the Cloud and can auto-upgrade themselves with new functionalities, even without any user action. Bots can network with one another to accomplish a series of actions in a workflow/sequence.

Bots are evolving

A bot is a piece of software designed to automate a specific task. When talked about in the context of conversation as a platform, a bot becomes the chat interface of a regular app. So, you should allow tasks that require full UI to be performed by the user only through conversation. We are at the early stages of a major evolving technology trend: the rise of conversation bots. Conversation bots can read and write messages just like a human would. Users will be able to interact with bots just as they interact with other humans using natural language.

Skype, WeChat, Kik, Facebook, GroupMe, Slack, Telegram, and so on are emerging conversation platforms, which help us in enabling interactions with any service from within the conversation platform. All these platforms enable developers to build conversation bots to provide a specific service. We can program bots to carry out specific automated actions. Conversation bots can initiate a definite action, and bots can respond to requests from other users as well as automate conversations and help complete transactions or implement workflows in the conversation.

Bots use cases

Let's look at some of the use cases where bots can enable users to have natural conversation to meet their needs:

- We can develop some e-commerce bots that enable us to buy goods and services through Skype, Slack, Facebook, and any other conversation platforms
- We can develop bots for restaurants to order food online or to make reservations at a restaurant
- We can develop content bots that share relevant content with you (such as news and weather)
- We can develop watcher/tracker bots that can notify us when specific events happen (such as when a flight is delayed, when your car needs servicing, and when your pizza order is ready for pickup)
- We can develop banking and stock trading bots that can provide financial services
- We can develop workflow bots that can automate business workflows in marketing, sales, operations, HR/admin, finance, payroll, and others
- When it comes to the IoT domain, bots are the best fit for IoT applications, which can connect to your smart homes, sensors, cars, and more

When you have so many bots, it makes sense to let your personal digital assistant (such as Cortana) manage the communication with the other bots for you, thus escalating only the high-priority requests for which you've trained it. We can develop a personal bot that can supervise all other bots on your behalf, as per your personal preferences (similar to Cortana in Windows OS). We can delegate authority to bots that act autonomously on our behalf. Most of our monitoring, shopping, tracking, scheduling, and other bots can be automated according to personal preferences, and our personal bot can even filter out advertising messages sent to you.

Developing your first bot

The Microsoft Bot Framework allows developers to develop code once and, using the Microsoft Bot Connector, deploy it onto multiple channels, including **SMS**, **Slack**, **Facebook Messenger**, **Skype**, **GroupMe**, and many other channels:

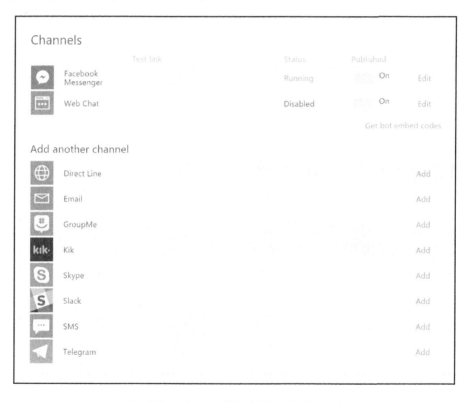

Figure 1: Various channels available in the Microsoft Bot Framework

The Microsoft Bot Framework has three main components:

- **Bot Connector**: This allows you to easily connect your bot to Slack or Skype, via SMS or the web
- **Bot Builder SDK**: An SDK that allows you to develop bots using C# .NET or Node.js, which is open source
- **Bot Directory**: A collection of all approved bots connected through the Bot Connector; it is a marketplace where users can search for bots to add in their chat applications

 It's really important for Visual Studio to be updated in order to use the Bot Directory, as well as download the web tools in the Visual Studio setup. Update all VS extensions to their latest versions by navigating to **Tools** | **Extensions and Updates** | **Updates**.

In this chapter, to get started with developing bots using the Microsoft Bot Framework, we will use the following:

- The Bot Connector
- The Bot Builder C#

We will build our bot using C#. However, in the Microsoft Bot Framework, bots can also be built in Node.js.

Creating our first bot

To develop a bot, perform the following steps:

1. Build a bot using the C# SDK.
2. Test it using the Bot Framework emulator.

Building a bot using the C# SDK

Let's go through the steps to create a bot application using the Bot Framework Connector SDK .NET template. They are as follows:

1. Open Visual Studio and navigate to **File** | **New** | **Project...** and select **Visual C#** from the left side **Templates** category. Then, from the **Templates** section, you will see the **Bot Application** template:

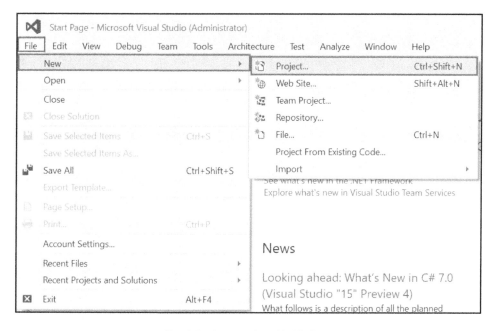

Figure 2: Creating a new project in Visual Studio IDE

Developing Your First Bot Using the Connector and Builder SDK

2. Select the **Bot Application** template, name the project `Hello World`, and then click on **OK**:

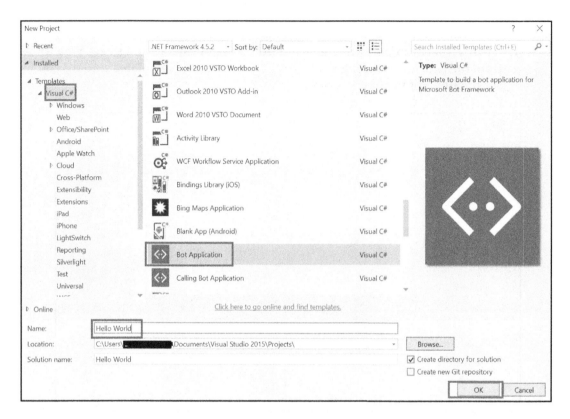

Figure 3: Selecting the Bot Application template and naming the project

A solution gets created with the `Hello World` project.

Let's go through the default files that were created by this **Bot Application** template in Visual Studio.

When we create a bot using the **Bot Application** template, it basically creates an ASP.NET Web API project, which contains all the Bot Framework SDKs and all the supporting files. The following are the files, by default:

- Properties\AssemblyInfo.cs
- References
- App_Start\WebApiConfig.cs
- Controllers\MessageController.cs
- default.htm
- Global.asax
- Packages.config
- Web.config

AssemblyInfo.cs

The main purpose of the AssemblyInfo.cs file is to store all information about the application assembly. General information about an assembly is controlled through the set of attributes that we see in the AssemblyInfo.cs class:

Figure 4: The AssemblyInfo.cs file in Solution Explorer

We can change these attribute values to modify the information associated with an assembly. It contains information about the project assembly, such as name, description, version number, loaded assemblies, and other information. If you remove the file from your project, then your project will be compiled with no information; that is, in the **Details** tab of the file properties, you will see no name, no description, version 0.0.0.0, and others.

If you open it, you can find one property called assembly:Guid--the value associated with it is the ID that will be used to identify the assembly if it is exposed as a COM object. So, if your assembly isn't COM-exposed, you don't need this. The GUID is generated by Visual Studio at the time of the project creation, and it will be generated randomly.

Developing Your First Bot Using the Connector and Builder SDK

The following is the default `AssemblyInfo.cs` class:

```
using System.Reflection;
using System.Runtime.CompilerServices;
using System.Runtime.InteropServices;

// General Information about an assembly is controlled through the following
// set of attributes. Change these attribute values to modify the information
// associated with an assembly.
[assembly: AssemblyTitle("Bot_Application2")]
[assembly: AssemblyDescription("")]
[assembly: AssemblyConfiguration("")]
[assembly: AssemblyCompany("")]
[assembly: AssemblyProduct("Bot_Application2")]
[assembly: AssemblyCopyright("Copyright ©  2015")]
[assembly: AssemblyTrademark("")]
[assembly: AssemblyCulture("")]

// Setting ComVisible to false makes the types in this assembly not visible
// to COM components.  If you need to access a type in this assembly from
// COM, set the ComVisible attribute to true on that type.
[assembly: ComVisible(false)]

// The following GUID is for the ID of the typelib if this project is exposed to COM
[assembly: Guid("a8ba1066-5695-4d71-abb4-65e5a5e0c3d4")]

// Version information for an assembly consists of the following four values:
//      Major Version
//      Minor Version
//      Build Number
//      Revision
// You can specify all the values or you can default the Revision and Build Numbers
// by using the '*' as shown below:
[assembly: AssemblyVersion("1.0.0.0")]
[assembly: AssemblyFileVersion("1.0.0.0")]
```

References

If you expand References, you will see all the required references for the ASP.NET application along with two new references for the Bot Framework:

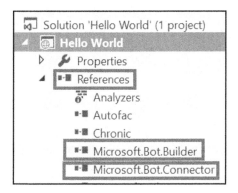

Figure 5: Various references needed to develop a bot in Solution Explorer

Microsoft Bot Builder

The Microsoft Bot Builder SDK/Framework provides very powerful features for developing bots. Using the Bot Builder Framework, we can build freeform interactive bots as well as guided bots where the features are shown to the user. Using this, we can build bots very easily in C#. This is one of the three main components of the Bot Framework.

Features included with the Bot Builder Framework are as follows:

- It provides dialogs with powerful systems that are composable and isolated.
- It also provides built-in dialogs with strings, enumeration, and yes/no functionalities. With built-in dialogs, we can use more powerful AI frameworks such as LUIS.
- It also is stateless, which helps us to scale bots.
- It provides form flow for automatically generating a bot from a C# class with such features as help, navigation, confirmation, and clarification.

Microsoft Bot Connector

This reference provides the Bot Framework Connector REST API services, which will be used for providing communication between your bot and many communication channels, such as Skype, Slack, Facebook, GroupMe, and so on.

The main function of the Bot Connector is that when you write a conversational bot that exposes a Microsoft Bot Framework-compatible API on the Internet, it will forward those messages from your bot to the user.

WebApiConfig.cs

This class provides the information for Web API-related configuration, including specific Web API routes, services, and other settings:

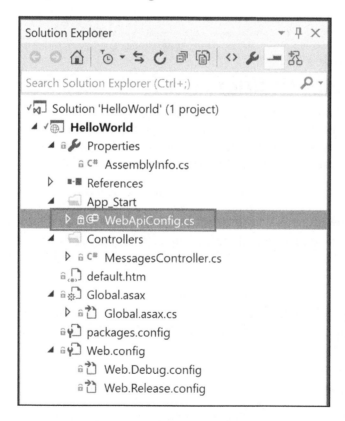

Figure 6: The WebApiConfig.cs file in Solution Explorer

Here, we will define how to handle null values at the time of the deserialization of objects and we will also define the routes. Instead of calling `Routes.MapRoutes`, as in the MVC `RouteConfig` class, we instead call `Config.Routes.MapHttpRoutes` using the following code:

```
// Web API routes
            config.MapHttpAttributeRoutes();

            config.Routes.MapHttpRoute(
            name: "DefaultApi",
            routeTemplate: "api/{controller}/{id}",
            defaults: new { id = RouteParameter.Optional }
            );
```

To allow the Web API to know which API the user is requesting and where it is located in the application, the `WebApiConfig.cs` file is where our Web API routing configuration takes place.

The following is the default `WebApiConfig.cs` class:

```
using Newtonsoft.Json;
using Newtonsoft.Json.Serialization;
using System;
using System.Collections.Generic;
using System.Linq;
using System.Web.Http;

namespace Bot_Application2
{
    public static class WebApiConfig
    {
        public static void Register(HttpConfiguration config)
        {
            // Json settings

            config.Formatters.JsonFormatter.
            SerializerSettings.NullValueHandling =
            NullValueHandling.Ignore;

            config.Formatters.JsonFormatter.
            SerializerSettings.ContractResolver = new
            CamelCasePropertyNamesContractResolver();

            config.Formatters.JsonFormatter.
            SerializerSettings.Formatting =
            Formatting.Indented;
```

```
                JsonConvert.DefaultSettings = () =>
                new JsonSerializerSettings()
            {
                ContractResolver = new
                CamelCasePropertyNamesContractResolver(),
                Formatting = Newtonsoft.Json.Formatting.Indented,
                NullValueHandling = NullValueHandling.Ignore,
            };

            // Web API configuration and services
            // Web API routes
            config.MapHttpAttributeRoutes();

            config.Routes.MapHttpRoute(
                name: "DefaultApi",
                routeTemplate: "api/{controller}/{id}",
                defaults: new { id = RouteParameter.Optional }
            );
        }
    }
}
```

MessageController.cs

This class is the *main* class, which handles communication between the bot and the user. This class contains a `Post` method, which will accept user messages, process them, and reply back with an appropriate message.

You can find this class under the `Controllers` folder as shown:

Figure 7: The MessagesController.cs file in Solution Explorer

The `MessagesController` class inherits from the `ApiController`. This means that the `MessagesController` is an API that can live on the web and be accessible from the outside world after we publish it.

If you observe closely, this class has an annotation called `[BotAuthentication]`, which means that only the bot can access the `MessageController` API. The `BotAuthentication` decoration on the method is used to validate your Bot Connector credentials over HTTPS.

This means that when we publish our service to a server, the Messages API can be accessed by the Bot Framework only from where our bot was registered.

The following is the default `MessagesController.cs` class:

```csharp
using System;
using System.Linq;
using System.Net;
using System.Net.Http;
using System.Threading.Tasks;
using System.Web.Http;
using System.Web.Http.Description;
using Microsoft.Bot.Connector;
using Microsoft.Bot.Connector.Utilities;
using Newtonsoft.Json;

namespace Bot_Application2
{
    [BotAuthentication]
    public class MessagesController : ApiController
    {
        // <summary>
        // POST: api/Messages
        // Receive a message from a user and reply to it
        // </summary>
        public async Task<Message> Post([FromBody]Message message)
        {
            if (message.Type == "Message")
            {
                // calculate something for us to return
                int length = (message.Text ?? string.Empty).Length;

                // return our reply to the user
                return message.CreateReplyMessage($"You sent {length} characters");
            }
            else
            {
```

```
                return HandleSystemMessage(message);
            }
        }

        private Message HandleSystemMessage(Message message)
        {
            if (message.Type == "Ping")
            {
                Message reply = message.CreateReplyMessage();
                reply.Type = "Ping";
                return reply;
            }
            else if (message.Type == "DeleteUserData")
            {
                // Implement user deletion here
                // If we handle user deletion, return a real message
            }
            else if (message.Type == "BotAddedToConversation")
            {
            }
            else if (message.Type == "BotRemovedFromConversation")
            {
            }
            else if (message.Type == "UserAddedToConversation")
            {
            }
            else if (message.Type == UserRemovedFromConversation")
            {
            }
            else if (message.Type == "EndOfConversation")
            {
            }

            return null;
        }
    }
}
```

Default.htm

This contains the default welcome page of our bot service, which will be displayed when we open the URL of the bot service. If you want to display the welcome text or give more information about your bot, here is the place you can design and display the information.

Global.asax

This file is an ASP.NET application file, which will be used to handle or respond to application level or session level events raised by HTTP modules. At runtime, it will automatically generate a framework file derived from the HTTP application when we compile the project. Due to this, any direct URL requests will be rejected automatically. This file is optional; you use it only when you want to handle application-level or session-level events.

The following is the default `Global.asax` file:

```
using System;
using System.Collections.Generic;
using System.Linq;
using System.Web;
using System.Web.Http;
using System.Web.Routing;

namespace Bot_Application2
{
    public class WebApiApplication : System.Web.HttpApplication
    {
        protected void Application_Start()
        {
            GlobalConfiguration.Configure(WebApiConfig.Register);
        }
    }
}
```

Packages.config

This file contains information about the references/packages used in the project, which will be helpful at the time of restoring them.

Web.config

This file is very important. It will hold all the required settings information about your application, which helps you to modify any settings value in the application without deploying the project again. Let's see what values we get by default when we create the project.

Under the `configuration` tag, `appSettings`, we have the following keys added by default:

```xml
<configuration>
  <appSettings>
    <!-- update these with your BotId, Microsoft App Id and your Microsoft App Password-->
    <add key="BotId" value="YourBotId" />
    <add key="MicrosoftAppId" value="" />
    <add key="MicrosoftAppPassword" value="" />
  </appSettings>
```

Figure 8: Figure showing Web.Config content and settings needed to configure bot

Post method

The `Post` method accepts messages from the user as an activity, which contains all conversation information between the user and our bot. Using this, we can ascertain what kind of information the user wants from the bot:

```
public async Task<HttpResponseMessage> Post([FromBody]Activity activity)
```

Here, we defined a sample bot that will reply back to the user with the same as what you say to it.

The Bot Framework provides many features that include how to identify the type of incoming message and based on that, your bot can respond to the user. To identify that, we have activity enum types, which will provide information about the conversation.

To identify and apply business logic to the message sent by the user, we will write the following code in the `Post` method:

```
if (activity.Type == ActivityTypes.Message)
            {
}
```

If the user is sending a message, it means they are requesting something to the bot. So, it will receive it, process it, apply some business logic, and will reply back to the user. To reply back to the user, we need a `ConnectorClient` object, which provides connector REST API services to forward messages from the bot to the user:

```
if (activity.Type == ActivityTypes.Message)
            {
                ConnectorClient connector = new ConnectorClient(new
                Uri(activity.ServiceUrl));
```

```csharp
            // calculate something for us to return
            int length = (activity.Text ?? string.Empty).Length;

            // return our reply to the user
            Activity reply = activity.CreateReply($"You sent
            {activity.Text} which was {length} characters");
            await
            connector.Conversations.ReplyToActivityAsync(reply);
        }
        else
        {
            HandleSystemMessage(activity);
        }
        var response = Request.CreateResponse(HttpStatusCode.OK);
        return response;
```

The following is the code for handling activity types other than the `message` type `activity`:

```csharp
    private Activity HandleSystemMessage(Activity message)
        {
            if (message.Type == ActivityTypes.DeleteUserData)
            {
                // Implement user deletion here
                // If we handle user deletion, return a real message
            }
            else if (message.Type == ActivityTypes.ConversationUpdate)
            {
                // Handle conversation state changes, like members
                  being added and removed
                // Use Activity.MembersAdded and
                    Activity.MembersRemoved and Activity.Action for info
                // Not available in all channels
            }
            else if (message.Type ==
                    ActivityTypes.ContactRelationUpdate)
            {
                // Handle add/remove from contact lists
                // Activity.From + Activity.Action represent what
                happened
            }
            else if (message.Type == ActivityTypes.Typing)
            {
                // Handle knowing that the user is typing
            }
            else if (message.Type == ActivityTypes.Ping)
            {
            }
```

```
            return null;
    }
```

We can reply to the user from the bot based on the activity done by the user with the help of the preceding code.

The `Post` method accepts an input as an `activity` type, which will hold all the information related to the conversation between the bot and the user. The `Activity` class is very important and is responsible for all chats/conversations between the bot and the user. The bot knows from which user it got the message because of the `activity` object. It holds complete information about the user, message information, previous conversations, and more.

When a user sends a message to the bot, the `Post` method receives that message along with all other information and saves it as an `activity` object. The following is the information that our `activity` object will have at the time of the POST request, in JSON format:

```
{
  "type": "message",
  "id": "c444400f077f4ce9a7b9cffbd398aa24",
  "timestamp": "2016-08-30T08:36:32.1399048Z",
  "serviceUrl": "http://localhost:9000/",
  "channelId": "emulator",
  "from": {
    "id": "2c1c7fa3",
    "name": "User1"
  },
  "conversation": {
    "isGroup": false,
    "id": "8a684db8",
    "name": "Conv1"
  },
  "recipient": {
    "id": "56800324",
    "name": "Bot1"
  },
  "text": "Hi John",
  "attachments": [],
  "entities": []
}
```

The `Post` method receives this in JSON format from the user as an `activity`. It contains the `type`, `serviceUrl` (which is the bot published URL), the `channelId` (Facebook, Slack, Skype, and so on), from whom we received the message, and conversation information. `text` means the message typed by the user. If it has any attachments, it will be under `attachments`. Based on this information, the bot will respond to the user.

BotID

This is the ID generated at the time of registering your bot at the `https://dev.botframework.com` site. It helps you to identify your bot.

Microsoft App ID

This also generates at the time of registering your bot at `https://dev.botframework.com`. It helps to authenticate your bot with a Microsoft application.

MicrosoftAppPassword

We have to generate this key after creating the Microsoft App ID. This is very important and provides `BotAuthentication` to your `MessagesController` class.

These three are the keys that will be used by the `BotAuthentication` class at the time of authenticating a request. So that all requests are received, the Bot Framework only accepts those from your bot. This way, the connector service will communicate to your user and respective channels.

To get these values, log in to your `dev.botframework.com` account, select the appropriate bot if already registered (if not, register one), and copy the Bot ID, Microsoft ID, and Microsoft App Password from there.

How to deploy and run the bot application in the Bot Framework emulator locally

To test and debug the bot application locally, we have the Bot Framework emulator, which will provide all the rich functionalities of the Bot Framework SDK.

Download the emulator and install it from https://emulator.botframework.com/. Now, go to Visual Studio and press *F5* to run and deploy the Hello World bot application locally in your browser. You will see the welcome page Default.htm of your bot as shown here:

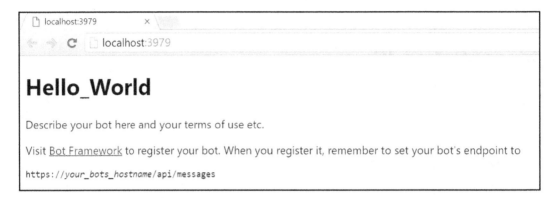

Figure 9: Your bot default page in the browser

Now, open the bot emulator that you installed in the first step. By default, the emulator sets the bot URL to localhost. Make sure that the bot application localhost port and the URL port in the emulator are the same. To check that, go to the browser where your bot application is running and open, and check the port number after the localhost word in that URL:

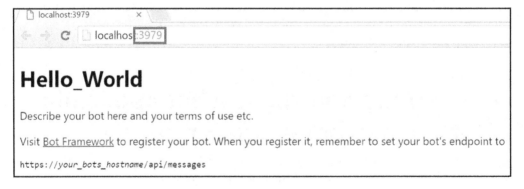

Figure 10: Your bot port number

For example, in the Hello World sample, the port number is 3979. Now, go to the bot emulator and check whether the bot URL has the same port number or not. We need to add the path /api/messages to the bot URL when using the bot application template:

Chapter 2

Figure 11: Your bot URL

Now, we are ready to test our Hello World bot application. The default bot application comes with a basic functionality, which will respond to users with a message. Whenever the user interacts with the bot, the Hello World bot responds back to the user with the same message that the user typed. This means that it is a simple *Echo Bot*. Open the `MessagesController.cs` class and replace the `Post` method with the following code, to make the code simple:

```csharp
0 references
public async Task<HttpResponseMessage> Post([FromBody]Activity activity)
{
    if (activity.Type == ActivityTypes.Message)
    {
        ConnectorClient connector = new ConnectorClient(new Uri(activity.ServiceUrl));

        // return our reply to the user
        Activity reply = activity.CreateReply($"Hello World:  {activity.Text}");
        await connector.Conversations.ReplyToActivityAsync(reply);
    }
    else
    {
        HandleSystemMessage(activity);
    }
    var response = Request.CreateResponse(HttpStatusCode.OK);
    return response;
}
```

Figure 12: The main logic of your bot code

Whenever a message is received by Hello World, it returns `Hello World: {text received from User}`.

Developing Your First Bot Using the Connector and Builder SDK

When a user sends a message, it holds it in the `activity` object. If it is of the `Message` type, then we will create a connector between the bot and the user with the help of the `ConnectorClient` class object, by passing `ServiceUrl` as a constructor parameter. This holds the connection that will be used at the time of replying back to the user:

```
ConnectorClient connector = new ConnectorClient(new
Uri(activity.ServiceUrl));
```

Once we have finished processing the user, we need to create a reply to the user. For that, we have to create a reference to the `Activity` class and create a reply with the help of the received `activity` object, as follows:

```
Activity reply = activity.CreateReply($"Hello World: {activity.Text}");
```

While replying, we are passing `Hello World: {received text from user}`.

After creating the reply, we need to send that reply back to the user. For that, we will use the `ConnectorClient` object, which we have just created:

```
await connector.Conversations.ReplyToActivityAsync(reply);
```

So, you will see the output in the emulator, as shown here:

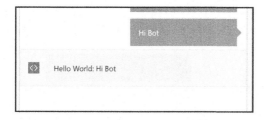

Figure 13: Your bot communication in the emulator

To test it, run the Hello World bot after making changes to your `Post` method, as we did in the preceding section. Then, open the emulator, type some message, and press *Enter*:

Chapter 2

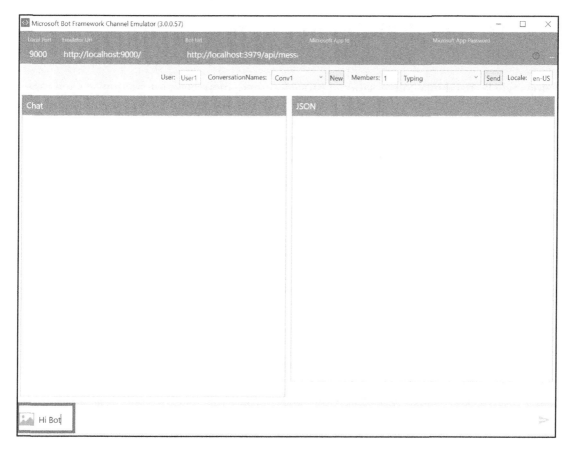

Figure 14: The bot emulator

Now, you will see a reply from the bot by appending Hello World to your message:

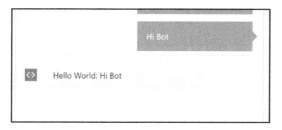

Figure 15: How bots communicate using messages inside the emulator

How to use dialogs in bot applications

Now, we will see how to use dialogs for the same Hello World bot application.

Dialogs will be used in a conversational process, where there is an interaction or exchange of messages between the user and the bot. Each dialog is an abstraction that encapsulates its own state in a C# class that implements `IDialog`. To work with dialogs, we need to import the `Microsoft.Bot.Builder.Dialogs` namespace. Add a C# class `HelloWorldDialog` into your project. To add a class, right-click on your project and navigate to **Add** | **Class...** from the menu:

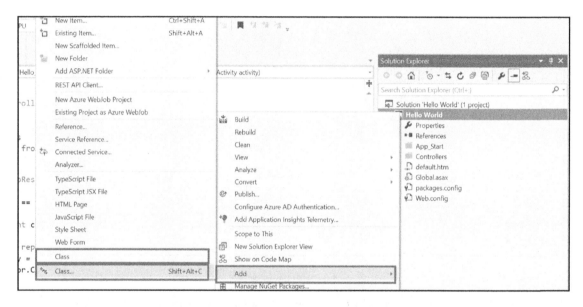

Figure 16: Using Visual Studio IDE to add a new class to an existing project

Give the **Name** as `HelloWorldDialog`:

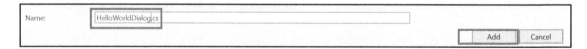

Figure 17: Using Visual Studio IDE to name a new class

In order to change the Hello World example, add the following code in `HelloWorldDialog`. To use the Bot Builder, we first need to import the required namespace:

```
using Microsoft.Bot.Builder.Dialogs;
```

Next, we need to add a C# class to represent our conversation. You can do this by adding this class to your `HelloWorldDialog.cs` file. Replace the code in the `HelloWorldDialog.cs` file with the following code:

```csharp
using Microsoft.Bot.Builder.Dialogs;
using Microsoft.Bot.Connector;
using System;
using System.Collections.Generic;
using System.Linq;
using System.Text;
using System.Threading.Tasks;

namespace Hello_World
{
    [Serializable]
    public class HelloWorldDialog : IDialog<object>
    {
        public async Task StartAsync(IDialogContext context)
        {
            context.Wait(MessageReceivedAsync);
        }

        public async Task MessageReceivedAsync(IDialogContext context,
        IAwaitable<IMessageActivity> argument)
        {
            var message = await argument;
            await context.PostAsync("Hello World: " + message.Text);
            context.Wait(MessageReceivedAsync);
        }
    }
}
```

Let's go through the `HelloWorldDialog.cs` class line by line.

To implement dialogs in the bot application, we need to create a class that inherits from `IDialog` and the class should be `Serializable`:

```csharp
[Serializable]
    public class HelloWorldDialog : IDialog<object>
```

Developing Your First Bot Using the Connector and Builder SDK

The `Dialog` class will have a `StartAsync` method, which receives the `activity` as `IDialogContext` and initiates the `MessageReceived` method whenever it receives a message from the user:

```
public async Task StartAsync(IDialogContext context)
    {
        context.Wait(MessageReceivedAsync);
    }
```

The `StartAsync` method will be an `async` method so that the requests will process asynchronously.

The `MessageReceived` method will accept the `context` and `MessageActivity` as arguments. Using these, we can process the user request the same way as we did in the `Post` method, but in a much richer way with the help of dialogs:

```
public async Task MessageReceivedAsync(IDialogContext context,
IAwaitable<IMessageActivity> argument)
    {
        var message = await argument;
        await context.PostAsync("Hello World: " + message.Text);
        context.Wait(MessageReceivedAsync);
    }
```

`IMessageActivity` is the interface implemented by the `Activity` class so that it can hold the activity in it.

Now, open the `MessagesController.cs` file and update the `Post` method with the following code:

```
public async Task<HttpResponseMessage> Post([FromBody]Activity activity)
    {
        if (activity.Type == ActivityTypes.Message)
        {
            await Conversation.SendAsync(activity, () => new
            HelloWorldDialog());
        }
        else
        {
            HandleSystemMessage(activity);
        }
        var response = Request.CreateResponse(HttpStatusCode.OK);
        return response;
    }
```

Now, in the `Post` method, we have to initiate the dialog class whenever it receives a message from the user. For that, we have the `Conversation` class, which initiates dialogs by accepting the `activity` and dialog class objects as parameters:

```
await Conversation.SendAsync(activity, () => new HelloWorldDialog());
```

The `Conversation` class is under the `Microsoft.Bot.Builder.Dialogs` namespace. The method is marked `async` because the Bot Builder makes use of the C# facilities for handling asynchronous communication. It returns a `Task`, which represents the task responsible for sending replies for the passed in `Message`. If there is an exception, the `Task` will contain the exception information. Within the `Post` method, we call `Conversation.SendAsync`, which is the root method for the Bot Builder SDK. It follows the **Dependency Inversion Principle** and performs the following steps:

1. Instantiates the required components.
2. Deserializes the dialog state (the dialog stack and each dialog's state) from the `IBotDataStore` (the default implementation uses the Bot Connector state API to back the `IBotDataStore`).
3. Resumes the conversation processes where the bot decided to suspend and wait for a message.
4. Sends the replies.
5. Serializes the updated dialog state and persists it back to the `IBotDataStore`.

When your conversation first starts, there is no dialog state in the `IBotDataStore` so the delegate passed to `Conversation.SendAsync` will be used to construct an `EchoDialog` and its `StartAsync` method will be called. In this case, `StartAsync` calls `IDialogContext.Wait` with the continuation delegate (our `MessageReceivedAsync` method) to call when there is a new message. In the initial case, there is an immediate message available (the one that launched the dialog), and it is immediately passed to `MessageReceivedAsync`.

Within `MessageReceivedAsync`, we wait for the message to come in and then post our response and wait for the next message. In this simple case, the next message would again be processed by `MessageReceivedAsync`. Every time we call `IDialogContext.Wait`, our bot is suspended and can be restarted on any machine that receives the message.

If you run and test this bot, it will behave exactly like the original one from the Bot Framework template. It is a little more complicated, but it allows you to compose together multiple dialogs into complex conversations without having to explicitly manage the state.

Now, run and deploy your bot application locally and test it in the bot emulator:

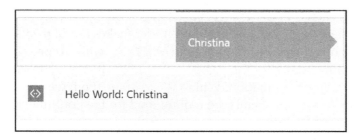

Figure 18: How to communicate with the bot using messages in the bot emulator

How to use FormFlow in the bot application

The main purpose of FormFlow is to provide more simplified, guided conversations. This gives more flexibility and avoids ambiguity in the conversation. It has helped to review the progress so far. It has limitations compared to dialogs, but in a way that requires less effort. With the combination of dialogs and LUIS dialogs, we can get the best of both worlds.

Dialogs can be are very powerful and flexible, but it can take lot of efforts in handling a guided conversation, like ordering a pizza. At any point in dialog one can contemplate various possibilities of what's next. You may be required to provide the clarification about an ambiguity, help options, go back, or display the progress.

In order to ease out the process of building the guided conversations, the framework comes with the powerful dialog building block known as **FormFlow**. Some of the flexibilities provided by dialogs is sacrificed by the FormFlow, but that is done to ease out the efforts. A combination of the FormFlow dialogs and other kinds of dialogs would prove beneficial. For example, A combination of FormFlow and LUIS dialogs could be made to get the best of both the worlds. A FormFlow dialog provides the guidance to the user in filling the form and provides guidance along the way through the conversation.

The simplest way to describe a form is through a C# class. Within a class, a field is any public field or property with one of the following types:

- Integral such as sbyte, byte, short, ushort, int, uint, long, or ulong
- Floating point such as float or double

- String
- DateTime
- Enum
- List of enums

The data types can be nullable, which provides a good way to model the field that does not have a value. If a field is not nullable and based on an enum, then the `0` value in the enum is considered to be null and it is required to start the enumeration at `1`. Any other fields, properties, or methods are ignored by the FormFlow code. It is required to create a form for the top level C# class in order to handle a list of complex objects and also one for the complex object. Forms can be composed together using the dialog system. Implementation of `Advanced.IField` or using `Advanced.Field` and populating the dictionaries within it. Makes the direct definition of the form possible. In order to better understand FormFlow and its capabilities, we will work through the following example.

Add a `HelloWorldFormFlow` C# class to your project. To add a class, right-click on your project and navigate to the **Add | Class...** option from the menu:

Figure 19: Using Visual Studio IDE to add a new class to an existing project

Replace the code in the `HelloWorldFormFlow.cs` file with the following code:

```
using Microsoft.Bot.Builder.FormFlow;
using System;
using System.Collections.Generic;
using System.Linq;
using System.Text;
using System.Threading.Tasks;

namespace Hello_World
{
    [Serializable]
    class HelloWorldFormFlow
    {
        [Prompt("Please enter name")]
        public string UserMessage;
        public static IForm<HelloWorldFormFlow> BuildForm()
        {
            OnCompletionAsyncDelegate<HelloWorldFormFlow> userMessage =
            async (context, state) =>
            {

                await context.PostAsync("Hello World:
                "+state.UserMessage);
            };
            return new FormBuilder<HelloWorldFormFlow>()
                    .Field(nameof(HelloWorldFormFlow.UserMessage))
                    .OnCompletion(userMessage)
                    .Build();
        }   };
}
```

Similar to dialogs, for FormFlow, we need to create a class and it should be serializable. Inside that class we have a method, which has a return type of IForm of the just created class itself:

```
public static IForm<HelloWorldFormFlow> BuildForm()
```

This example is a very simple one, which will just return the message by appending Hello World to the user message.

For that, we have a `FormBuilder` class that is responsible for processing the user request in the form of a flow, based on the properties defined in the `Form` class. For example, here we have defined the `UserMessage` property:

```
[Prompt("Please enter name")]
        public string UserMessage;
```

When the user sends a message to the bot, the `FormBuilder` runs the form and sends a message to the user saying **Please enter name**. This happens because in the `return` method of the `FormBuilder`, the first step is `Field` and specifies the field name. So, the `FormBuilder` knows that the field expects a string and we defined a prompt message to that field, and the bot sends that prompt message back to the user:

```
return new FormBuilder<HelloWorldFormFlow>()
                .Field(nameof(HelloWorldFormFlow.UserMessage))
```

Now, the user will respond back with the name. Finally, the `FormBuilder` will call the `OnComplete` delegate method, which will send the message to the user as `Hello World: {user message}`:

```
OnCompletionAsyncDelegate<HelloWorldFormFlow> userMessage = async (context, state) =>
            {
                await context.PostAsync("Hello World: "+state.UserMessage);
            };
```

So, it just receives the message from the user, appends the Hello World to it, and sends it back to the user:

```
.OnCompletion(userMessage)
            .Build();
```

Now, open the `MessagesController.cs` file and update the `Post` method with the following code:

```
internal static IDialog<HelloWorldFormFlow> MakeRootDialog()
        {
            return Chain.From(() =>
            FormDialog.FromForm(HelloWorldFormFlow.BuildForm));
        }
        /// <summary>
        /// POST: api/Messages
        /// Receive a message from a user and reply to it
        /// </summary>
        [ResponseType(typeof(void))]
        public async Task<HttpResponseMessage> Post([FromBody]Activity activity)
        {
            if (activity.Type == ActivityTypes.Message)
            {
                await Conversation.SendAsync(activity, MakeRootDialog);
```

```
        }
        else
        {
            HandleSystemMessage(activity);
        }
        var response = Request.CreateResponse(HttpStatusCode.OK);
        return response;
    }
```

To initiate the `FormBuilder` from your Bot Framework, we need to do two things. One is to create a static method of having the return type of `IDialog` in the `MessagesController` class, which has a functionality to initiate FormFlow using the `Chain` class:

```
internal static IDialog<HelloWorldFormFlow> MakeRootDialog()
    {
        return Chain.From(() =>
        FormDialog.FromForm(HelloWorldFormFlow.BuildForm));
    }
```

The second is to call that method from the `Post` method:

```
await Conversation.SendAsync(activity, MakeRootDialog);
```

Now, run and deploy your bot application locally and test it in the bot emulator:

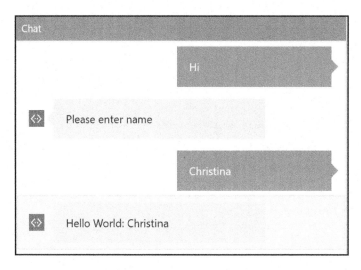

Figure 20: How to communicate with the bot using messages in the bot emulator

By default, FormFlow supports a set of commands such as **Help**, **Back**, **Quit**, **Reset**, and **Status**:

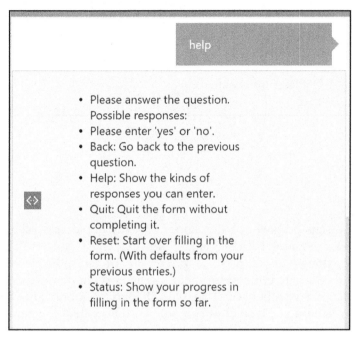

Figure 21: FormFlow commands in the bot emulator

If we type **Back** and send it to our bot, we will get the following reply:

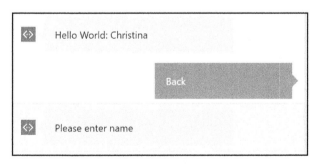

Figure 22: FormFlow commands in the bot emulator

If we type **Quit**, it stops the FormFlow. If we type **reset**, it starts FormFlow:

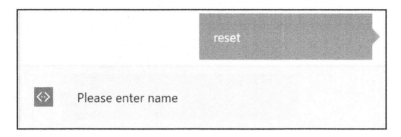

Figure 23: FormFlow commands in the bot emulator

Summary

In this chapter, we discussed how to build a bot by locally deploying a simple Hello World bot application. You also learned about Visual Studio, C# .NET, the Bot Framework, and the related technologies along with all the steps for creating projects. We also discussed the bot emulator and how it relates to bot development. In the next chapter, we will see how to develop a fully functional weather bot. Also, we will learn about how the bot communicates about the current weather in a given city. You will learn how the bot interacts with Skype or any other channel to know the current weather.

3
Developing WeatherBot Using Dialogs and LUIS

In previous chapters, we have gone through some of the concepts involved in developing and publishing bot applications. In this chapter, we will develop a bot called WeatherBot, show you how to use LUIS in dialogs and how to use third-party APIs from a bot. This involves some additional coding efforts to develop the weather bot. We will build a weather bot that is able to understand and respond to various commands, such as *What's the weather like in New York?*, *Get Weather in Seattle*, and so on. The bot will use LUIS to identify the intent of the user and reply with the appropriate message.

Before jumping into writing code, we need to configure LUIS for WeatherBot. Here, we will go through the steps on how the user gets weather data for a given location when requested by the user. We will see how LUIS can help us make the conversation between the user and your bot in more natural language, similar to how we interact with humans.

The WeatherBot will have intelligence, which will help users to interact with it, similar to how we interact with humans (in natural language). The following are some examples:

- What will the weather be like in Ashburn?
- Get weather in Seattle
- Weather in Seattle
- Hi, what is the current weather in Ashburn?

We will achieve this with the help of **Natural Language Processing** (**NLP**) using *Microsoft Cognitive Services'* LUIS.

Language Understanding Intelligent Service (LUIS)

Language Understanding Intelligent Service (**LUIS**) is one of the services in **Microsoft Cognitive Services** provided by Microsoft. As mentioned earlier, natural language is a fundamental element in developing bot applications. As a result, the technology industry has seen a direct correlation between the evolution of bot platforms and NLP platforms. Although the evolution of bot technologies has been predominantly driven by messaging platform providers such as Slack or Facebook, the main advancements in NLP technologies seem to be coming from cloud platform providers such as Microsoft. As a result, to take advantage of the NLP and **Natural Language Understanding** (**NLU**) algorithms, most bot developers spend time integrating their bot applications with NLP services provided by platforms such as LUIS from Microsoft. LUIS can process natural language using pre-built or custom-trained language models.

Microsoft's LUIS is a component of the Microsoft Cognitive Services Suite that helps in creating and processing natural language models. LUIS provides a sophisticated toolset that allows developers to develop and train the platform in new conversation models. LUIS can also be used in conjunction with other text processing APIs in the Microsoft Cognitive Services Suite, such as text analytics and many other services. The LUIS platform provides a deep integration with Microsoft Bot Framework technology and can be used by other bot platforms.

Here are some of the salient features of LUIS:

Language Understanding (LUIS)

- Create language understanding models
- Add conversational intelligence
- Pre-built, world class models (Bing & Cortana)
- Action fulfillment capabilities
- Deploy to HTTP
- Activate on any device
- Maintain with ease

Chapter 3

Let's perform the following steps to sign up for Microsoft Cognitive Services and learn how to use LUIS:

1. Go to `https://www.microsoft.com/cognitive-services` and select the **APIs** option on the home page:

2. Under the **APIs** menu, select the **Language Understanding** option:

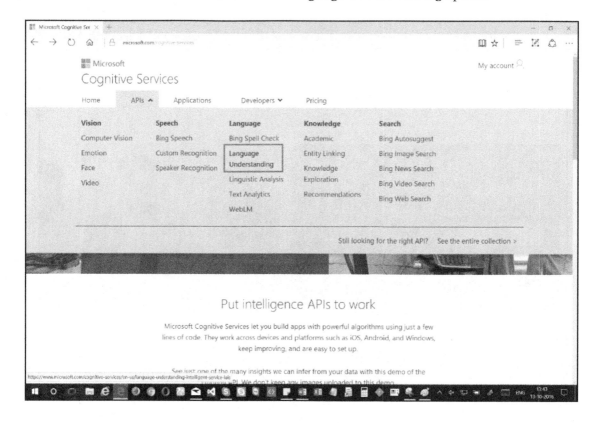

3. On the **Language Understanding Intelligent Service (LUIS)** page, click on **Get started for free**:

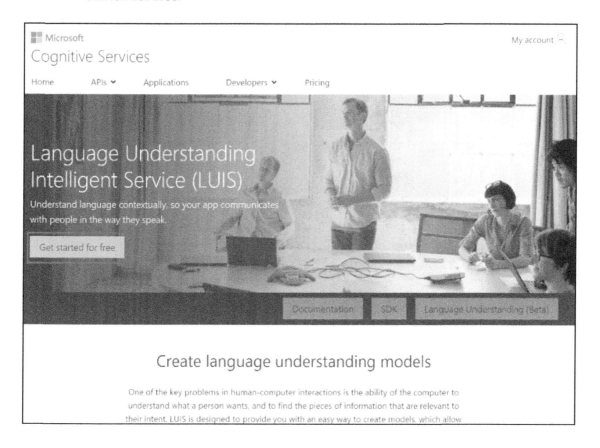

4. It will navigate to https://www.luis.ai/, the home page of LUIS. Click on **Sign in or create an account**:

5. On the **Sign In Options** popup, select **Sign in using a Microsoft account (most users)**:

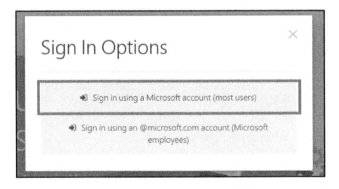

6. It will open an OAuth flow to authenticate your Microsoft account. Once you are successfully authenticated, it will ask you to grant permissions to access your profile information; click on **Yes**:

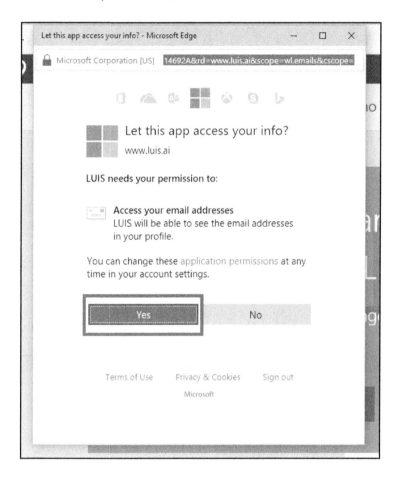

Developing WeatherBot Using Dialogs and LUIS

7. Now LUIS will ask you to give a little more information about your country and company. After entering all the required information, click on the **Continue** button:

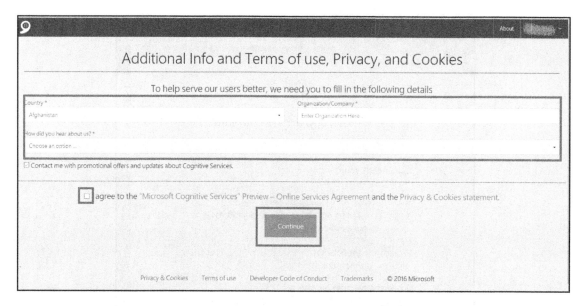

8. The following is the page where you will see all the LUIS apps, that you create:

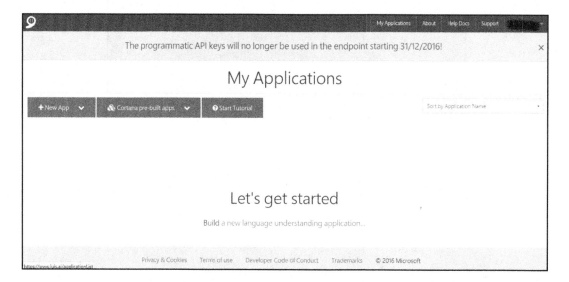

Now we are ready to create and build LUIS models. With the help of LUIS, we can build more complex NLP models, but for the weather bot, we will use basic and pre-built features. Before building your model, you should know what an Intent is and what an Entity is.

Intents and Entities

When a user enters a sentence, LUIS will interpret it and parse out the Intent and Entities. An **Intent** is an action the user wants to perform, and **Entities** are the subjects for the Intent. For example, if someone asks, *Hi, what is the current weather in Seattle?*, the Intent could be knowing weather and the entity is Seattle. Based on the complexity and requirement, you can define multiple Intents in LUIS and perform respective actions. Now, let's create an app for your WeatherBot:

1. Click on **New App**:

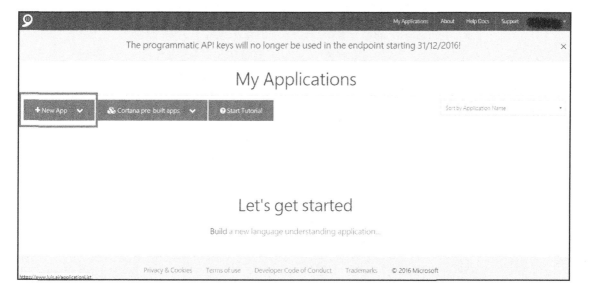

Developing WeatherBot Using Dialogs and LUIS

2. On the **New App** dropdown, select **New Application**:

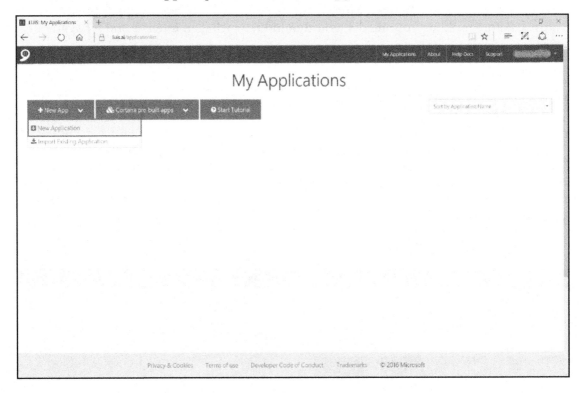

Chapter 3

3. On the **Add a new application** popup, enter the application name, the application usage scenario as **Bot**, and select the category as **Weather**:

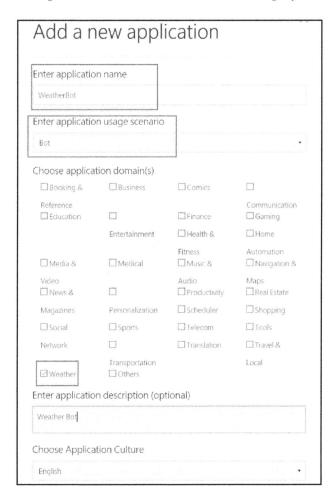

Developing WeatherBot Using Dialogs and LUIS

4. Finally, click on the **Add App** button:

5. After the successful creation of the app, open it and click on the + icon of the **Intents** section from the left-hand side menu:

6. Enter the name for your Intent and click on the **Save** button:

7. Now, add an Entity. From the left-hand side menu, click on the + icon of **Pre-built Entities**:

8. Select **geography** as the Entity:

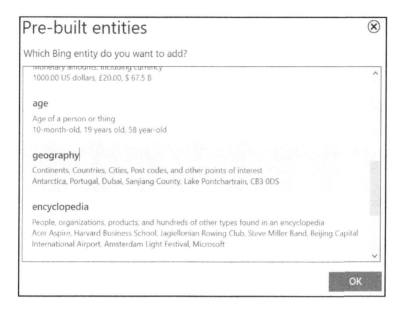

The reason why we use a pre-built entity is that LUIS already contains geography that has complete information about the locations. If you want to use a custom Entity for the location, then you have to provide all the cities/locations information to LUIS, otherwise LUIS cannot identify the location from the given sentence.

Now we have an Intent and an Entity:

Training your bot using utterances

Now you have to train your app using utterances to get the appropriate results from LUIS. An **utterance** is nothing but the sentence typed/asked by the user of your bot, such as *What is the current weather in Ashburn, Virginia?*. You have to enter as many utterances as possible with your bot.

Some examples of utterances include the following:

- What is the current weather in Ashburn, Virginia?
- Get weather in Boston
- Get weather in Miami

To train your app, you have to add different types of utterances in LUIS. Let's perform the following steps to add new utterances:

1. Select the **New utterances** section and then add the new utterance in the textbox:

2. After entering the utterance, press *Enter*. LUIS will automatically highlight the geography in your text, as shown in the following screenshot:

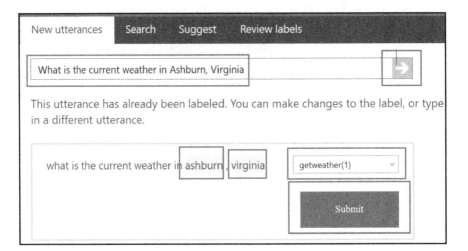

3. Before clicking on **Submit**, make sure that the sentence is identified correctly and if it shows the Intent as **getweather** or not. If the sentence is correct and is asking about the weather, then manually select the **getweather** Intent from the drop-down menu. Before submitting, check whether **geography** is highlighted or not. If not, then manually highlight it and submit.

4. Now, click on **Submit**. Repeat this for some possible combinations of statements.

5. After entering some utterances, click on the **Train** option, which is located in the bottom-left corner of the page. If you don't train your LUIS, then you will not get proper results, so make sure that you have trained every time you submit new utterances. You also have to add the minimum number of utterances to your app so that LUIS can give accurate results:

6. Now publish your LUIS app. For that, click on the **Go to Preview** option at the top of the page:

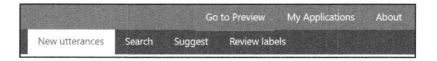

7. Then, click on the **Publish** option on the left-hand side menu. The **Publish** button is enabled only in the preview mode:

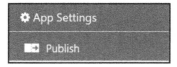

Developing WeatherBot Using Dialogs and LUIS

8. Now click on **Publish web service button/Update published application**:

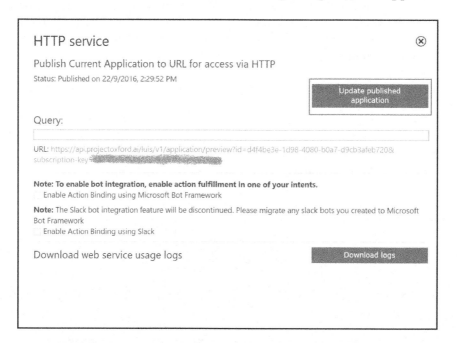

Testing your LUIS app

We need to test before using our LUIS app to make sure that it correctly identifies the Intents and Entities present in a sentence, as we configured in the preceding steps. Let's say, for example, the user typed *Get weather in Seattle*. For this sentence, the Intent knows weather information and the Entity is Seattle (**geography**). When we enter a query such as `Get weather in Seattle` in the **Query** text box and press the *Enter* button, we're redirected to another window, which displays the results shown in the following screenshot:

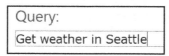

If you observe in the JSON result, the `topScoringIntent` is `getweather` and the `entity` is `seattle` of the `geography.city` type. This way, we can test before integrating LUIS into our bot:

```
{
  "query": "Get weather in Seattle",
  "topScoringIntent": {
    "intent": "getweather",
    "score": 0.9999995
  },
  "entities": [
    {
      "entity": "seattle",
      "type": "builtin.geography.city",
      "startIndex": 15,
      "endIndex": 21,
      "score": 0.9073885
    }
  ]
}
```

If the results are not as expected, then go back to the LUIS app and train it with more utterances.

Copy the URL to query and save it in a safe place; we will need it in later steps:

URL: https://api.projectoxford.ai/luis/v1/application/preview?id=d4f4be3e-1d98-4080-b0a7-d9cb3afeb720&subscription-key=...&q=

Development of WeatherBot code

We have completed setting up LUIS. Now let's develop a bot for knowing the weather of a given geography. We will also see how LUIS can help us in identifying the geography of a given sentence.

Developing WeatherBot Using Dialogs and LUIS

This guide is for C# using the Bot Framework Connector SDK .NET template:

1. Open Visual Studio and navigate to **New** | **Project**:

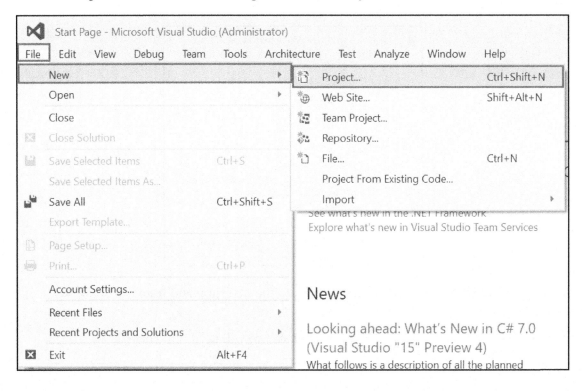

Chapter 3

2. Select **Visual C#** from the left-hand side template category. From the templates section, you will see the **Bot Application** template:

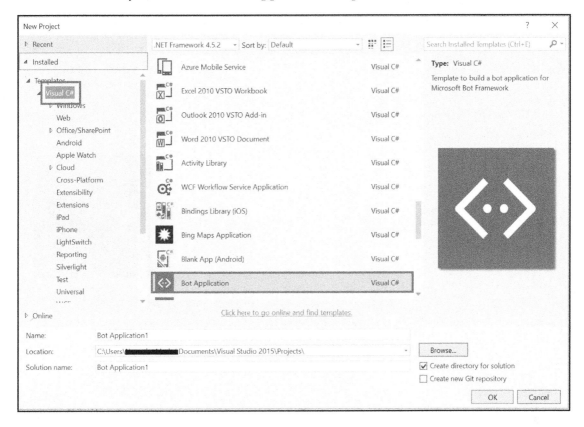

3. Select the **Bot Application** template, name the project WeatherBot, and then click on **OK**:

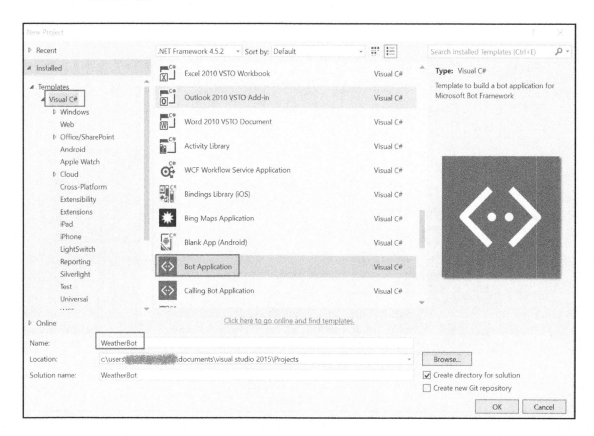

Chapter 3

4. Select the `MessagesController.cs` file, which is located under the `Controllers` folder:

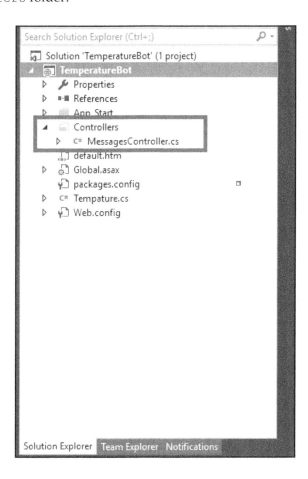

5. Update the `Post` method to call the `Dialogs`. For that, add a class called `WeatherDialog.cs` in to your solution and extend it with `IDialog`. For that, you have to right-click on your project and select **Add | Class...**:

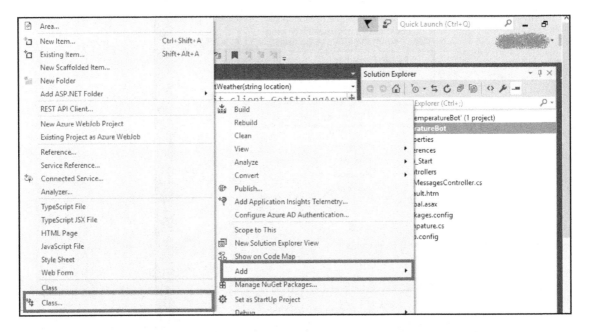

6. Extend the class with `IDialog`, implement its interface method, `StartAsync()`, and also decorate the class with a `Serializable` annotation:

```
[Serializable]
public class WeatherDialog: IDialog<object>
{
    public async Task StartAsync(IDialogContext context)
    {
        context.Wait(MessageReceivedAsync);
    }
```

Chapter 3

The core functionality of the bot template is all in the `Post` function within `Controllers\MessagesController.cs`.

In this case, the code takes the message text from the user and then creates a reply message using the `CreateReplyMessage` function. The `BotAuthentication` decoration on the method is used to validate your Bot Connector credentials over HTTPS. If you choose to operate over HTTP, you will need to remove the `BotAuthentication` decoration. Update your `Post` method in `MessagesController.cs` with the following code to call `WeatherDialog`:

```
public async Task<HttpResponseMessage> Post([FromBody]Activity
    activity)
    {
        try
        {
            ConnectorClient connector = new ConnectorClient(new
            Uri(activity.ServiceUrl));
            if (activity != null && activity.Type ==
            ActivityTypes.Message)
            {
                var text = (activity.Text).ToLower();
                await Conversation.SendAsync(activity, () => new
                WeatherDialog());
            }
            else
            {
                HandleSystemMessage(activity);
            }

            return new
            HttpResponseMessage
            (System.Net.HttpStatusCode.Accepted);
        }
        catch (Exception ex)
        {
            var content = new StringContent(ex.Message);
            var responseMessage = new HttpResponseMessage
            (System.Net.HttpStatusCode.InternalServerError);
            responseMessage.Content = content;
            return responseMessage;
        }
    }
```

[87]

Developing WeatherBot Using Dialogs and LUIS

The method is marked `async` because the Bot Builder makes use of the C# facilities for handling asynchronous communication. It returns a `Task`, which represents the task responsible for sending replies for the passed in `Message`. If there is an exception, the `Task` will contain the exception information. Within the `Post` method, we call `Conversation.SendAsync`, which is the root method for the Bot Builder SDK. It follows the dependency inversion principle and performs the following steps:

- It instantiates the required components
- It deserializes the dialog state (the dialog stack and each dialog's state) from `IBotDataStore` (the default implementation uses the Bot Connector state API as backing `IBotDataStore`)
- It resumes the conversation processes where the bot decided to suspend and wait for a message
- It sends the replies
- It serializes the updated dialog state and persists it back to `IBotDataStore`
- It awaits `Conversation.SendAsync (activity, () => new WeatherDialog());`

When your conversation first starts, there is no dialog state in `IBotDataStore`, so the delegate passed to `Conversation.SendAsync` will be used to construct a `WeatherDialog` and its `StartAsync` method will be called. In this case, `StartAsync` calls `IDialogContext.Wait` with the continuation delegate (our `MessageReceivedAsync` method) to call when there is a new message. In the initial case, there is an immediate message available (the one that launched the dialog), and it is immediately passed to `MessageReceivedAsync`:

```
public async Task StartAsync(IDialogContext context)
{
    context.Wait(MessageReceivedAsync);
}
```

Now, go to the `WeatherDialog.cs` file and generate a method for `MessageReceivedAsync` under the `StartAsync` method:

```
public async Task StartAsync(IDialogContext context)
{
    context.Wait(MessageReceivedAsync);
}
```

Within `MessageReceivedAsync`, we wait for the message to come in and then post our response and wait for the next message:

```
private async Task MessageReceivedAsync(IDialogContext context,
IAwaitable<Object> argument)
{
    context.Wait(MessageReceivedAsync);
}
```

In this simple case, the next message would again be processed by `MessageReceivedAsync`. Every time we call `IDialogContext.Wait`, our bot is suspended and can be restarted on any machine that receives the message.

Calling LUIS from the bot

To incorporate a call to LUIS, we can start by adding this function. It simply calls LUIS and returns the city, state, or country names if the message is a weather query mentioning state and country.

Create a method in the `WeatherDialog.cs` class as follows; we will call this method from the `MessageReceivedAsync` method by passing the sentence asked by the user to your bot:

```
private static async Task<string> IdentifyCityUsingLUIS(string message)
{
}
```

Now do a GET request to your LUIS app using the LUIS URL, which you saved in an earlier step, as follows:

```
var responseInString = await
httpClient.GetStringAsync(@"REPLACE_WITH_YOUR_URL_HERE&q="
        + System.Uri.EscapeDataString(message));
            dynamic response = JObject.Parse(responseInString);
```

Once you get a response from LUIS, try to parse it and identify whether the sentence contains the required Intent and Entities. For that, write the following code:

```
var intent = response.intents?.First?.intent;
            string city="",state="",country="";
            if (intent == "getweather")
            {
                foreach(var entity in response.entities)
                {
```

```
                if (entity.type == "builtin.geography.city")
                {
                    if(city=="")
                    city= entity.entity;
                    else
                    {
                        if(city==state)
                        {
                            city = entity.entity;
                        }
                        else if(entity.entity == state)
                        {

                        }
                    }
                }
                else if (entity?.type ==
                "builtin.geography.us_state")
                {
                    state= entity.entity;
                }
                else if (entity?.type ==
                "builtin.geography.country")
                {
                    country= entity.entity;
                }

        }
        if (city != "" && state != "" && country != "")
            return city + "," + state + "," + country;
        else if(city != "" && state != "")
            return city + "," + state;
        else if (city != "" && country != "")
            return city + "," + country;
        else if (state != "" && country != "")
            return state + "," + country;
        else if (city != "")
            return city;
        else if (state != "")
            return state;
        else if (country != "")
            return country;
        else
            return null;
    }
```

Now update your `MessageReceivedAsync` method to call the just created method and receive the city information from it:

```
private async Task MessageReceivedAsync(IDialogContext context,
IAwaitable<Object> argument)
    {
        var activity = await argument as Activity;
        string queryText = activity.Text;
        var locationInfo = await IdentifyCityUsingLUIS(queryText);
        context.Wait(MessageReceivedAsync);
    }
}
```

Now we have the location information with the help of LUIS; we will get the weather information for the identified location with the help of the Weather API.

Calling the Weather API

There are many APIs available for getting weather information for a given city. As of now, we'll use Weather Underground.

Before using it, we'll need an API key. So, sign up for a free account to get a key from Weather Underground at `https://www.wunderground.com/`.

Now that we have an API key, add the following method in the `WeatherDialog` class:

```
private static async Task<dynamic> GetCurrentWeatherUsingAPI(string
    location)
        {
            using (var client = new HttpClient())
            {
                try
                {
                    var escapedLocation = Regex.Replace(location,
                    @"\W+", "_");
                    var jsonString = await
                    client.GetStringAsync($"http://api.wunderground.com
                    /api/ENTER_YOUR_KEY_HERE/conditions/q/
                    {escapedLocation}.json");
                    dynamic response = JObject.Parse(jsonString);

                    dynamic observation = response.current_observation;
                    dynamic results = response.response.results;

                    if (observation != null)
                    {
                        return observation;
```

Developing WeatherBot Using Dialogs and LUIS

```
                    }
                    else if (results != null)
                    {
                        return null;
                    }
                }
                catch (Exception ex)
                {
                }

                return null;
            }
        }
```

This gets the current weather for the specified city as a string. If the API indicates that the city is ambiguous (it returns multiple results), the bot informs the message to the user. If there is an issue, the bot returns null.

Now update your `MessageReceivedAsync` method and call the `GetCurrentWeatherUsingAPI` method by passing the location for the one we got from the LUIS method:

```
    private async Task MessageReceivedAsync(IDialogContext context,
        IAwaitable<Object> argument)
        {
            var activity = await argument as Activity;
            string queryText = activity.Text;
            var locationInfo = await IdentifyCityUsingLUIS(queryText);
            var currentObservation = await
            GetCurrentWeatherUsingAPI(locationInfo);
            string displayLocation =
            currentObservation.display_location?.full;
            decimal tempC = currentObservation.temp_c;
            string weather = currentObservation.weather;
            var weatherInfo = $"It is {weather} and {tempC} degrees
            in {displayLocation}.";
            string icon = currentObservation.icon;
            context.Wait(MessageReceivedAsync);
        }
```

From the Weather API, we will get `currentObservation` of a city/location.

Using cards

Now we know the weather information of a city/location in the `currentObservation` variable; to display the information to your user on a channel in rich UI, we have **cards** in the Bot Builder.

To display weather information in the cards, we will go through the steps on how to use thumbnail cards, as the following describes.

The **thumbnail card** is a multipurpose card; it primarily hosts a single small image, a button, and a `tap action`, along with text content to display on the card. The following is sample code on how to create a thumbnail card:

```
List<CardImage> cardImages = new List<CardImage>();
            cardImages.Add(new CardImage(url:
            "http://icons.wxug.com/i/c/g/" + icon + ".gif"));
            ThumbnailCard plCard = new ThumbnailCard()
            {
                Text = weatherInfo,
                Title = "Current Weather",
                Images = cardImages,

            };
            Attachment plAttachment = plCard.ToAttachment();
```

After creating a thumbnail card, we need to pass it as an `Attachment` in the `Activity` reply, as follows:

```
Activity replyToConversation = activity.CreateReply($"Weather report in
{locationInfo} is");
replyToConversation.Type = "message";
replyToConversation.Attachments = new List<Attachment>();
replyToConversation.Attachments.Add(plAttachment);
```

Using all the concepts explained in this chapter, the following is the code we will write in the `MessageReceivedAsync` method so that a bot can communicate the weather to the users:

```
private async Task MessageReceivedAsync(IDialogContext context,
   IAwaitable<Object> argument)
        {
            var activity = await argument as Activity;
            string queryText = activity.Text;
            var locationInfo = await IdentifyCityUsingLUIS(queryText);
            var currentObservation = await
            GetCurrentWeatherUsingAPI(locationInfo);
```

```csharp
            if (currentObservation != null)
            {
                string displayLocation =
                currentObservation.display_location?.full;
                decimal tempC = currentObservation.temp_c;
                string weather = currentObservation.weather;
                var weatherInfo = $"It is {weather} and {tempC} degrees
                in {displayLocation}.";
                string icon = currentObservation.icon;
                //string rfc822DateTime =
                currentObservation.observation_time_rfc822;
                //var observationTime = DateTime.Parse(rfc822DateTime);
                //var dayOrNight = observationTime.Hour;

                Activity replyToConversation =
                activity.CreateReply($"Weather report in {locationInfo}
                is");
                replyToConversation.Type = "message";
                replyToConversation.Attachments = new List<Attachment>
                ();
                List<CardImage> cardImages = new List<CardImage>();
                cardImages.Add(new CardImage(url:
                "http://icons.wxug.com/i/c/g/" + icon + ".gif"));
                ThumbnailCard plCard = new ThumbnailCard()
                {
                    Text = weatherInfo,
                    Title = "Current Weather",
                    Images = cardImages,

                };
                Attachment plAttachment = plCard.ToAttachment();
                replyToConversation.Attachments.Add(plAttachment);
                await context.PostAsync(replyToConversation);
            }
            else
            {
                await context.PostAsync($"There is more than one
                '{locationInfo}'. Can you be more specific?");
            }
            context.Wait(MessageReceivedAsync);
}
```

Run the WeatherBot and test it in the emulator. You will have output as follows:

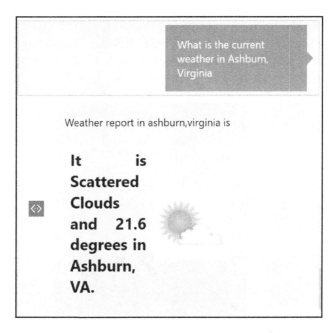

Natural speech and Intent processing bot using Microsoft Cognitive Services

As LUIS is a new concept, we will go through one more project to understand the concepts better. This project is for understanding how to use **Cortana Intelligence Services** and **Rich Text Messaging** technology. This bot identifies the concepts and actions in the text that is sent to the bot with part-of-speech tagging, finds phrases and concepts using natural language parsers, and returns all the identified Intents, which are created and trained in the custom LUIS app. For example, if you say *Hi John, am going to New York tonight*, the bot will return part-of-speech tagging as well as parsing data for natural speech and Intent processing to know the name and location:

- Name: John
- Place: New York

Developing WeatherBot Using Dialogs and LUIS

Whether you're mining customer feedback, interpreting user commands, or consuming web text, understanding the structure of the text is a critical first step, and this chapter teaches you that. Before starting the tutorial, you should know about Microsoft Cognitive Services (**Cortana Intelligence Services**), which helps you to build applications using very complex and powerful algorithms just using a few lines of code. You can build applications for any platform and they are easy to configure. It's free to sign up, and it also has paid plans which are currently in preview:

1. To sign up, go to Microsoft Cognitive Services (`https://www.microsoft.com/cognitive-services/en-us/`) and click on the **Get started for free** button on the page:

2. On the next page, click on the **Let's go** button:

3. Alternatively, you can also click on the **My account** option on the right-top side of the page and log in using your Microsoft account:

    My account

4. After a successful sign-in, you have to subscribe each and every API individually by checking the check box of each API. Select all and click on the **Subscribe** option. Now you are ready to use Cognitive Services:

My free subscriptions (15)   Request new trials

Product	Description	Keys	State	Created	Quota		
Recommendations - Preview	10,000 transactions per month.	Key 1: XXXXXXXXXXXXXXXXXXXXXXXXX Regenerate | Show | Copy Key 2: XXXXXXXXXXXXXXXXXXXXXXXXX Regenerate | Show | Copy	active	6/4/2016 7:01:59 PM	Show Quota	Buy On Azure	Cancel
Text Analytics - Preview	5,000 transactions per month.	Key 1: XXXXXXXXXXXXXXXXXXXXXXXXX Regenerate | Show | Copy Key 2: XXXXXXXXXXXXXXXXXXXXXXXXX Regenerate | Show | Copy	active	6/4/2016 7:01:59 PM	Show Quota	Buy On Azure	Cancel
Academic - Preview	10,000 transactions per month, 3 per second for interpret, 1 per second for evaluate, 6 per minute for calcHistogram.	Key 1: XXXXXXXXXXXXXXXXXXXXXXXXX Regenerate | Show | Copy Key 2: XXXXXXXXXXXXXXXXXXXXXXXXX Regenerate | Show | Copy	active	6/4/2016 7:01:58 PM	Show Quota	Buy On Azure	Cancel

5. Open Visual Studio, click on **New** | **Project...**, and select **Visual C#** from the left-hand side template category. From the templates section, you will see the **Bot Application** template:

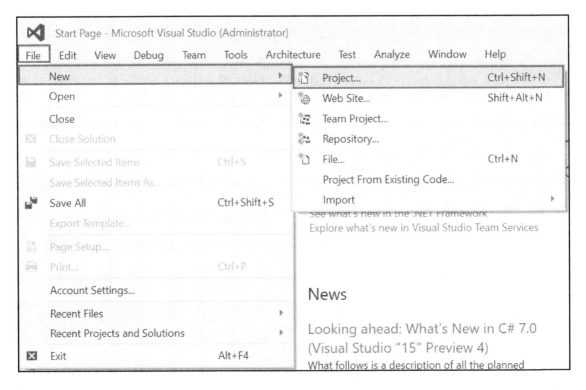

6. Select the **Bot Application** template, name the project `IntentProcessing`, and then click on **OK**:

Chapter 3

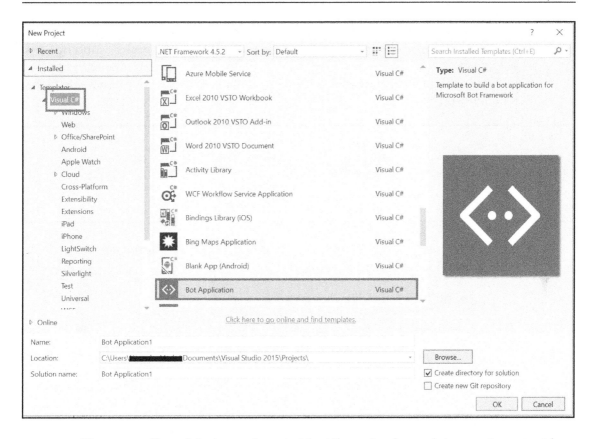

Here, we will explain to you how to identify parts of speech in a sentence sent by a user to a bot. For this, we will use Cognitive Services. In Cognitive Services, we have the **Linguistic Analysis API**, which is responsible for knowing the structure of a sentence.

As mentioned on the Microsoft Azure website, *The Linguistic API uses advanced linguistic analysis tools for NLP, giving you access to part-of-speech tagging and parsing. These tools allow you to hone in on important concepts and actions.*

The API can tap into traditional linguistic analysis tools that allow you to identify the concepts and actions in your text with part-of-speech tagging, and find phrases and concepts using natural language parsers. Whether you're mining customer feedback, interpreting user commands, or consuming web text, understanding the structure of the text is a critical first step.

For more details on the preceding information, please refer: https://www.microsoft.com/cognitive-services/en-us/linguistic-analysis-api

[99]

Now we will use the Linguistic Analysis API in our bot to *identify the parts of speech* in a sentence entered by the user. Go to the Cognitive Services subscriptions page (https://www.microsoft.com/cognitive-services/en-us/subscriptions), under the Linguistic Analysis API section, copy the key, and save it in a safe place for later use:

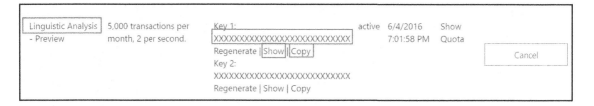

7. Go back to the `IntentProcessing` solution in Visual Studio and add the following helper classes in to your solution:

   - Add the following code in `Analyzer.cs`:

     ```
     public class Analyzer
     {
         /// <summary>
         /// Unique identifier for this analyzer used to
         communicate with the service
         /// </summary>
         public Guid Id { get; set; }

         /// <summary>
         /// List of two letter ISO language codes for which
         this analyzer is available. e.g. "en" represents
         "English"
         /// </summary>
         public string[] Languages { get; set; }

         /// <summary>
         /// Description of the type of analysis used here,
         such
         as Constituency_Tree or POS_tags.
         /// </summary>
         public string Kind { get; set; }

         /// <summary>
         /// The specification for how a human should
         produce ideal output for this task. Most use the
         specification from the Penn Teeebank.
     ```

```csharp
/// </summary>
public string Specification { get; set; }
/// <summary>
/// Description of the implementation used in this
analyzer.
/// </summary>
public string Implementation { get; set; }
}
```

- Add the following code in `AnalyzerTextRequest.cs`:

```csharp
public class AnalyzeTextRequest
    {
        /// <summary>
        /// Two letter ISO language code, e.g. "en" for
        "English"
        /// </summary>
        public string Language { get; set; }

        /// <summary>
        /// List of IDs of the analyzers to be used on the
        given input text; see Analyzer for more
        information.
        /// </summary>
        public Guid[] AnalyzerIds { get; set; }

        /// <summary>
        /// The raw input text to be analyzed.
        /// </summary>
        public string Text { get; set; }
    }

AnalyzeTextResults
public class AnalyzeTextResult
    {
        /// <summary>
        /// The unique ID of the analyzer; see Analyzer
        for more information.
        /// </summary>
        public Guid AnalyzerId { get; set; }

        /// <summary>
        /// The resulting analysis, encoded as JSON. See
        the documentation for the relevant analyzer kind
        for more information on formatting.
        /// </summary>
        public object Result { get; set; }
    }
```

- Add the following code in `JsonConversionClasses.cs`:

```csharp
public class RootObject
{
    public string analyzerId { get; set; }
    public List<object> result { get; set; }
}

public class Token
{
    public int Len { get; set; }
    public string NormalizedToken { get; set; }
    public int Offset { get; set; }
    public string RawToken { get; set; }
}

public class TokenRootObject
{
    public int Len { get; set; }
    public int Offset { get; set; }
    public List<Token> Tokens { get; set; }
}

public class Tree
{
    public List<string> Nodes { get; set; }
}

public class Intent
{
    public string intent { get; set; }
    public double score { get; set; }
}

public class Entity
{
    public string entity { get; set; }
    public string type { get; set; }
    public int startIndex { get; set; }
    public int endIndex { get; set; }
    public double score { get; set; }
}

public class LuisResponse
{
    public string query { get; set; }
    public List<Intent> intents { get; set; }
    public List<Entity> entities { get; set; }
```

Chapter 3

```
            }
            enum EtityType
            {
                Location,
                Name,
                Company
            }
```

8. Now open the `MessagesController.cs` class file. Add the following required variables in the class level, which are used while calling the Linguistic API:

```
#region private members

/// <summary>
/// The Default Service Host
/// </summary>
private const string DefaultServiceHost =
"https://api.projectoxford.ai/linguistics/v1.0";

/// <summary>
/// The JSON content type header.
/// </summary>
private const string JsonContentTypeHeader =
"application/json";

/// <summary>
/// The subscription key name.
/// </summary>
private const string SubscriptionKeyName = "ocp-apim-
subscription-key";

/// <summary>
/// The ListAnalyzers.
/// </summary>
private const string ListAnalyzersQuery = "analyzers";

/// <summary>
/// The AnalyzeText.
/// </summary>
private const string AnalyzeTextQuery = "analyze";

/// <summary>
/// The default resolver.
/// </summary>
private static readonly CamelCasePropertyNamesContractResolver
defaultResolver = new CamelCasePropertyNamesContractResolver();
```

```
/// <summary>
/// The settings
/// </summary>
private static readonly JsonSerializerSettings settings = new
JsonSerializerSettings()
{
    DateFormatHandling = DateFormatHandling.IsoDateFormat,
    NullValueHandling = NullValueHandling.Ignore,
    ContractResolver = defaultResolver
};

/// <summary>
/// The service host.
/// </summary>
private string serviceHost;

/// <summary>
/// The HTTP client
/// </summary>
private HttpClient httpClient;

#endregion
```

9. `DefaultServiceHost` is just API URL. `Analyzers` are used to analyze the text in all available analyzer formats. `SubscriptionKeyName` is just the HTTP header key name, which we will mention in HTTP `DefaultRequestHeaders`, with the value as your Linguistic API key.

10. Next, create the `HttpClient` object and set the `DefaultRequestHeader` as shown:

    ```
    httpClient = new HttpClient();

    httpClient.DefaultRequestHeaders.Add(SubscriptionKeyName,
    "ENTER_YOUR_LINGUISTIC_API_KEY");
    ```

11. Next, get all analyzers supported by the API by requesting the Linguistic API, as follows:

    ```
    // List analyzers
    Analyzer[] supportedAnalyzers = null;
    try
    {
        var requestUrl = $"
        {this.serviceHost}/{ListAnalyzersQuery}";

        supportedAnalyzers = await SendRequestAsync<object,
    ```

```
            Analyzer[]>(HttpMethod.Get, requestUrl);
            var analyzersAsJson =
            JsonConvert.SerializeObject(supportedAnalyzers,
            Formatting.Indented, jsonSerializerSettings);
            //Console.WriteLine("Supported analyzers: " +
            analyzersAsJson);
        }
        catch (Exception e)
        {
            //Console.Error.WriteLine("Failed to list supported
            analyzers: " + e.ToString());
            Environment.Exit(1);
        }
```

12. Each analyzer name contains four parts: ID, kind, a specification, and an implementation. We use the ID for identifying each analyzer. Next, each analyzer is a kind. This defines in very broad terms the type of analysis returned and should uniquely define the data structure used to represent that analysis.

13. Next, create an `AnalyzeTextRequest` by passing all supported analyzer IDs and the sentence sent by the user to it:

```
    // Analyze text with all available analyzers
        var analyzeTextRequest = new AnalyzeTextRequest()
        {
            Language = "en",
            AnalyzerIds = supportedAnalyzers.Select(analyzer =>
            analyzer.Id).ToArray(),
            Text = messagetext
        };
```

14. Next, send a request to the Linguistic API to analyze the sentence by passing the `AnalyzeTextRequest`:

```
object in request body.
try
    {
        var requestUrl = $"
        {this.serviceHost}/{AnalyzeTextQuery}";

        var analyzeTextResults = await
        this.SendRequestAsync<object, AnalyzeTextResult[]>
        (HttpMethod.Post, requestUrl, analyzeTextRequest);

        resultsAsJson =
        JsonConvert.SerializeObject(analyzeTextResults,
        Formatting.Indented, jsonSerializerSettings);
```

Developing WeatherBot Using Dialogs and LUIS

```
            //Console.WriteLine("Analyze text results: " +
            resultsAsJson);
            var insightproperties = new Dictionary<string, string>
            { {"Page Name","MessagesController" }, {"Method
            Name","Post" },
            { "Session Id",telemetry.Context.Session.Id }, {"Json
            Result",resultsAsJson } };

            telemetry.TrackEvent("Post Event Views",
            insightproperties);
        }
        catch (Exception e)
        {
            //Console.Error.WriteLine("Failed to list supported
            analyzers: " + e.ToString());
            Environment.Exit(1);
        }
```

15. The following is the code for sending a request to the Linguistic API:

```
private async Task<TResponse> SendRequestAsync<TRequest,
TResponse>(HttpMethod httpMethod, string requestUrl, TRequest
requestBody = default(TRequest))
    {
        var request = new HttpRequestMessage(httpMethod,
        requestUrl);
        if (requestBody != null)
        {
            request.Content = new
            StringContent(JsonConvert.SerializeObject(requestBody,
            settings), Encoding.UTF8, JsonContentTypeHeader);
        }

        HttpResponseMessage response = await
        httpClient.SendAsync(request);
        if (response.IsSuccessStatusCode)
        {
            string responseContent = null;
            if (response.Content != null)
            {
                responseContent = await
                response.Content.ReadAsStringAsync();
            }

            if (!string.IsNullOrWhiteSpace(responseContent))
            {
                return JsonConvert.DeserializeObject<TResponse>
                (responseContent, settings);
```

```
            }

            return default(TResponse);
        }
        else
        {
            if (response.Content != null &&
            response.Content.Headers.ContentType
            .MediaType.Contains(JsonContentTypeHeader))
            {
                var errorObjectString = await
                response.Content.ReadAsStringAsync();
                ClientError errorCollection =
                JsonConvert.DeserializeObject<ClientError>
                (errorObjectString);
                if (errorCollection != null)
                {
                    throw new ClientException(errorCollection,
                    response.StatusCode);
                }
            }

            response.EnsureSuccessStatusCode();
        }

        return default(TResponse);
    }
```

16. After getting a response from the API, deserialize it:

    ```
    var data = JsonConvert.DeserializeObject<List<RootObject>>
    (resultsAsJson);
    ```

In response, you will get all the supported analyzer's results. These include tokens, POS tags, and the constituency tree:

- **Tokens**: In the first step of analysis, Linguistic will separate sentences and tokens. The next task is to break sentences in to tokens. By default, English tokens are *delimited* by *white space*. In the first step, punctuation should often be split away from the surrounding context. Secondly, English has contractions, such as *didn't* or *it's*, where words have been compressed and abbreviated into smaller pieces. The goal of the tokenizer is to break the character sequence into words.

- **Parts-of-speech tags**: After the separation of sentences and tokens, the next step is to identify parts-of-speech.
- **Constituency parsing (tree)**: The purpose of constituency parsing is to identify phrases. This helps to identify the key phrases from a large given text. To a linguist, a phrase is more than just a sequence of words. To be a phrase, a group of words has to come together to play a specific role in the sentence. That group of words can be moved together or replaced as a whole, and the sentence should remain fluent and grammatical.

The result of the parsing will look as shown here:

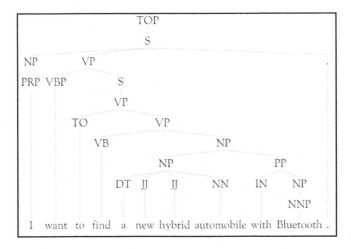

17. From the response, you will get all three lists. The following is the code for that:

```
var jsonTreeList = data[0].result.ToArray();
    string jsonTree = jsonTreeList.Count() > 0 ? "{Nodes:"
+ jsonTreeList[0].ToString() + "}" : null;
//jsonTree = "{Nodes:" + jsonTree;
var posTags = JsonConvert.DeserializeObject<Tree>
(jsonTree);

    var jsonTreeView = data[1].result.ToArray();

    var tokenList = data[2].result.ToArray();
for (int i = 0; i < posTags.Nodes.Count; i++)
    {
        if (posTags.Nodes[i] == "NNP")
        {
```

```
            botOutputString += tokenData.Tokens[i].RawToken
            + " is Noun" + " \r \n";
        }
        else if (posTags.Nodes[i] == "VBG" ||
        posTags.Nodes[i] == "VB")
        {
            botOutputString += tokenData.Tokens[i].RawToken
            + " is Verb" + " \r \n";
        }
        else if (posTags.Nodes[i] == "WRB")
        {
            botOutputString += tokenData.Tokens[i].RawToken
            + " is Adverb" + " \r \n";
        }
        else if (posTags.Nodes[i] == "WP")
        {
            botOutputString += tokenData.Tokens[i].RawToken
            + " is Pronoun" + " \r \n";
        }
        else if (posTags.Nodes[i] == "JJ" ||
        posTags.Nodes[i] == "JJR" || posTags.Nodes[i] ==
        "JJS")
        {
            botOutputString += tokenData.Tokens[i].RawToken
            + " is Adjective" + " \r \n";
        }
        else if (posTags.Nodes[i] == "IN")
        {
            botOutputString += tokenData.Tokens[i].RawToken
            + " is Preposition" + " \r \n";
        }
}

botOutputString = botOutputString != "" ? "Speech and
Natural Language Processing \r \n" + botOutputString :
"";
```

Developing WeatherBot Using Dialogs and LUIS

Identifying the name of a person, place, and company using LUIS

Now we will create a custom LUIS app to return all the identified Intents that are created and trained. For example, if you say *Hi John, am going to New York tonight*, the LUIS app will return natural speech and intent processing to know the name, location, and other things, such as John as name and New York as place:

1. After logging into LUIS in `luis.ai`, create an app for your `IntentProcessing`. To do that, click on **New App** and select **New Application**:

2. Enter the application's name, the usage as `Bot`, and select the category. Finally, click on the **Add App** button:

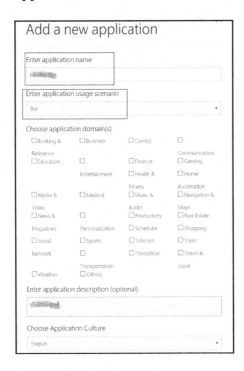

Chapter 3

3. After successful creation of the app, open it and click on the **+** icon of the **Intents** section from the left-hand side of the menu:

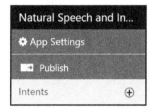

4. Enter the name for your Intent and click on the **Save** button:

5. Now add a custom entity from the left-hand side menu, click on the + icon of the Entity, and enter the name:

6. Repeat the preceding step for Entity `Company`:

7. Now add an Entity. From the left-hand side menu, click on the **+** icon of **Pre-Built Entities**:

8. Select **geography** as the Entity:

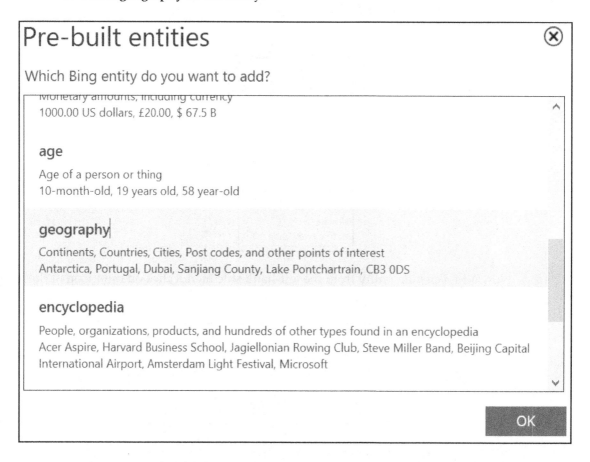

9. The reason why we use the pre-built Entity is that LUIS already contains geography, which has complete information about the locations. If you want to use a custom Entity for the location, then you will have to provide all the cities/locations information to LUIS, otherwise LUIS cannot identify the location from the given sentence.

10. Now we have an Intent and an Entity:

Training your app

Now you have to train your app using utterances to get the appropriate results from LUIS.

Some examples of utterances include the following:

- I am John living in Ashburn, Virginia and working at Microsoft
- Jim lives in Princeton, New Jersey and works at Google

Developing WeatherBot Using Dialogs and LUIS

Go through the training process as we explained in previous sections:

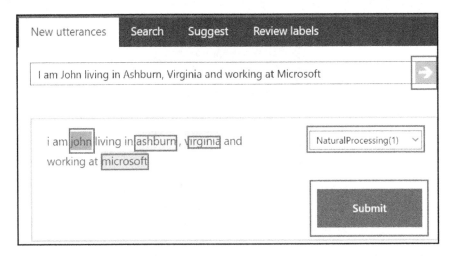

Before clicking on **Submit**, make sure that the sentence is identified correctly and shows the Intent as `NaturalProcessing(my intent name)`. If the name did not get highlighted, then manually click on the name. It will open a popup; select **Name** as the Entity. For example, here in my case, **john** was not highlighted by default, so I selected it manually and clicked on the **Name** Intent. The same applies for the company as well:

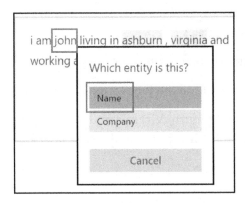

Chapter 3

Now publish your LUIS. Click on the **Publish** option on the left-hand side menu:

Now click on the **Publish web service/Update published application**:

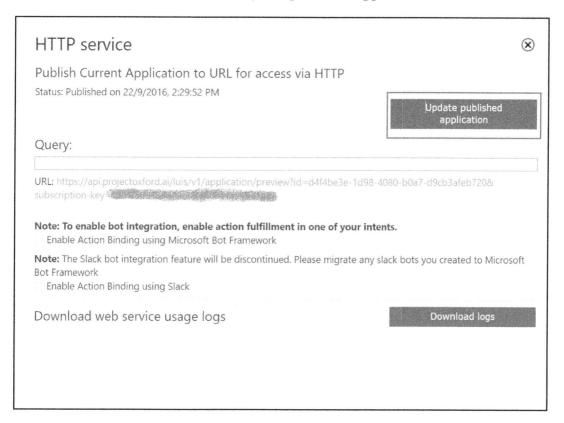

Copy the URL up to query and save it in a safe place. We will need it for later steps:

URL: https://api.projectoxford.ai/luis/v1/application/preview?id=d4f4be3e-1d98-4080-b0a7-d9cb3afeb720&
subscription-key=███████████████████████&q=

[115]

Now come back to Visual Studio, open the `MessagesController.cs` file and, under the `Post` method, write the code to get the LUIS results:

Calling LUIS from the bot

To incorporate a call to LUIS, we can start by adding this function. It simply calls LUIS and returns the phrases identified by LUIS, such as name, city, company name, and so on.

Place your LUIS app endpoint URL, which you copied from the preceding step, in to the following variable in your code:

```
var luisRequestURL =
"https://api.projectoxford.ai/luis/v1/application?id=
fbec04e7-8bda-4160-a059-a8f8b995184b&subscription-
key=ENTER_KEY_HERE";
```

Next, append the user message, which we get from the user to the `luisRequestUrl` and do a `Get` request:

```
httpClient = new HttpClient();
HttpResponseMessage response = await
httpClient.GetAsync(luisRequestURL + "&q=" + messagetext);

string luisResponseString = await
response.Content.ReadAsStringAsync();
```

Deserialize the LUIS response and parse it to identify the Intents and Entities:

```
            var luisResponse =
            JsonConvert.DeserializeObject<LuisResponse>
            (luisResponseString);

            if (luisResponse.entities.Count > 0)
            {
                foreach (var entity in luisResponse.entities)
                {
                    if (entity.type.Contains("geography"))
                    {
                        if(!luisOutputString.ToLower().
                        Contains(entity.entity.ToLower()))
                        luisOutputString +=
                        entity.type.Replace("builtin.geography.", "")+"
                        : " + entity.entity + " \r \n";
                    }
```

```
                    else if (entity.type == "Name")
                    {
                        luisOutputString += "Name: " + entity.entity +
                        " \r \n";
                    }
                    else if (entity.type == "Company")
                    {
                        luisOutputString += "Company: " + entity.entity
                        + " \r \n";
                    }
                    else
                    {
                        luisOutputString += entity.type + " " +
                        entity.entity + " \r \n";
                    }
                }
            }
            else
            {
                luisOutputString = "No matching found for Intent and
                Language Understanding Intelligence Service
                Processing";
            }

            if (botOutputString == "")
            {
                botOutputString = "No matching found for Natural Speech
                and Intent Processing";
            }
```

The complete code of the Post method will be as follows:

```
public async Task<Message> Post([FromBody]Message message)
    {
        var properties = new Dictionary<string, string> { {"Page
        Name","MessagesController" }, {"Method Name","Post" },
        { "Session Id",telemetry.Context.Session.Id }, {"User
        Spoken Message Json",message.ToString() } };

        telemetry.TrackEvent("Post Event Views", properties);

        string messagetext = message.Text;
        var aiproperties = new Dictionary<string, string> { {"Page
        Name","MessagesController" }, {"Method Name","Post" },
        { "Session Id",telemetry.Context.Session.Id }, {"User
        Spoken Message",messagetext } };
```

```csharp
telemetry.TrackEvent("Post Event Views", aiproperties);

string resultsAsJson = "", botOutputString = "";
this.serviceHost = string.IsNullOrWhiteSpace(serviceHost) ?
DefaultServiceHost : serviceHost.Trim();

httpClient = new HttpClient();
httpClient.DefaultRequestHeaders.Add(SubscriptionKeyName,
"b7ba08bf576747728ad0a74af2d5718f");

// List analyzers
Analyzer[] supportedAnalyzers = null;
try
{
    var requestUrl = $"
    {this.serviceHost}/{ListAnalyzersQuery}";

    supportedAnalyzers = await SendRequestAsync<object,
    Analyzer[]>(HttpMethod.Get, requestUrl);
    var analyzersAsJson =
    JsonConvert.SerializeObject(supportedAnalyzers,
    Formatting.Indented, jsonSerializerSettings);
    //Console.WriteLine("Supported analyzers: " +
    analyzersAsJson);
}
catch (Exception e)
{
    //Console.Error.WriteLine("Failed to list supported
    analyzers: " + e.ToString());
    Environment.Exit(1);
}

// Analyze text with all available analyzers
var analyzeTextRequest = new AnalyzeTextRequest()
{
    Language = "en",
    AnalyzerIds = supportedAnalyzers.Select(analyzer =>
    analyzer.Id).ToArray(),
    Text = messagetext
};

try
{
    var requestUrl = $"
    {this.serviceHost}/{AnalyzeTextQuery}";

    var analyzeTextResults = await
    this.SendRequestAsync<object, AnalyzeTextResult[]>
```

```csharp
            (HttpMethod.Post, requestUrl, analyzeTextRequest);

        resultsAsJson =
        JsonConvert.SerializeObject(analyzeTextResults,
        Formatting.Indented, jsonSerializerSettings);

        //Console.WriteLine("Analyze text results: " +
        resultsAsJson);

    }
    catch (Exception e)
    {
        //Console.Error.WriteLine("Failed to list supported
        analyzers: " + e.ToString());
        Environment.Exit(1);
    }

    var data = JsonConvert.DeserializeObject<List<RootObject>>
    (resultsAsJson);

    if (data.Count == 3)
    {
        var jsonTreeList = data[0].result.ToArray();
        string jsonTree = jsonTreeList.Count() > 0 ? "{Nodes:"
        + jsonTreeList[0].ToString() + "}" : null;
        //jsonTree = "{Nodes:" + jsonTree;
        var posTags = JsonConvert.DeserializeObject<Tree>
        (jsonTree);


        var jsonTreeView = data[1].result.ToArray();

        var tokenList = data[2].result.ToArray();
        string tokenJson = tokenList.Count() > 0 ?
        tokenList[0].ToString() : null;
        var tokenData =
        JsonConvert.DeserializeObject<TokenRootObject>
        (tokenJson);

        for (int i = 0; i < posTags.Nodes.Count; i++)
        {
            if (posTags.Nodes[i] == "NNP")
            {

                botOutputString += tokenData.Tokens[i].RawToken
                + " is Noun" + " \r \n";
            }
            else if (posTags.Nodes[i] == "VBG" ||
```

```csharp
                posTags.Nodes[i] == "VB")
                {
                    botOutputString += tokenData.Tokens[i].RawToken
                    + " is Verb" + " \r \n";
                }
                else if (posTags.Nodes[i] == "WRB")
                {
                    botOutputString += tokenData.Tokens[i].RawToken
                    + " is Adverb" + " \r \n";
                }
                else if (posTags.Nodes[i] == "WP")
                {
                    botOutputString += tokenData.Tokens[i].RawToken
                    + " is Pronoun" + " \r \n";
                }
                else if (posTags.Nodes[i] == "JJ" ||
                posTags.Nodes[i] == "JJR" || posTags.Nodes[i] ==
                "JJS")
                {
                    botOutputString += tokenData.Tokens[i].RawToken
                    + " is Adjective" + " \r \n";
                }
                else if (posTags.Nodes[i] == "IN")
                {
                    botOutputString += tokenData.Tokens[i].RawToken
                    + " is Preposition" + " \r \n";
                }
            }

            botOutputString = botOutputString != "" ? "Speech and
            Natural Language Processing \r \n" + botOutputString :
            "";

            var insightproperties = new Dictionary<string, string>
            { {"Page Name","MessagesController" }, {"Method
            Name","Post" },
            { "Session Id",telemetry.Context.Session.Id }, {"Result
            From Linguistic API",botOutputString } };

            telemetry.TrackEvent("Post Event Views",
            insightproperties);

    }
    else
    {
        botOutputString = "";
    }
```

```csharp
//To identify name of a person, place and Company - Using
LUIS
var luisOutputString = "Intent and Language Understanding
Intelligence Service Processing results are \r \n";
var luisRequestURL =
"https://api.projectoxford.ai/luis/v1/application?
id=fbec04e7-8bda-4160-a059-a8f8b995184b&subscription-
key=d14817bff85b4de0af2cc701b2e5de70";
httpClient = new HttpClient();
HttpResponseMessage response = await
httpClient.GetAsync(luisRequestURL + "&q=" + messagetext);

string luisResponseString = await
response.Content.ReadAsStringAsync();

var insightsproperties = new Dictionary<string, string> {
{"Page Name","MessagesController" }, {"Method Name","Post"
},
{ "Session Id",telemetry.Context.Session.Id }, {"Json
Result From LUIS",luisResponseString } };

telemetry.TrackEvent("Post Event Views",
insightsproperties);

var luisResponse =
JsonConvert.DeserializeObject<LuisResponse>
(luisResponseString);

if (luisResponse.entities.Count > 0)
{
    foreach (var entity in luisResponse.entities)
    {
        if (entity.type.Contains("geography"))
        {
            if(!luisOutputString.ToLower().
            Contains(entity.entity.ToLower()))
            luisOutputString +=
            entity.type.Replace("builtin.geography.", "")+"
            : " + entity.entity + " \r \n";
        }
        else if (entity.type == "Name")
        {
            luisOutputString += "Name: " + entity.entity +
            " \r \n";
        }
        else if (entity.type == "Company")
        {
            luisOutputString += "Company: " + entity.entity
```

```
                    + " \r \n";
            }
            else
            {
                luisOutputString += entity.type + " " +
                entity.entity + " \r \n";
            }
        }
    }
    else
    {
        luisOutputString = "No matching found for Intent and
        Language Understanding Intelligence Service
        Processing";
    }

    if (botOutputString == "")
    {
        botOutputString = "No matching found for Natural Speech
        and Intent Processing";
    }

    var appinsightsproperties = new Dictionary<string, string>
    { {"Page Name","MessagesController" }, {"Method
    Name","Post" },
    { "Session Id",telemetry.Context.Session.Id }, {"Final
    Result From LUIS",luisOutputString } };

    telemetry.TrackEvent("Post Event Views",
    appinsightsproperties);

    return message.CreateReplyMessage(botOutputString + " \r \n
    \r \n \r \n \r \n" + luisOutputString);
}
```

Run the `IntentProcessing` bot and ask any sentence. You will get output as shown here:

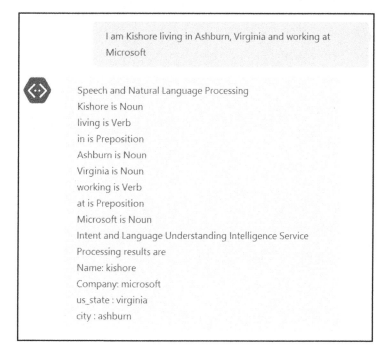

Summary

In this chapter, we have learned the following:

- **Bot dialogs**: The `Dialogs` model is a conversational process, where the exchange of messages between the bot and the user is the primary channel for interaction with the outside world
- **LUIS**: Creating language understanding models, training, and deploying/publishing a model to an endpoint
- **Cognitive Services**: Linguistic API, an advanced linguistic analysis tool for NLP, giving you access to part-of-speech tagging and parsing

4
Natural Speech and Intent Processing Bot Using Microsoft Cognitive Services

This chapter is for understanding how to use **Microsoft Cognitive Services**. The bot identifies the concepts and actions in the message that is sent to the bot with part-of-speech tagging, and finds phrases and concepts using **natural language parsers**. Also, it returns all the identified intents that were created and trained in the custom LUIS app. For example, if you say "Hi John, am going to New York tonight", the bot will return part-of-speech tagging as well as parses data for natural speech and Intent Processing to know the name and location--that is, Name: John, Place: New York, and so on.

You may be mining customer feedback of your application since you want to know whether the user has given a positive or negative feedback, or you may need to identify what your user is trying to communicate with your bot by interpreting user commands, such as identifying what action mentioned in the text the user wants to perform. To achieve this, first you need to have an understanding of the structure of the text, which is a critical first step, and this chapter teaches you how to achieve the previous mentioned scenarios.

Before starting with this chapter, you should know about **Microsoft Cognitive Services** (**Cortana Intelligence Services**), which helps you to build applications using very complex and powerful algorithms just through a few lines of code.

Microsoft Cognitive Services

Initially, Microsoft Cognitive Services was known as **Microsoft Project Oxford**. It is also known as **suite of intelligent APIs** and works across platforms which provide facial recognition in images, voice recognition of speakers, language processing, Academic Knowledge, and more. All these APIs are RESTful services. Owing to REST services, you can develop and integrate with any programming language; here, we use C#.

You must try out all the APIs that are available and just play around. For example, APIs such as Face, Emotion, and Speaker recognition will always return a confidence rating/value for each emotion identified in a given image from Face & Emotion APIs. In the case of Speaker recognition, it will tell you how much it accurately matches the voice to your previously registered voice. The best machine learning example API is **Language Understanding Intelligent Service** (**LUIS**). It has a potential for a much better text parser. To use this in an app, you'll need a Microsoft account to log in and get API keys. You can build an application for any platform that is easy to configure. It's free to sign up and they have paid plans, which are currently in preview.

Signing up for Microsoft Cognitive Services

Now, let's take a look at the following steps that we need to carry out while signing up for Microsoft Cognitive Services:

1. Go to **Microsoft Cognitive Services** (https://www.microsoft.com/cognitive-services/en-us/) and click on the **Get started for free** button at the following page:

2. On the next page, click on the **Let's go** button:

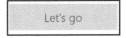

3. Alternatively, you can also click on the **My account** option in the top-right corner of the page and log in using Microsoft Account:

4. After a successful sign in, you have to subscribe to each and every API individually by checking the checkbox of each API. Select all and click on the **Subscribe** option. Now you are ready to use Cognitive Services:

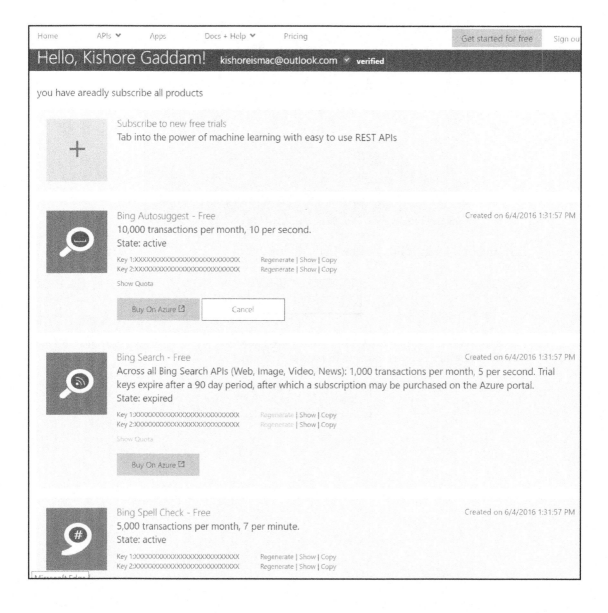

Now you are ready to build applications that use Cognitive Services using the respective API keys. In the next steps, we will walk-through how to use the API keys in a bot application.

Building a bot application using Cognitive Services APIs

Let's perform the following steps to build a bot application using Cognitive Services APIs:

1. Open Visual Studio, click on **New** | **Project**, and select **Visual C#** from the left side template category; then, you will see Bot Application template under the templates section:

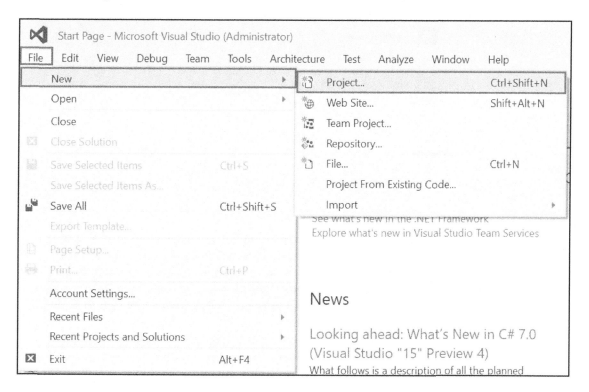

Natural Speech and Intent Processing Bot Using Microsoft Cognitive Services

2. Select **Bot Application template**, name the project as `IntentProcessing`, and then click on **OK**:

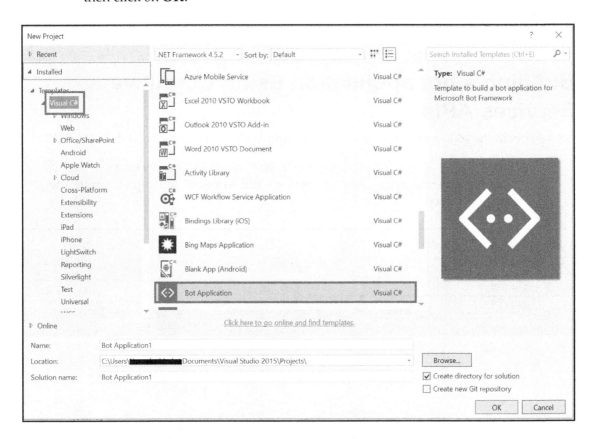

Here, we will explain to you how to identify parts of speech in a sentence sent by a user to the bot. For this, we will use Cognitive Services. In Cognitive Services, we have the Linguistic Analysis API, which is responsible for knowing the structure of a sentence. The Linguistic API uses advanced linguistic analysis tools for Natural Language Processing, giving you access to part-of-speech tagging and parsing. These tools allow you to hone in on important concepts and actions.

The API can tap into traditional linguistic analysis tools that allow you to identify the concepts and actions in your text with part-of-speech tagging and find phrases and concepts using natural language parsers. Whether you're mining customer feedback, interpreting user commands, or consuming web text, understanding the structure of the text is a critical first step.

Chapter 4

3. Now we will use the Linguistic Analysis API in our bot to identify the parts of speech in a sentence entered by the user.
4. Go to the Cognitive Services subscriptions page (https://www.microsoft.com/cognitive-services/en-US/sign-up?ReturnUrl=/cognitive-services/en-us/subscriptions). Under the **Linguistic Analysis** API section, copy the key and save it in a safe place for later use:

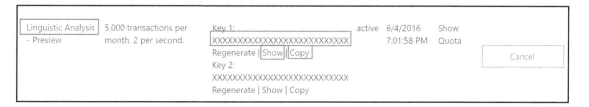

5. Return to `IntentProcessing` solution in Visual Studio and add the following helper classes into your solution.

6. We use the `Analyzer.cs` class to communicate with the API respective specifications, such as the language analyzer we will use, the type of analysis-- whether it is a constituency tree or POS tags, and on what specification it should produce the output:

```
Analyzer.cs

public class Analyzer
    {
        /// <summary>
        /// Unique identifier for this analyzer used to
        communicate with the service
        /// </summary>
        public Guid Id { get; set; }

        /// <summary>
        /// List of two letter ISO language codes for which this
        analyzer is available. e.g. "en" represents "English"
        /// </summary>
        public string[] Languages { get; set; }

        /// <summary>
        /// Description of the type of analysis used here, such
        as Constituency_Tree or POS_tags.
        /// </summary>
```

[131]

```csharp
        public string Kind { get; set; }

        /// <summary>
        /// The specification for how a human should produce
        /// ideal output for this task. Most use the specification
        /// from the Penn Treebank.
        /// </summary>
        public string Specification { get; set; }
        /// <summary>
        /// Description of the implementation used in this
        /// analyzer.
        /// </summary>
        public string Implementation { get; set; }
    }
```

7. The following class is used to send the request to the Linguistic API to process the text received from your user:

```
AnalyzerTextRequest.cs
```

```csharp
public class AnalyzeTextRequest
    {
        /// <summary>
        /// Two letter ISO language code, e.g. "en" for "English"
        /// </summary>
        public string Language { get; set; }

        /// <summary>
        /// List of IDs of the analyers to be used on the given
        /// input text; see Analyzer for more information.
        /// </summary>
        public Guid[] AnalyzerIds { get; set; }
        /// <summary>
        /// The raw input text to be analyzed.
        /// </summary>
        public string Text { get; set; }
    }
```

8. Once we receive the results from the API, we will store those results using the following helper class:

```
AnalyzeTextResults

public class AnalyzeTextResult

    {

        /// <summary>
        /// The unique ID of the analyzer; see Analyzer for more
        information.
        /// </summary>
        public Guid AnalyzerId { get; set; }

        /// <summary>
        /// The resulting analysis, encoded as JSON. See the
        documentation for the relevant analyzer kind for more
        information on formatting.
        /// </summary>
        public object Result { get; set; }
    }
```

9. We will receive the result from the API in JSON text; later, we will parse and convert it into an object. The following helper classes will be used to save the JSON response:

```
JsonConversionClasses

public class RootObject
    {
        public string analyzerId { get; set; }
        public List<object> result { get; set; }
    }

    public class Token
    {
        public int Len { get; set; }
        public string NormalizedToken { get; set; }
        public int Offset { get; set; }
        public string RawToken { get; set; }
    }

    public class TokenRootObject
    {
```

```csharp
        public int Len { get; set; }
        public int Offset { get; set; }
        public List<Token> Tokens { get; set; }
    }

    public class Tree
    {
        public List<string> Nodes { get; set; }
    }

    public class Intent
    {
        public string intent { get; set; }
        public double score { get; set; }
    }

    public class Entity
    {
        public string entity { get; set; }
        public string type { get; set; }
        public int startIndex { get; set; }
        public int endIndex { get; set; }
        public double score { get; set; }
    }
    public class LuisResponse
    {
        public string query { get; set; }
        public List<Intent> intents { get; set; }
        public List<Entity> entities { get; set; }
    }
    enum EtityType
    {
        Location,
        Name,
        Company
    }
```

10. Now, open the `MessagesController.cs` class file. Add the following required variable in class level, which is used while calling the Linguistic API:

    ```csharp
    #region private members

            /// <summary>
            /// The Default Service Host
            /// </summary>
            private const string DefaultServiceHost =
            "https://api.projectoxford.ai/linguistics/v1.0";
    ```

```csharp
/// <summary>
/// The JSON content type header.
/// </summary>
private const string JsonContentTypeHeader =
"application/json";

/// <summary>
/// The subscription key name.
/// </summary>
private const string SubscriptionKeyName = "ocp-apim-
subscription-key";

/// <summary>
/// The ListAnalyzers.
/// </summary>
private const string ListAnalyzersQuery = "analyzers";

/// <summary>
/// The AnalyzeText.
/// </summary>
private const string AnalyzeTextQuery = "analyze";

/// <summary>
/// The default resolver.
/// </summary>
private static readonly
CamelCasePropertyNamesContractResolver defaultResolver =
new CamelCasePropertyNamesContractResolver();
/// <summary>
/// The settings
/// </summary>
private static readonly JsonSerializerSettings settings =
new JsonSerializerSettings()
{
    DateFormatHandling =
    DateFormatHandling.IsoDateFormat,
    NullValueHandling = NullValueHandling.Ignore,
    ContractResolver = defaultResolver
};

/// <summary>
/// The service host.
/// </summary>
private string serviceHost;

/// <summary>
/// The HTTP client
/// </summary>
```

Natural Speech and Intent Processing Bot Using Microsoft Cognitive Services

```
        private HttpClient httpClient;

    #endregion
```

11. `DefaultServiceHost` is nothing but the API URL. `Analyzers` are used to analyze the text in all available analyzer formats. `SubscriptionKeyName` is nothing but the HTTP header key name, which we will mention in HTTP `DefaultRequestHeaders` with the value as your Linguistic API key. Next, create an `HttpClient` object and set the `DefaultRequestHeader` as follows:

```
httpClient = new HttpClient();
    httpClient.DefaultRequestHeaders.Add(SubscriptionKeyName,
    "ENTER_YOUR_LINGUISTIC_API_KEY");
```

12. Next, get all the `Analyzers` supported by the API by requesting the Linguistic API, as follows:

```
// List analyzers
        Analyzer[] supportedAnalyzers = null;
        try
        {
            var requestUrl = $"
            {this.serviceHost}/{ListAnalyzersQuery}";
        supportedAnalyzers = await SendRequestAsync<object,
        Analyzer[]>(HttpMethod.Get, requestUrl);
            var analyzersAsJson =
            JsonConvert.SerializeObject(supportedAnalyzers,
            Formatting.Indented, jsonSerializerSettings);
            //Console.WriteLine("Supported analyzers: " +
            analyzersAsJson);
        }
        catch (Exception e)
        {
            //Console.Error.WriteLine("Failed to list
            supported analyzers: " + e.ToString());
            Environment.Exit(1);
        }
```

13. Each `Analyzers` name contains four parts:
    - ID
    - Kind
    - Specification
    - Implementation

    We use an ID for identifying each analyzer; each analyzer is a kind. This defines in very broad terms the type of analysis returned, and should uniquely define the data structure used to represent that analysis.

14. Next, create an `AnalyzeTextRequest` by passing all supported Analyzer IDs and the sentence sent by the user in it:

    ```
    // Analyze text with all available analyzers
            var analyzeTextRequest = new AnalyzeTextRequest()
            {
                Language = "en",
                AnalyzerIds = supportedAnalyzers.Select(analyzer
                => analyzer.Id).ToArray(),
                Text = messagetext
            };
    ```

15. Next, send a request to the Linguistic API to analyze the sentence by passing the `AnalyzeTextRequest` object in its request body:

    ```
    try
            {
                var requestUrl = $"
                {this.serviceHost}/{AnalyzeTextQuery}";

                var analyzeTextResults = await
                this.SendRequestAsync<object,
                AnalyzeTextResult[]>(HttpMethod.Post, requestUrl,
                analyzeTextRequest);

                resultsAsJson =
                JsonConvert.SerializeObject(analyzeTextResults,
                Formatting.Indented, jsonSerializerSettings);

                //Console.WriteLine("Analyze text results: " +
                resultsAsJson);
                var insightproperties = new Dictionary<string,
                string> { {"Page Name","MessagesController" },
    ```

```
            {"Method Name","Post" },
            { "Session  Id",telemetry.Context.Session.Id },
            {"Json Result",resultsAsJson } };

            telemetry.TrackEvent("Post Event Views",
            insightproperties);
    }
    catch (Exception e)
    {
        //Console.Error.WriteLine("Failed to list
        supported analyzers: " + e.ToString());
        Environment.Exit(1);
    }
```

16. The following is the code for sending the request to the Linguistic API:

```
private async Task<TResponse> SendRequestAsync<TRequest,
TResponse>(HttpMethod httpMethod, string requestUrl, TRequest
requestBody = default(TRequest))
        {
        var request = new HttpRequestMessage(httpMethod,
        requestUrl);
        if (requestBody != null)
        {
            request.Content = new
            StringContent(JsonConvert.SerializeObject
            (requestBody, settings), Encoding.UTF8,
            JsonContentTypeHeader);
        }

        HttpResponseMessage response = await
        httpClient.SendAsync(request);
        if (response.IsSuccessStatusCode)
        {
            string responseContent = null;
            if (response.Content != null)
            {
                responseContent = await
                response.Content.ReadAsStringAsync();
            }

            if (!string.IsNullOrWhiteSpace(responseContent))
            {
                return
                JsonConvert.DeserializeObject<TResponse>
                (responseContent, settings);
            }
```

```
            return default(TResponse);
        }
        else
        {
            if (response.Content != null &&
            response.Content.Headers.ContentType
            .MediaType.Contains(JsonContentTypeHeader))
            {
                var errorObjectString = await
                response.Content.ReadAsStringAsync();
                ClientError errorCollection =
                JsonConvert.DeserializeObject
                <ClientError>(errorObjectString);
                if (errorCollection != null)
                {
                    throw new
                    ClientException(errorCollection,
                    response.StatusCode);
                }
            }
          response.EnsureSuccessStatusCode();
        }

        return default(TResponse);
    }
```

17. After getting a response from the API, deserialize it:

    ```
    var data = JsonConvert.DeserializeObject<List<RootObject>>
    (resultsAsJson);
    ```

Analyzer's results

In response to the code mentioned in the preceding section, you will get all the supported Analyzer's results. This includes tokens, POS tags, and the Constituency Parsing tree:

- **Tokens**: In the first step of analysis, linguistic will separate the sentences and tokens. The next task is to break the sentences into tokens. By default, in English, tokens are delimited by white space.
  In the first step, punctuation often should be split away from its surrounding context. Secondly, English has contractions, such as didn't or it's, where words have been compressed and abbreviated into smaller pieces. The goal of the tokenizer is to break the character sequence into words.

- **Parts-of-Speech Tags**: After the separation of sentences and tokens, the next step is to identify parts-of-speech, also called POS tagging. It is nothing but the tagging of each word in the sentence with respective parts of speech. The following is a list of supported POS tags:

Tag	Description	Example words
$	dollar	$
``	opening quotation mark	` ``
''	closing quotation mark	' ''
(	opening parenthesis	([{
)	closing parenthesis	)] }
,	comma	,
--	dash	--
.	sentence terminator	. ! ?
:	colon or ellipsis	: ; ...
CC	conjunction, coordinating	and but or yet
CD	numeral, cardinal	nine 20 1980 '96
DT	determiner	a the an all both neither
EX	existential there	there
FW	foreign word	enfant terrible hoi polloi je ne sais quoi
IN	preposition or subordinating conjunction	in inside if upon whether
JJ	adjective or numeral, ordinal	ninth pretty execrable multimodal
JJR	adjective, comparative	better faster cheaper
JJS	adjective, superlative	best fastest cheapest
LS	list item marker	(a) (b) 1 2 A B A. B.
MD	modal auxiliary	can may shall will could might should ought
NN	noun, common, singular or mass	potato money shoe

Tag	Description	Example words
NNP	noun, proper, singular	Kennedy Roosevelt Chicago Weehauken
NNPS	noun, proper, plural	Springfields Bushes
NNS	noun, common, plural	pieces mice fields
PDT	pre-determiner	all both half many quite such sure this
POS	genitive marker	' 's
PRP	pronoun, personal	she he it I we they you
PRP$	pronoun, possessive	hers his its my our their your
RB	adverb	clinically only
RBR	adverb, comparative	further gloomier grander graver greater grimmer harder harsher healthier heavier higher however larger later leaner lengthier less-perfectly lesser lonelier longer louder lower more
RBS	adverb, superlative	best biggest bluntest earliest farthest first furthest hardest heartiest highest largest least less most nearest second tightest worst
RP	particle	on off up out about
SYM	symbol	% &
TO	"to" as preposition or infinitive marker	to
UH	interjection	uh hooray howdy hello
VB	verb, base form	give assign fly
VBD	verb, past tense	gave assigned flew
VBG	verb, present participle or gerund	giving assigning flying
VBN	verb, past participle	given assigned flown
VBP	verb, present tense, not 3rd person singular	give assign fly
VBZ	verb, present tense, 3rd person singular	gives assigns flies
WDT	WH-determiner	that what which

Tag	Description	Example words
WP	WH-pronoun	who whom
WP$	WH-pronoun, possessive	whose
WRB	WH-adverb	how however whenever where

- **Constituency Parsing tree**: The purpose of constituency parsing is to identify the phrases. This helps to identify the key phrases from a given big text. To a linguist, a phrase is more than just a sequence of words. To be a phrase, a group of words has to come together to play a specific role in a sentence. That group of words can be moved together or replaced as a whole, and the sentence should remain fluent and grammatical. The result of the parsing looks as follows:

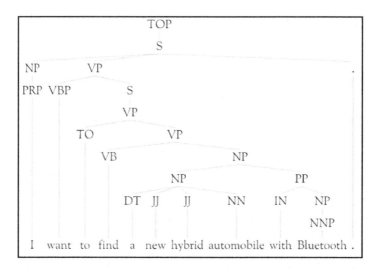

From the response, you will get all three lists; the following is the code for that:

```
var jsonTreeList = data[0].result.ToArray();
            string jsonTree = jsonTreeList.Count() > 0 ? "{Nodes:"
            + jsonTreeList[0].ToString() + "}" : null;
            //jsonTree = "{Nodes:" + jsonTree;
            var posTags = JsonConvert.DeserializeObject<Tree>
            (jsonTree);
            var jsonTreeView = data[1].result.ToArray();

            var tokenList = data[2].result.ToArray();
            for (int i = 0; i < posTags.Nodes.Count; i++)
            {
                if (posTags.Nodes[i] == "NNP")
```

```
            {
                botOutputString += tokenData.Tokens[i].RawToken
                + " is Noun" + " \r \n";
            }
            else if (posTags.Nodes[i] == "VBG" ||
            posTags.Nodes[i] == "VB")
            {
                botOutputString += tokenData.Tokens[i].RawToken
                + " is Verb" + " \r \n";
            }
            else if (posTags.Nodes[i] == "WRB")
            {
                botOutputString += tokenData.Tokens[i].RawToken
                + " is Adverb" + " \r \n";
            }
            else if (posTags.Nodes[i] == "WP")
            {
                botOutputString += tokenData.Tokens[i].RawToken
                + " is Pronoun" + " \r \n";
            }
            else if (posTags.Nodes[i] == "JJ" ||
            posTags.Nodes[i] == "JJR" || posTags.Nodes[i] ==
            "JJS")
            {
                botOutputString += tokenData.Tokens[i].RawToken
                + " is Adjective" + " \r \n";
            }
            else if (posTags.Nodes[i] == "IN")
            {
               botOutputString += tokenData.Tokens[i].RawToken
               + " is Preposition" + " \r \n";
            }
      }
botOutputString = botOutputString != "" ? "Speech and
Natural Language Processing \r \n" + botOutputString :
"";
```

So far, you have learned how to parse the text and identify the POS tags called Speech and Natural Language Processing. In the next step, you will learn how to do Intent Processing using LUIS.

Identifying the name of a person, place, and company using LUIS

In this step, you will learn how to identify the intent in a sentence. Identifying intent is very important, and helps you to understand what users want to do with your bot. Once you know the intent, you can interpret the sentence based on it and identify the actions from it:

1. After logging in to LUIS at `luis.ai`, create an app for your `IntentProcessing`. To do that, click on **New App** and select **New Application**:

2. Enter the name of your application, the usage as Bot, and select a category. Finally, click on the **Add App** button:

Chapter 4

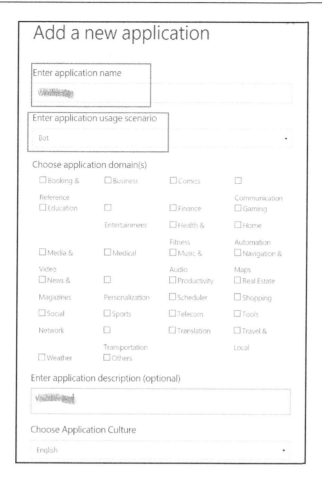

3. After the successful creation of the app, open it and click on the + icon of the **Intents** section from the left side menu:

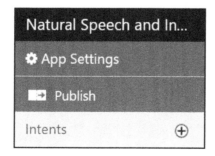

[145]

4. Enter a name for your intent and click on the **Save** button:

5. Now, add a custom entity, and from the left side menu, click on the + icon of Entity and enter **Name**:

6. Repeat the above step for the company entity:

7. Now, add an entity, and from the left side menu, click on the + icon of **Pre-built Entities**:

8. Select **geography** as the entity:

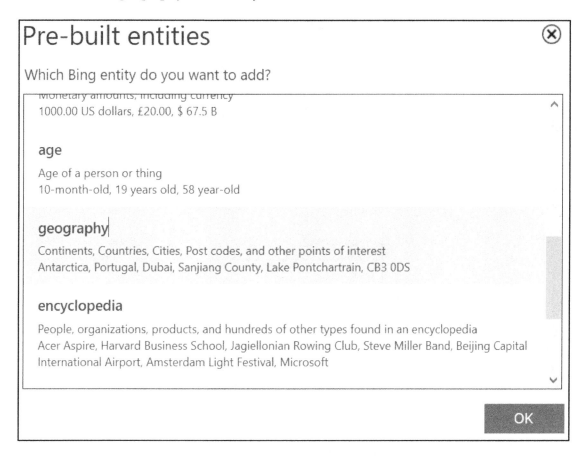

9. The reason why we use the pre-built entity is that LUIS already contains geography, which has the complete information about the locations. If you want to use a custom entity for location, then you have to provide all of the cities/locations information to LUIS, otherwise LUIS cannot identify the location from the given sentence.

10. Now we have an intent and an entity:

Training your app using utterances

Now, let's train your app using utterances for getting the appropriate results from the **Language Understanding Intelligent Service** (**LUIS**). To train, you have to add different types of utterances in your LUIS app. For this, select the **New utterances** section and then add the new utterance:

Utterance is nothing but the sentence typed/asked by the user to your bot, such as "I am Kishore living in Ashburn, Virginia and working at Microsoft." You have to enter as many utterances as possible with your bot.

Some examples of an utterance are as follows:

- I am John living in Ashburn, Virginia and working at Microsoft
- Jim lives in Princeton, New Jersey and works at Google

1. After entering the utterance, press *Enter*; now, LUIS will automatically highlight the geography and the name of the person and company in your text, as shown in the following image:

2. Before clicking on **Submit**, ensure that the sentence is identified correctly and showing Intent as Natural Processing (my intent name). If the name is not highlighted then manually click on the name. It will open a popup; then select Name as the entity. For example, here in my case, john was not highlighted by default, so I selected it manually and clicked on the Name intent. Do the same thing for the company as well:

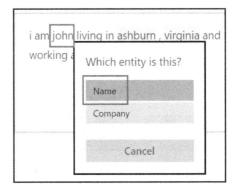

3. Now, click on **Submit**. Repeat this for more combinations of sentences.

4. After entering some utterances, click on the **Train** option, which is located in the bottom-left corner of the page. If you don't train your LUIS, you will not get proper results; so, ensure that you train every time you submit new utterances. Also, you have to add the minimum number of utterances to your app, only then can LUIS give accurate results:

5. Now, publish your LUIS app. For that, click on the **Go to Preview** option at the top of the page:

Chapter 4

6. Then, click on the **Publish** option on the left side menu. The publish button is enabled only in Preview mode:

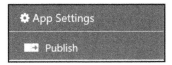

7. Now, click on the Publish web service button / **Update published application**:

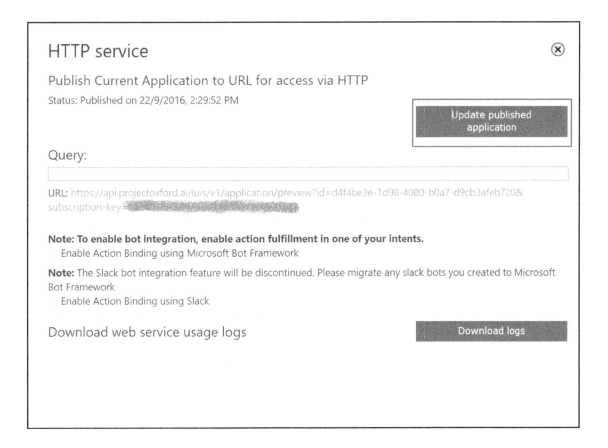

[151]

8. To test your LUIS app, enter the query in the Query text box and press the *Enter* button. It redirects to another window and displays the following result:

```
{
  "query": "John lives in Princeton, NewJersy and works at Microsoft",
  "intents": [
    {
      "intent": "NaturalProcessing",
      "score": 0.995691538
    },
    {
      "intent": "None",
      "score": 0.008353699
    }
  ],
  "entities": [
    {
      "entity": "newjersy",
      "type": "builtin.geography.us_state",
      "startIndex": 25,
      "endIndex": 32
    },
    {
      "entity": "princeton",
      "type": "builtin.geography.city",
      "startIndex": 14,
      "endIndex": 22,
      "score": 0.752777755
    },
    {
      "entity": "microsoft",
      "type": "Company",
      "startIndex": 47,
      "endIndex": 55,
      "score": 0.999907
    },
    {
      "entity": "john",
      "type": "Name",
      "startIndex": 0,
      "endIndex": 3,
      "score": 0.996062934
    }
  ]
}
```

9. Copy the URL upto the query and save it in a safe place; we will need it in later steps:

URL: https://api.projectoxford.ai/luis/v1/application/preview?id=d4f4be3e-1d98-4080-b0a7-d9cb3afeb720&subscription-key=▓▓▓▓▓▓▓▓▓▓▓▓▓▓▓▓▓▓▓▓&q=

Calling LUIS from the bot

In the previous step, we set up and configured the LUIS app and also trained it. Now, let's see how you can use the LUIS app in a bot application. To incorporate a call to LUIS, we can start by adding the mentioned function. It simply calls LUIS REST API and returns the phrases and intents we set up in LUIS, for example, name, city, company name, and so on.

Return to Visual Studio and open the `MessagesController.cs` file; under the `Post` method, update the code to get the LUIS results, as follows:

```
var luisOutputString = "Intent and Language Understanding Intelligence
  Service Processing results are \r \n";
```

The following line of code is where we frame a LUIS app REST API URL--if you observe, we are passing the LUIS app ID and LUIS subscription key; this is the URL you copied from the above step, publishing settings of the LUIS app:

```
var luisRequestURL =
"https://api.projectoxford.ai/luis/v1/application?
  id=fbec04e7-8bda-4160-a059-a8f8b995184b&subscription-
  key=ENTER_KEY_HERE";
httpClient = new HttpClient();
HttpResponseMessage response = await
httpClient.GetAsync(luisRequestURL + "&q=" + messagetext);

string luisResponseString = await
  response.Content.ReadAsStringAsync();
```

After getting a LUIS response (in JSON), we will parse/deserialize it, as follows:

```
var luisResponse =
JsonConvert.DeserializeObject<LuisResponse>
(luisResponseString);

if (luisResponse.entities.Count > 0)
```

```
        {
            foreach (var entity in luisResponse.entities)
            {
                if (entity.type.Contains("geography"))
                {
                    if(!luisOutputString.ToLower().
                        Contains(entity.entity.ToLower()))
                    luisOutputString +=
                    entity.type.Replace("builtin.geography.", "")+"
                    : " + entity.entity + " \r \n";
                }
                else if (entity.type == "Name")
                {
                    luisOutputString += "Name: " + entity.entity +
                    " \r \n";
                }
                else if (entity.type == "Company")
                {
                    luisOutputString += "Company: " + entity.entity
                    + " \r \n";
                }
                else
                {
                    luisOutputString += entity.type + " " +
                    entity.entity + " \r \n";
                }
            }
        }
        else
        {
            luisOutputString = "No matching found for Intent and
            Language Understanding Intelligence Service
            Processing";
        }

        if (botOutputString == "")
        {
            botOutputString = "No matching found for Natural Speech
            and Intent Processing";
        }
```

Finally, we will return the `botOutputString` value to our user as a reply.

Refer to the *How to deploy and run the bot application in the Bot Framework emulator locally* section in `Chapter 2`, *Developing Your First Bot Using the Connector and Builder SDK*, to learn how to run and debug the bot application locally.

Run the `IntentProcessing` bot and ask any sentence; you will get the following output in the Bot emulator:

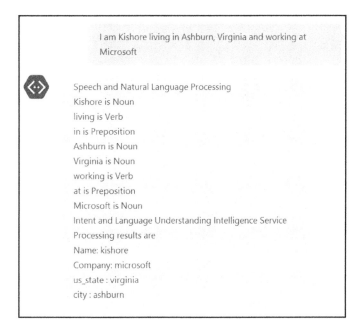

Summary

In this chapter, we have learned the following:

- **Cognitive Services**: Linguistic API, advanced linguistic analysis tools for natural language processing, giving you access to part-of-speech tagging and parsing

- **LUIS**: Creating Language Understanding Models and Training and deploying/Publishing model to an Endpoint

In the next chapter, you will learn about developing bots using LUIS Prompt Dialogs with State and Nearby Bot using custom APIs.

If you feel like publishing your bot to other channels, refer to `Chapter 9`, *Publishing a bot to Skype, Slack, Facebook, and the GroupMe Channel*, for how to publish our bot to Skype, Slack, Facebook, and so on.

5
Developing Bots Using LUIS Prompt Dialogs with State and Nearby Bot Using Custom APIs

In this chapter, we will discuss and develop two bots. One is the Employee Enroll bot using LUIS prompt dialogs and the other is the Nearby Bot using custom APIs. Enroll bot is a basic employee registration kind of bot that will prompt users to enter their first name, last name, designation, and department. If any value is not supplied, then LUIS will prompt the user to enter the missing values. We will also discuss the implementation of bot state. Secondly, we will develop the Nearby Bot to know the attractions near you using a third-party API. So, let's get started.

Employee Enroll bot using LUIS prompt dialogs

The following steps will guide you to create the Enroll bot:

1. Login to `https://www.luis.ai/`; for more information on activating or signing up for Cognitive Services, check out `Chapter 4`, *Natural Speech and Intent Processing Bot Using Microsoft Cognitive Services*.

2. Click on **New App**:

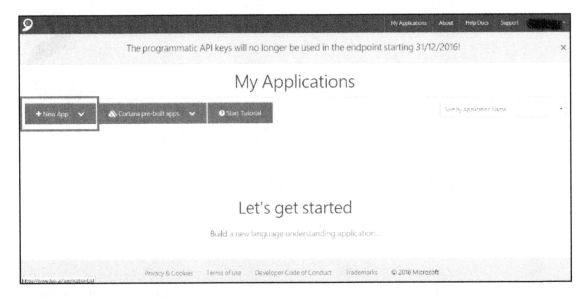

3. On the **New App** drop-down menu, select **New Application**:

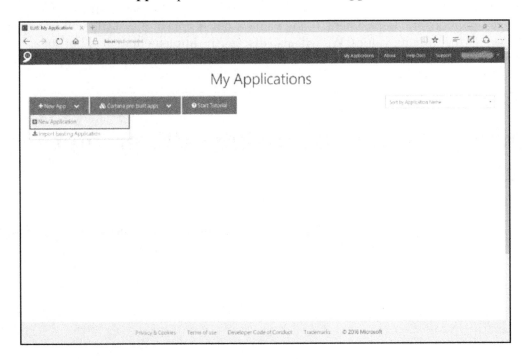

4. It opens an **Add a new application** popup; enter the application name, the application usage scenario as Bot, and select the category related to your bot. Finally, click on the **Add App** button:

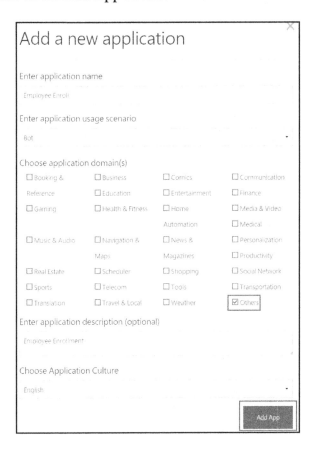

5. The following application will be created:

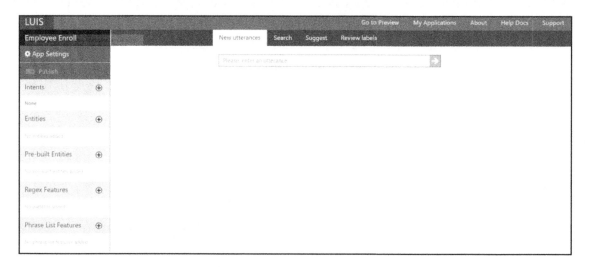

6. Our application will need to detect three entities, namely employee name (composed of first name and last name that we will define as children in the next steps), department, and location.
7. To create these, click on the plus sign next to **Entities**:

8. Enter **Employee Name** for the entity, then click on the checkbox of **Include children,** and select **Hierarchical** as the option:

9. Now, click on the plus sign next to **Entity Children**, as shown in the following screenshot:

10. Enter the first name in the children name box and again click on the plus icon near **Entity Children** to add the last name as another child; click on **Save**:

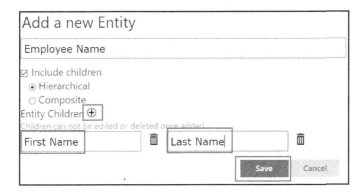

11. The **Employee Name** will be created; you can click on the downward arrow next to it to display its children:

12. Similarly, add a **Department** and **Designation** entity:

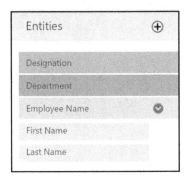

13. You can also help LUIS by entering common keywords in the **Phrase List Features** section. In the bottom-left corner of the LUIS app page you will find the phrase list:

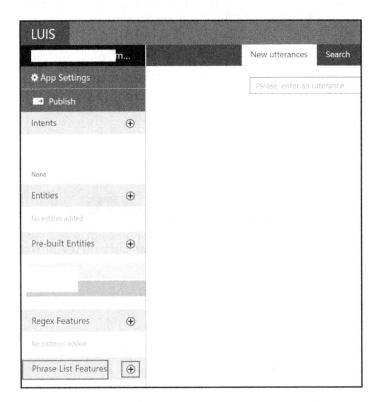

14. Click on the **+** sign and add **Departments,** and name all possible Department names with comma (,) separated words:

15. Give the list a name.
16. Insert the phrases (separated by commas) and click on **Save**.
17. Note that **Exchangeable** means that what it learns about one phrase will be automatically applied to the others.
18. Repeat the previous steps for **Designations** as well.
19. Our application will require to detect an intent to enroll. To create this, click on the plus sign next to **Intents**:

20. Enter `Enrol` for the **Intent name** and a sample phrase:

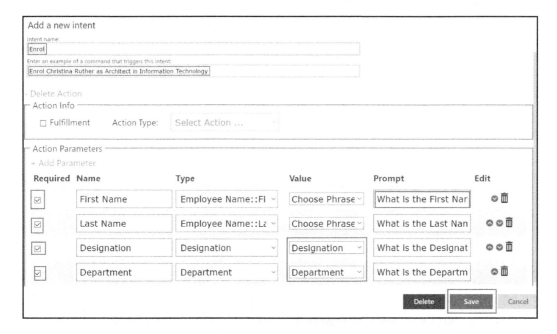

21. Click on the **Save** button:

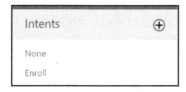

Training the service

Now we have to train the LUIS app to identify the first name, last name, designation, and department. The following steps will help you train your LUIS app:

1. Select the **New utterances** tab, enter a phrase in the box, and click on the arrow button to process it:

    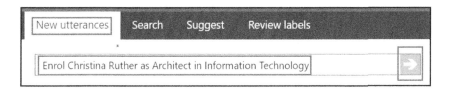

2. The result will be as shown in the following screenshot; it will detect the intent (**Enroll**), but it will not detect the entities:

    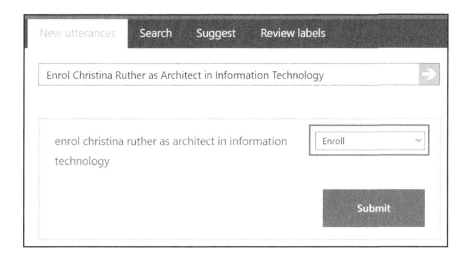

3. Click on the name **christina** and a popup will appear. Expand **Employee Name** and select **First Name** (to indicate that LUIS should learn that this is the first name):

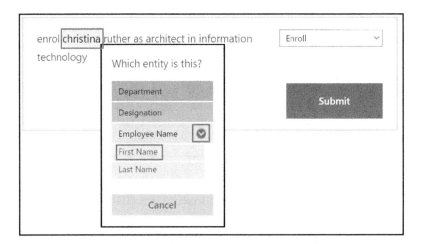

4. Now, select **ruther** and repeat the preceding step:

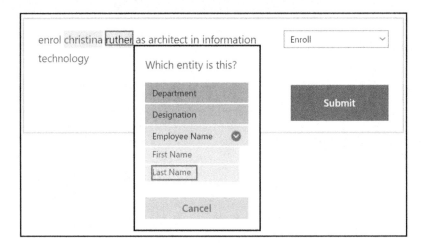

5. Now select **architect,** and select **Designation** from the popup:

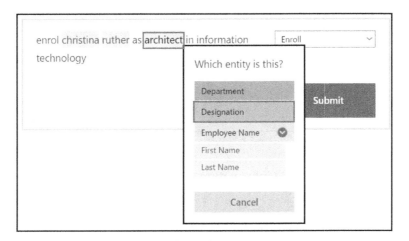

6. Now select **information technology,** and select **Department** from the popup:

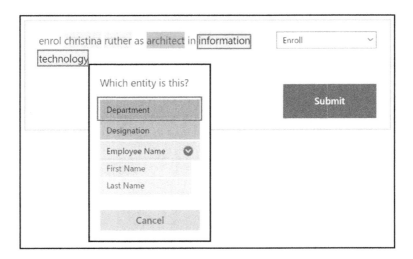

7. Click on each element and label it.

8. When you are done, click on the **Submit** button:

9. This is how you provide information to help train LUIS:

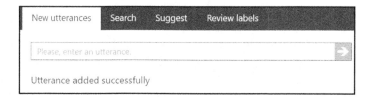

10. Continue to train the service by giving more utterances. You will note that eventually it will start detecting the entities on its own. However, many times you will still have to correct it. Enter and correct at least nine different utterances.
11. You can review and correct labels for utterances on the **Review labels** tab:

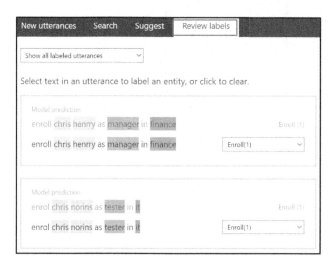

Training and publishing

Once you are done with all the possible utterances, train the app so that we can publish the latest changes to the LUIS endpoint. Let's check out the steps to train the app:

1. Click the **Train** button in the bottom left-hand corner of the LUIS app to train the model:

2. Now, publish your LUIS app. To do so, click on the **Go to Preview** option at the top of the page:

   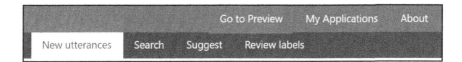

3. Then, click on the **Publish** option on the left-hand side menu.

    The **Publish** button is enabled only in preview mode.

4. Now, click on **Update published application** as shown in the following screenshot:

5. To test your LUIS app, enter the query in the **Query** textbox and press the *Enter* button. It's redirected to another window, and the results are displayed as follows:

```
{
    "query": "Enroll Kishore Gaddam as Architect in IT",
    "intents": [
        {
            "intent": "Enroll",
            "score": 0.999999046
        },
        {
            "intent": "None",
            "score": 0.239324629
        }
    ],
    "entities": [
        {
            "entity": "it",
            "type": "Department",
            "startIndex": 38,
            "endIndex": 39,
            "score": 0.9971673
        },
        {
            "entity": "architect",
            "type": "Designation",
            "startIndex": 25,
            "endIndex": 33,
            "score": 0.843642235
        },
        {
            "entity": "kishore",
            "type": "Employee Name::First Name",
            "startIndex": 7,
            "endIndex": 13,
            "score": 0.9482315
        },
        {
            "entity": "gaddam",
            "type": "Employee Name::Last Name",
            "startIndex": 15,
            "endIndex": 20,
            "score": 0.919439
        }
    ]
}
```

Chapter 5

6. Make a note of the **URL**, **App ID**, and **subscription-key** shown in the following screenshot. You will need to use these in the application that will be created later:

 For a production application, after LUIS is out of preview, you will obtain your subscription key from Azure.

Creating the C# class for LUIS response

For the application, we will have to create C# classes to hold the expected results of the LUIS output.

In the following steps, when you test the LUIS endpoint as in the fifth step of the preceding section, it generates a JSON output; simply select all the contents and copy them:

1. Go to http://json2csharp.com/ or http://jsonutils.com/, or use JSON C# Class Generator at https://jsonclassgenerator.codeplex.com/ and paste the contents of the JSON, then click on **Generate**. These services are used to generate C# classes from a given JSON text.

[171]

2. **Copy** the results:

```
"score": 0.9482315
},
{
    "entity": "qaddam",
    "type": "Employee Name::Last Name",
    "startIndex": 15,
    "endIndex": 20,
    "score": 0.919439
}
]
}
```

```csharp
public class Intent
{
    public string intent { get; set; }
    public double score { get; set; }
}

public class Entity
{
    public string entity { get; set; }
    public string type { get; set; }
    public int startIndex { get; set; }
    public int endIndex { get; set; }
    public double score { get; set; }
}

public class RootObject
{
    public string query { get; set; }
    public List<Intent> intents { get; set; }
    public List<Entity> entities { get; set; }
}
```

Creating the bot application

Let's take a look at the mentioned steps to create the bot application:

1. Open Visual Studio, navigate to **New** | **Project...**, and select **Visual C#** from the left side template category. Then, from the templates section, you will see the **Bot Application** template:

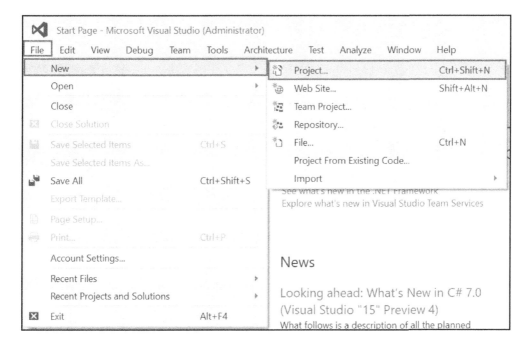

2. Select the **Bot Application** template, name the project `EmployeeEnrolBot`, and then click on **OK**:

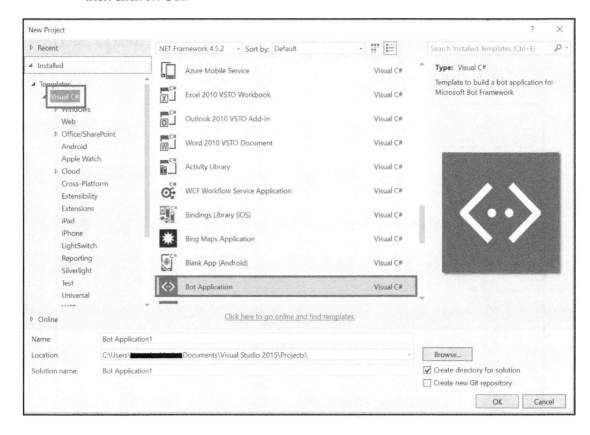

3. Add a new class and name the class `LUIS`. Then, paste the C# classes that you generated for LUIS in the preceding step. Rename the `RootObject` class to `LUIS`:

```csharp
namespace EmployeeEnrolBot
{
    public class Intent
    {
        public string intent { get; set; }
        public double score { get; set; }
    }

    public class Entity
    {
        public string entity { get; set; }
        public string type { get; set; }
        public int startIndex { get; set; }
        public int endIndex { get; set; }
        public double score { get; set; }
    }

    public class LUIS
    {
        public string query { get; set; }
        public List<Intent> intents { get; set; }
        public List<Entity> entities { get; set; }
    }
}
```

4. Add the following class into the file:

```
public class Query
    {
        public string FirstName { get; set; }
        public string LastName { get; set; }
        public string Class { get; set; }
        public string Period { get; set; }
    }
```

This class will be used to display the final results on the bot.

5. Open the Web.Config file and add the following keys in to it:

```xml
<add key="LUIS_Url" value="https://api.projectoxford.ai/luis/v1/application" />
<add key="LUIS_APP_Id" value="" />
<add key="LUIS_Subscription_Key" value="" />
</appSettings>
```

6. Now, open the MessagesController.cs file and add the following method into it:

```csharp
private static async Task<LUIS> QueryLUIS(string Query)
    {
            LUIS LUISResult = new LUIS();
            var LUISQuery = Uri.EscapeDataString(Query);

            using (System.Net.Http.HttpClient client = new
            System.Net.Http.HttpClient())
            {
                // Get key values from the web.config
                string LUIS_Url =
                ConfigurationManager.AppSettings["LUIS_Url"];
                string LUIS_Id =
                ConfigurationManager.AppSettings["LUIS_APP_Id"];
                string LUIS_Subscription_Key =
                ConfigurationManager.AppSettings
                ["LUIS_Subscription_Key"];

                string RequestURI = String.Format("{0}?id=
                {1}&subscription-key={2}&q={3}",
                LUIS_Url, LUIS_Id, LUIS_Subscription_Key,
                LUISQuery);

                System.Net.Http.HttpResponseMessage msg = await
```

```
                    client.GetAsync(RequestURI);

                    if (msg.IsSuccessStatusCode)
                    {
                        var JsonDataResponse = await
                        msg.Content.ReadAsStringAsync();
                        LUISResult =
                        JsonConvert.DeserializeObject<LUIS>
                        (JsonDataResponse);
                    }
                }
                return LUISResult;
        }
```

7. Modify the `Post` method in the `MessagesController.cs` file as follows:

```
     public async Task<HttpResponseMessage> Post([FromBody]Activity
activity)
                {
                if (activity.Type == ActivityTypes.Message)
                {
                    ConnectorClient connector = new
                    ConnectorClient(new
                    Uri(activity.ServiceUrl));
                    var messageText = activity.Text;
                    string list = "";
                    var rootObject = new RootObject();
                    try
                    {
                        var http = new HttpClient();

                        HttpResponseMessage placesResponse = await
                        http.GetAsync(new
                        Uri("https://maps.googleapis.com/maps/api
                        /place/textsearch/json?query=" + messageText
                        +
                        "&key=AIzaSyBjjWqN7J444VbwbpOukC-
                          9MAjqFYHBiCM"));

                        var jsonResponse = await
                        placesResponse.Content.ReadAsStringAsync();

                        if (jsonResponse != null && jsonResponse !=
                        "")
                        {
                            rootObject =
                            JsonConvert.DeserializeObject<RootObject>
                            (jsonResponse);
```

```csharp
            }
        }
        catch (Exception ex)
        {

            // return our reply to the user
            Activity reply =
            activity.CreateReply("Oops....
            Something went wrong please try again.
            "+ex.Message);
            await
            connector.Conversations.ReplyToActivityAsync
            (reply);
        }
        if (rootObject.results.Count > 0)
        {
            foreach (var item2 in rootObject.results)
            {

                list += item2.name + "," + "\r \n";
            }

            // return our reply to the user
            Activity reply = activity.CreateReply(list);
            await
           connector.Conversations.ReplyToActivityAsync
           (reply);
        }
        else
        {
            // return our reply to the user
            Activity reply = activity.CreateReply("Sorry
            we are unable to find the results for " +
            "'" + messageText + "'" + "Please make sure
            that you have typed correct phrase..." + "\r
            \n" + " some examples are..." + "\r \n" +
            "'" + "Restaurants in Albany" + "'" + "\r
            \n" + "(or)" + "\r \n" + "'" + "show me book
            stores in Norwich" + "'" + "'" + "\r \n" +
            "(or)" + "\r \n" + "'" + "Parking near
            Norwich" + "'" + "'" + "\r \n" + "(or)" +
            "\r \n" + "'" + "atms surrounding Norwich" +
            "'" + "'");
            await
            connector.Conversations.ReplyToActivityAsync
            (reply);

        }
```

Chapter 5

```
        }
        else
        {
            HandleSystemMessage(activity);
        }

        var response =
        Request.CreateResponse(HttpStatusCode.OK);
        return response;
    }
```

8. Press *F5* in Visual Studio to run the bot:

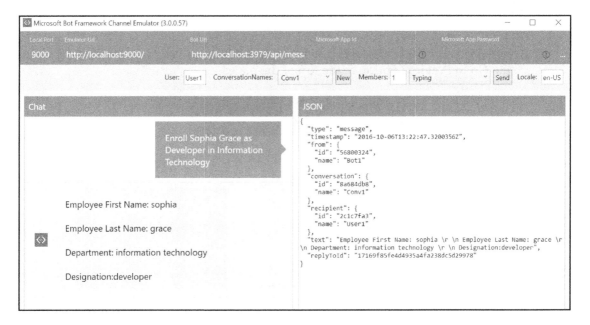

So far, if the LUIS service recognized the intent and the values for all required entities entered by the end user, all was well. However, if all the values for the required entities were not recognized (or they were not supplied), the end user was simply stuck.

[179]

Now we will see how we can overcome the problem posed when a user does not supply all entities; when a user has missed any entity then LUIS will ask the user for the missing entity using dialogs. Then, the user enters only the missing entity and LUIS will process the response to complete it.

To use dialogs, we need to make some changes in the LUIS app. Let's look at those changes:

1. Go to the LUIS app and click on your **Intent (Enroll)**.

 At the time of writing this book, the features described were in preview.

2. If you do not see the features described, switch to preview mode by clicking on the **Go to Preview** option at the top of the page:

3. Now, open the **Enroll** intent:

4. When the intent opens, click on **Add Action** and then on **Add Parameter**, and add the following parameters:

```
Name: First Name
Type: Employee Name::First Name
Prompt: What is the First Name?

Name: Last Name
Type: Employee Name::Last Name
Prompt: What is the Last Name?

Name: Designation
Type: Designation
Phrase List: Designation
```

[180]

```
Prompt: What is the Designation?

Name: Department
Type: Department
Phrase List: Department
Prompt: What is the Department?
```

5. Mark them all as required.
6. When you are done, click on the **Save** button:

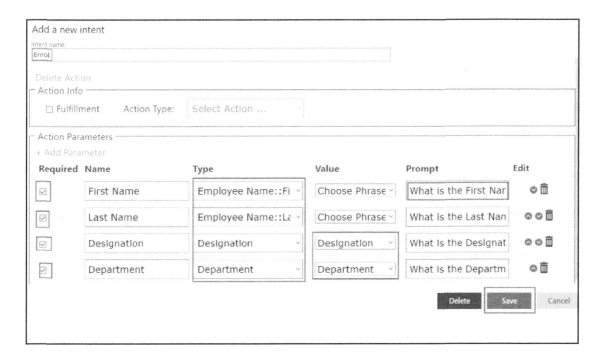

7. Click on **Train** and publish the LUIS app again:

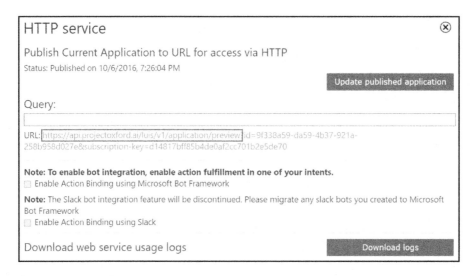

8. Update the URL of the LUIS app in your bot application's `Web.config` file.

9. On the publish page, enter **Query** and press *Enter* for the JSON content of the updated LUIS app:

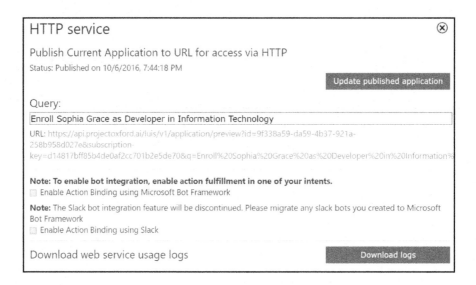

10. Using the JSON content, generate C# classes again and then add the updated and newly generated classes to the `LUIS.cs` file:

```
using System;
using System.Collections.Generic;
using System.Linq;
using System.Text;
using System.Threading.Tasks;

namespace EmployeeEnrolBot
{

    public class Value
    {
        public string entity { get; set; }
        public string type { get; set; }
        public Resolution resolution { get; set; }
    }

    public class Parameter
    {
        public string name { get; set; }
        public bool required { get; set; }
        public List<Value> value { get; set; }
    }

    public class Action
    {
        public bool triggered { get; set; }
        public string name { get; set; }
        public List<Parameter> parameters { get; set; }
    }

    public class TopScoringIntent
    {
        public string intent { get; set; }
        public double score { get; set; }
        public List<Action> actions { get; set; }
    }

    public class Entity
    {
        public string entity { get; set; }
        public string type { get; set; }
        public int startIndex { get; set; }
        public int endIndex { get; set; }
```

```
            public double score { get; set; }
            public Resolution resolution { get; set; }
        }
        public class Dialog
        {
            public string prompt { get; set; }
            public string parameterName { get; set; }
            public string parameterType { get; set; }
            public string contextId { get; set; }
            public string status { get; set; }
        }

        public class LUIS
        {
            public string query { get; set; }
            public TopScoringIntent topScoringIntent { get; set;
}
            public List<Entity> entities { get; set; }
            public Dialog dialog { get; set; }
        }

        public class Resolution
        {
        }
        public class Query
        {
            public string FirstName { get; set; }
            public string LastName { get; set; }
            public string Designation { get; set; }
            public string Department { get; set; }
        }
    }
```

When LUIS has a question, it places it in the dialog property along with a `ContextId` that is used to track the exchange. In the code, we save the `ContextId` in bot state using the bot state service.

Bot state service

The key to good bot design is to do the following:

- Make the web service stateless so that it can be scaled
- Make it track the context of a conversation

Since all bots have these requirements, the Bot Framework has a service for storing bot state. This lets your bot track things such as *what was the last question I asked them?*

In our case, we want to save the `contextId` of the LUIS to exchange the missed information to the LUIS app from our bot.

To do that, first we need to create `BotStateClient`.

Creating a state client

The default state client is stored in a central service. For some channel IDs, you may want to use a state API hosted in the channel itself (for example, with the *emulator* channel) so that the state can be stored in a compliant store that the channel supplies.

We have provided a helper method on the `activity` object, which makes it easy to get an appropriate `StateClient` for a given message:

```
StateClient stateClient = activity.GetStateClient();
```

After getting the state client, we can now save our `contextId` to it. When your bot sends a reply, you simply set your object in one of the `BotData` records properties, and it will be persisted and played back to you on future messages when the context is the same. Your bot may store data for a user, a conversation, or a single user within a conversation (called *private* data). Each payload may be up to 32 KB in size. The data may be removed by the bot or upon a user's request, for example, if the user requests the channel to inform the bot (and therefore, the Bot Framework) to delete the user's data.

Get/SetProperty methods

The C# library has helper methods called `SetProperty()` and `GetProperty()`, which make it easy to get and set any type of data from a `BotData` record, including complex objects.

In this application, first we will try to get the `contextId` from the `BotState` using the following code--if we already have a `ContextId` then we will request the LUIS along with the `contextId`, which we saved previously; based on the `ContextId`, LUIS will process the complete sentence and return the entities:

```
string strContextId = "";
            BotData userData = await
            stateClient.BotState.GetUserDataAsync
```

[185]

Developing Bots Using LUIS Prompt Dialogs with State and Nearby Bot Using Custom APIs

```
                    (activity.ChannelId, activity.From.Id);

                    if (userData.GetProperty<string>
                    ("contextId")!=null)
                    {
                        // If we have a ContextId saved in TempData
                        // retrieve it
                        strContextId = userData.GetProperty<bool>
                        ("contextId").ToString();
                    }
    LUIS objLUISResult = await QueryLUIS(activity.Text,strContextId);
```

If LUIS identifies that the user missed some information, then it sends a question to the `Prompt` variable of the `Dialog` class. Based on that, we can identify the missed entity and prompt the user to enter it.

The LUIS app prompts a question of missed information/action along with the `ContextId`. We will save it into a bot state using the following code:

```
    LUIS objLUISResult = await QueryLUIS(activity.Text,strContextId);
                    if (objLUISResult.dialog.prompt != null)
                    {
                        // If there is a question ask it
                        Result.Question =
                        objLUISResult.dialog.prompt;
                        // Set the ContextID
                        userData.SetProperty<string>("contextId",
                        objLUISResult.dialog.contextId);
                        await
                        stateClient.BotState.SetUserDataAsync
                        (activity.ChannelId, activity.From.Id,
                        userData);

                        // return our reply to the user
                        Activity reply =
                        activity.CreateReply(Result.Question);
                        await
                        connector.Conversations.ReplyToActivityAsync
                        (reply);
                    }
```

After the question is answered, we retrieve the `ContextId` from `BotState` and then pass it to LUIS along with the reply to the question.

We append the `ContextId` to the query sent to LUIS as follows:

```
string RequestURI = String.Format("{0}?id={1}&subscription-
key={2}&q={3}&contextId={4}",
            LUIS_Url, LUIS_Id, LUIS_Subscription_Key,
            LUISQuery, contextId);

        System.Net.Http.HttpResponseMessage msg = await
        client.GetAsync(RequestURI);
```

Updating your Post method

Let's use the following code to update your `Post` method:

```
public async Task<HttpResponseMessage> Post([FromBody]Activity activity)
    {
        if (activity.Type == ActivityTypes.Message)
        {
            ConnectorClient connector = new ConnectorClient(new
            Uri(activity.ServiceUrl));
            StateClient stateClient = activity.GetStateClient();
            Query Result = new Query();

            try
            {
                if (activity.Text != null)
                {
                    string strContextId = "";
                    BotData userData = await
                    stateClient.BotState.GetUserDataAsync
                    (activity.ChannelId, activity.From.Id);

                    if (userData.GetProperty<string>
                    ("contextId")!=null)
                    {
                        // If we have a ContextId saved in TempData
                        // retrieve it
                        strContextId = userData.GetProperty<string>
                        ("contextId").ToString();
                    }

                    LUIS objLUISResult = await
                    QueryLUIS(activity.Text,strContextId);
```

```csharp
if (objLUISResult.dialog.prompt != null)
{
    // If there is a question ask it
    Result.Question =
    objLUISResult.dialog.prompt;
    // Set the ContextID
    userData.SetProperty<string>("contextId",
    objLUISResult.dialog.contextId);
    await
    stateClient.BotState.SetUserDataAsync
    (activity.ChannelId, activity.From.Id,
     userData);

    // return our reply to the user
    Activity reply =
    activity.CreateReply(Result.Question);
    await
   connector.Conversations.ReplyToActivityAsync
    (reply);
}
else
{
    userData.SetProperty<string>("contextId",
    "");
    await stateClient.BotState.SetUserDataAsync
    (activity.ChannelId, activity.From.Id,
    userData);
    foreach (var item in
    objLUISResult.topScoringIntent.actions)
    {
        // Loop through the parameters
        foreach (var parameter in
        item.parameters)
        {
            if (parameter.value[0].type ==
            "Employee Name::First Name")
            {
                Result.FirstName =
                parameter.value[0].entity;
            }

            if (parameter.value[0].type ==
            "Employee Name::Last Name")
            {
                Result.LastName =
                parameter.value[0].entity;
            }
```

```
                            if (parameter.value[0].type ==
                            "Department")
                            {
                                Result.Department =
                                parameter.value[0].entity;
                            }

                            if (parameter.value[0].type ==
                            "Designation")
                            {
                                Result.Designation =
                                parameter.value[0].entity;
                            }
                        }
                    }
                    // return our reply to the user
                    Activity reply =
                    activity.CreateReply($"Employee First Name:
                    {Result.FirstName} \r \n Employee Last
                    Name: {Result.LastName} \r \n Department:
                    {Result.Department} \r \n Designation:
                    {Result.Designation}");
                    await
                    connector.Conversations.ReplyToActivityAsync
                    (reply);
                }
            }
        }
        catch (Exception ex)
        {
            // return our reply to the user
            Activity reply = activity.CreateReply($"Something
            went wrong. \r \n"+ex.Message);
            await
            connector.Conversations.ReplyToActivityAsync
            (reply);
        }

    }
    else
    {
        HandleSystemMessage(activity);
    }
    var response = Request.CreateResponse(HttpStatusCode.OK);
    return response;
}
```

Updating your QueryLUIS method

Now, let's move on to update your `QueryLUIS` method:

```
private static async Task<LUIS> QueryLUIS(string Query, string contextId)
{
    // Create a new LUIS class
    LUIS LUISResult = new LUIS();

    using (System.Net.Http.HttpClient client = new System.Net.Http.HttpClient())
    {
        // Get key values from the web.config
        string LUIS_Url =
            ConfigurationManager.AppSettings["LUIS_Url"];
        string LUIS_Id =
            ConfigurationManager.AppSettings["LUIS_APP_Id"];
        string LUIS_Subscription_Key =

        ConfigurationManager.AppSettings
        ["LUIS_Subscription_Key"];

        // Get the text of the query entered by the user
        var LUISQuery = Uri.EscapeDataString(Query);

        // Send Query to LUIS and get response
        string RequestURI = String.Format("{0}?id={1}&subscription-key={2}&q={3}&contextId={4}",
            LUIS_Url, LUIS_Id, LUIS_Subscription_Key,
            LUISQuery, contextId);

        System.Net.Http.HttpResponseMessage msg = await
        client.GetAsync(RequestURI);

        if (msg.IsSuccessStatusCode)
        {
            var JsonDataResponse = await
            msg.Content.ReadAsStringAsync();
            LUISResult = JsonConvert.DeserializeObject<LUIS>
              (JsonDataResponse);
        }
    }

    return LUISResult;
}
```

Once we've updated the QueryLUIS, let's take a look at the further steps:

1. Run the bot application, go to the bot emulator, and enter the sentence without entering the department:

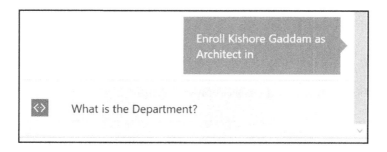

2. Now, enter the department:

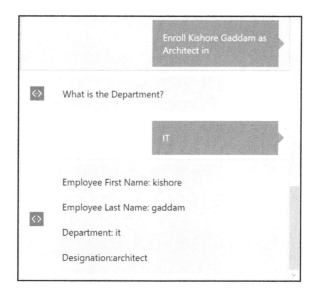

Developing a Nearby Bot using custom APIs

So far, you have learned about bot application creation using *Visual Studio*, publishing to *Azure*, *Bot* registration at dev.Botframework.com, and connecting to channels. In this Nearby Bot tutorial, we will explain how to use third-party APIs from your bot.

The main purpose of this bot is to provide information about the nearby amenities of a given place--for example, if you want to know the top restaurants near New York.

 This guide is for C# using the Bot Framework Connector SDK .NET template.

Let's look at the steps:

1. Open Visual Studio and click on **New** | **Project...**:

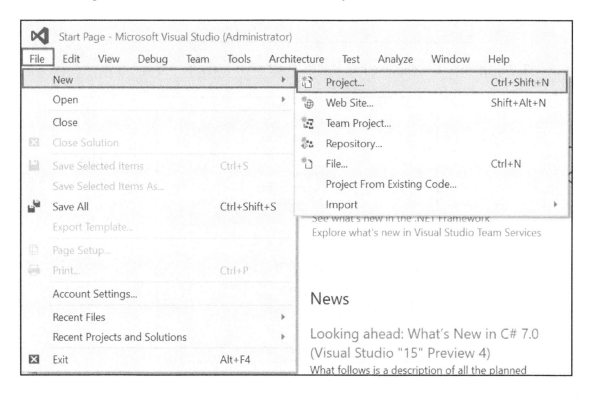

Chapter 5

2. Select **Visual C#** from the left side template category; then, from the templates section, you will see the **Bot Application** template:

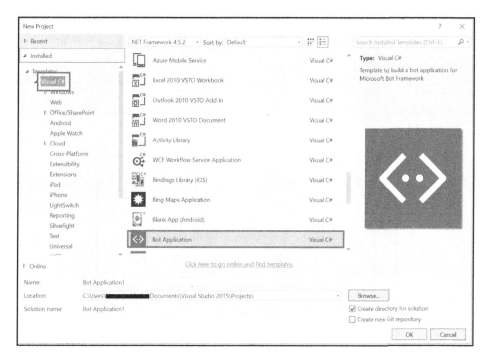

3. Select the **Bot Application** template, name the project `NearbyBot`, and then click on **OK**.

Before we jump into the code, first we will explain how to get the nearby places information of a given place using third-party APIs. We will do this by using the *Google Places API*. If you want to use the Google Places API, you need to have an **API key**--for that, follow the following instructions:

1. Go to the **Google Places API** page at `https://developers.google.com/places/web-service/search`:

[193]

2. The page looks as follows. Click on the **GET A KEY** button, which is on the top-right side of the page:

3. On the next page, sign in using your Google account. If you don't have one, then it's time to create one:

Chapter 5

4. Once you have successfully signed in, click on the **GET A KEY** button again. Now the site will prompt you to **Select or Create a project**, as shown. Select the **Create a new project** option:

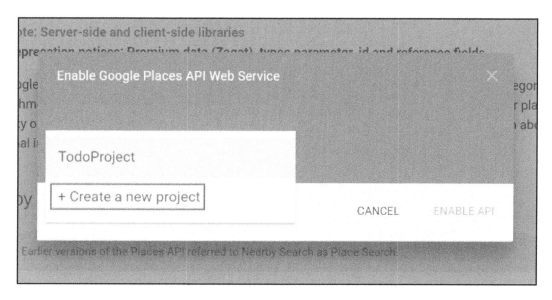

5. Enter a name for the project and then click on the **CREATE AND ENABLE API** option:

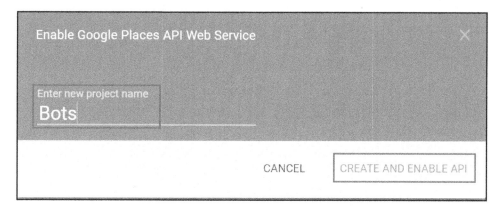

[195]

6. On the next page, you will see a key that you will need to copy to a safe place, as we will use it in later steps. After that, click on the **GO TO DOCS** option on the popup:

7. On the API documentation page, select the **Place Searches** link:

Chapter 5

8. On the **Place Searches** page, scroll down to the **Text Search Requests** API documentation and copy the API usage and URL:

Text Search Requests

The Google Places API Text Search Service is a web service that returns information about a set of places based on a string — for example "pizza in New York" or "shoe stores near Ottawa". The service responds with a list of places matching the text string and any location bias that has been set. The search response will include a list of places, you can send a Place Details request for more information about any of the places in the response.

 The Google Places search services share the same usage limits. However, the Text Search service is subject to a 10-times multiplier. That is, each Text Search request that you make will count as 10 requests against your quota. If you've purchased the Google Places API as part of your Google Maps APIs Premium Plan contract, the multiplier may be different. Please refer to the Google Maps APIs Premium Plan documentation for details.

A Text Search request is an HTTP URL of the following form:

```
https://maps.googleapis.com/maps/api/place/textsearch/output?parameters
```

9. The following is the example request:

```
https://maps.googleapis.com/maps/api/place/textsearch/json?query=restaurants+in+Sydney&key=YOUR_API_KEY
```

[197]

10. Copy the request URL and replace `YOUR_API_KEY` with the key you copied/generated in earlier steps; then, paste it in a browser address bar and press *Enter*. You should be able to see the API result in JSON format, as follows:

```
{
  "html_attributions" : [],
  "next_page_token" : "CvQB4gAAABorcOSmxFenwL02ikVLvrxPoH2YNMqSDL31dfKr7dZmhVEDdHmjdP4ibg9jowkElTq5k1A8jfUZ_avMoj1DciSFc8LDb_HgGgptJ_DBok22uao47nk0g31EwAcEymw7OZ1X6R8Mo0VPKNbJxGNN5Q1KoC2R27_xRBdWoKUaVQXWLSfca7WyGz0R89skHoVeUWfUqreddxTxMg9A",
  "results" : [
    {
      "formatted_address" : "529 Kent St, Sydney NSW 2000, Australia",
      "geometry" : {
        "location" : {
          "lat" : -33.875154,
          "lng" : 151.204976
        },
        "viewport" : {
          "northeast" : {
            "lat" : -33.87498464999999,
            "lng" : 151.20556445
          },
          "southwest" : {
            "lat" : -33.87521045,
            "lng" : 151.20477985
          }
        }
      },
      "icon" : "https://maps.gstatic.com/mapfiles/place_api/icons/restaurant-71.png",
      "id" : "827f1ac561d72ec25897df088199315f7cbbc8ed",
      "name" : "Tetsuya's Restaurant",
      "opening_hours" : {
        "open_now" : false,
        "weekday_text" : []
```

11. Now we need to generate the C# classes to hold the respective JSON result.

12. Go to `http://json2csharp.com/` or `http://jsonutils.com/`, or use the JSON Class Generator at `https://jsonclassgenerator.codeplex.com/`.

13. Paste the contents of the JSON, and then click on **Generate** and copy the results:

json2csharp

generate c# classes from json

developed by Jonathan Keith
with thanks to the JSON C# Class Generator project
and James Newton-King's Json.NET

```
      "score": 0.9482315
    },
    {
      "entity": "gaddam",
      "type": "Employee Name::Last Name",
      "startIndex": 15,
      "endIndex": 20,
      "score": 0.919439
    }
  ]
}
```

Generate   ? ! @

```
public class Intent
{
    public string intent { get; set; }
    public double score { get; set; }
}

public class Entity
{
    public string entity { get; set; }
    public string type { get; set; }
    public int startIndex { get; set; }
    public int endIndex { get; set; }
    public double score { get; set; }
}

public class RootObject
{
    public string query { get; set; }
    public List<Intent> intents { get; set; }
    public List<Entity> entities { get; set; }
}
```

Close Copy

14. Now, go back to the project and create a `HelperClasses.cs` file and paste the generated classes in it:

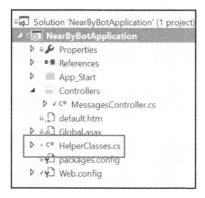

15. Helper classes should contain the following classes:

```
using System;
using System.Collections.Generic;
using System.Linq;
using System.Text;
using System.Threading.Tasks;

namespace NearByBotApplication
{
    public class Location
    {
        public double lat { get; set; }
        public double lng { get; set; }
    }

    public class Northeast
    {
        public double lat { get; set; }
        public double lng { get; set; }
    }

    public class Southwest
    {
        public double lat { get; set; }
        public double lng { get; set; }
    }

    public class Viewport
    {
```

```csharp
            public Northeast northeast { get; set; }
            public Southwest southwest { get; set; }
        }

        public class Geometry
        {
            public Location location { get; set; }
            public Viewport viewport { get; set; }
        }

        public class OpeningHours
        {
            public bool open_now { get; set; }
            public List<object> weekday_text { get; set; }
        }

        public class Photo
        {
            public int height { get; set; }
            public List<string> html_attributions { get; set; }
            public string photo_reference { get; set; }
            public int width { get; set; }
        }

        public class Result
        {
            public string formatted_address { get; set; }
            public Geometry geometry { get; set; }
            public string icon { get; set; }
            public string id { get; set; }
            public string name { get; set; }
            public OpeningHours opening_hours { get; set; }
            public List<Photo> photos { get; set; }
            public string place_id { get; set; }
            public int price_level { get; set; }
            public double rating { get; set; }
            public string reference { get; set; }
            public List<string> types { get; set; }
        }

        public class RootObject
        {
            public List<object> html_attributions { get; set; }
            public string next_page_token { get; set; }
            public List<Result> results { get; set; }
            public string status { get; set; }
        }
    }
```

16. Now open the `MessagesController.cs` file, which is located under the `Controllers` folder:

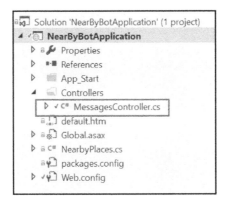

17. When the user asks Nearby Bot about restaurants in New York, under the `Post` method we will send that text to the Text Search Request API to get the list of restaurants in New York. For that, first we need to create an object for the HTTP client:

    ```
    var http = new HttpClient();
    ```

18. Now carry out a GET request to the Text Search Request API, as follows:

    ```
    HttpResponseMessage response = await http.GetAsync(new
    Uri("https://maps.googleapis.com/maps/api/place/textsearch/json?
    query=" + messageText + "&key=YOUR_KEY"));
    ```

19. The message is nothing but the text received by the bot from the user.

20. Next, read the response from the response content using the following code:

    ```
    var jsonResponse = await response.Content.ReadAsStringAsync();
    ```

21. Now deserialize the JSON response, using the following code to parse the list of results:

    ```
    if (jsonResponse!= null && jsonResponse!= "")
                {
                        rootObject =
                        JsonConvert.DeserializeObject<RootObject>
                        (jsonResponse);
    ```

Chapter 5

}

22. Now, parse and format the results and send a reply to the user with the help of the rich text format, as follows:

```
if (rootObject.results.Count > 0)
    {
        foreach (var item2 in rootObject.results)
        {
            list += item2.name + "," + "\r \n";
        }

        // return our reply to the user
        Activity reply = activity.CreateReply(list);
        await
        connector.Conversations.ReplyToActivityAsync
        (reply);
    }
    else
    {
        // return our reply to the user
        Activity reply = activity.CreateReply("Sorry
        we are unable to find the results for " +
        "'" + messageText + "'" + "Please make sure
        that you have typed correct phrase..." + "\r
        \n" + " some examples are..." + "\r \n" +
        "'" + "Restaurants in Albany" + "'" + "\r
        \n" + "(or)" + "\r \n" + "'" + "show me book
        stores in Norwich" + "'" + "'" + "\r \n" +
        "(or)" + "\r \n" + "'" + "Parking near
        Norwich" + "'" + "'" + "\r \n" + "(or)" +
        "\r \n" + "'" + "atms surrounding Norwich" +
        "'" + "'");
        await
        connector.Conversations.ReplyToActivityAsync
        (reply);

    }
```

23. The following is the complete code for the Post method:

```
public async Task<HttpResponseMessage> Post([FromBody]Activity
activity)
        {
            if (activity.Type == ActivityTypes.Message)
            {
```

[203]

```csharp
ConnectorClient connector = new
ConnectorClient(new
Uri(activity.ServiceUrl));
var messageText = activity.Text;
string list = "";
var rootObject = new RootObject();
try
{

    var http = new HttpClient();

    HttpResponseMessage placesResponse = await
    http.GetAsync(new
    Uri("https://maps.googleapis.com/maps/
    api/place/textsearch/json?query=" +
    messageText +
    "&key=AIzaSyBjjWqN7J444VbwbpOukC
    -9MAjqFYHBiCM"));

    var jsonResponse = await
    placesResponse.Content.ReadAsStringAsync();

    if (jsonResponse != null && jsonResponse !=
    "")
    {
        rootObject =
        JsonConvert.DeserializeObject<RootObject>
        (jsonResponse);

    }
}
catch (Exception ex)
{

    // return our reply to the user
    Activity reply =
    activity.CreateReply("Oops....
    Something went wrong please try again.
    "+ex.Message);
    await
    connector.Conversations.ReplyToActivityAsync
    (reply);
}
if (rootObject.results.Count > 0)
{
    foreach (var item2 in rootObject.results)
    {
```

```csharp
                    list += item2.name + "," + "\r \n";
                }

                // return our reply to the user
                Activity reply = activity.CreateReply(list);
                await
                connector.Conversations.ReplyToActivityAsync
                (reply);
            }
            else
            {
                // return our reply to the user
                Activity reply = activity.CreateReply("Sorry
                we are unable to find the results for " +
                "'" + messageText + "'" + "Please make sure
                that you have typed correct phrase..." + "\r
                \n" + " some examples are..." + "\r \n" +
                "'" + "Restaurants in Albany" + "'" + "\r
                \n" + "(or)" + "\r \n" + "'" + "show me book
                stores in Norwich" + "'" + "'" +
                "\r \n" + "(or)" + "\r \n" + "'" + "Parking
                near Norwich" + "'" + "'" + "\r \n" + "
                (or)" + "\r \n" + "'" + "atms surrounding
                Norwich" + "'" + "'");
                await
                connector.Conversations.ReplyToActivityAsync
                (reply);

            }
        }
        else
        {
            HandleSystemMessage(activity);
        }

        var response =
        Request.CreateResponse(HttpStatusCode.OK);
        return response;
    }
}
```

24. Now run the Nearby Bot locally in the bot emulator:

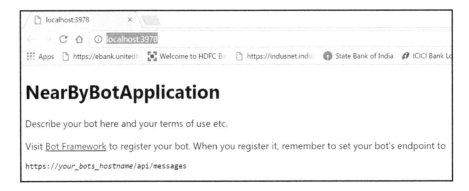

25. Open the emulator and type a phrase, as shown in the following screenshot:

26. You should get all the top restaurants in Sydney, as shown in the following screenshot:

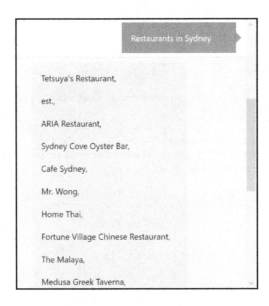

Summary

In this chapter, we have learned the following:

- **LUIS prompt dialogs**: Using this feature, we can make our bot more mature by identifying the missing / expecting entities in a given sentence, which gives a more natural way of conversation with users.
- **Third-party APIs**: These are used for calling third-party APIs from the bot.
- **Bot state**: This will help us to store information about the user and important information in the last conversation. Based on the last conversation, we can communicate with users in a more natural way, like how we did in the Employee Enroll bot.

6
Developing an IVR Bot for a Bank Using Advanced Microsoft Bot Framework Technologies

The Bank **Interactive Voice Response (IVR)** bot is like phone banking you can do bank transactions from within the bot itself. This bot will have options such as create account, balance enquiry, credit card payment, and delete account. The Bank IVR bot can tell you the balance of your account. It can also pay your credit card bill as well, by just selecting a few options.

In this bot, we will mainly use the **Conversation Concept** using **FormFlow** and dialogs. For example, whenever a user enters some text, the bot will immediately send a response message and also remember the entire conversation. Unlike dialogs, FormFlow helps to handle guided conversations such as ordering a sandwich, booking a movie ticket, setting up an appointment with a doctor, and so on. These types of scenarios need lots of effort.

High-level architectural diagram

The following is the architecture diagram for the Bank IVR bot. These are the descriptions of the numbers:

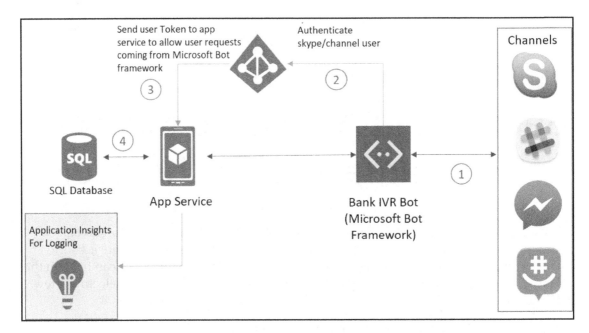

1. We have the Bank IVR bot registered with Microsoft Bot Framework and configured to channels.
2. We have an AAD authentication.
3. App service is where we publish our Bot--it requests a token to allow user requests coming from Microsoft Bot Framework (from channels).
4. We also have a SQL database connected to App service.
5. For logging/tracking user operations, we use Application Insights.

As mentioned in preceding architecture, you need to develop a Bot Application first. Perform the steps mentioned in the next section to develop a Bot Application using Visual Studio.

Let's start coding

Perform the following steps to create the bot application:

1. Create a new C# project using the new **Bot Application** template.
2. Navigate to **New** | **Project...** in Visual Studio 2015; it will open the following window:

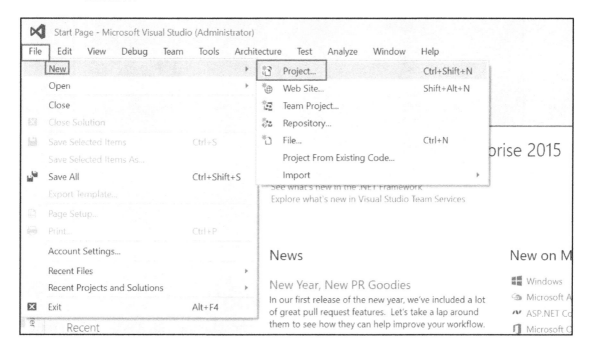

Developing an IVR Bot for a Bank Using Advanced Microsoft Bot Framework Technologies

3. Select the **Bot Application** template, give it a name, and click on **OK**:

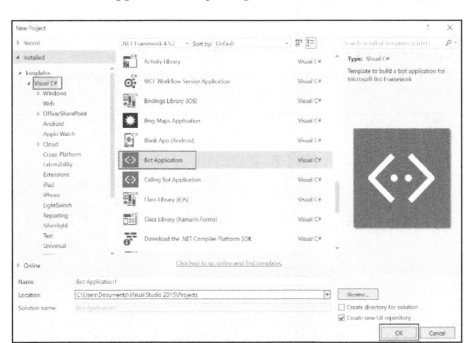

Creating an account with the bot

Here, I will explain how to build a FormFlow to create an account with this bot. To start the FormFlow and create an account, you need to create a C# class to define the form you want the information to be completed.

Create an enum with all the options we are going to implement, as shown here:

```
public enum Options
{
    CreateAccount,
    [Terms(new string[] { "savings balance", "Savings Account Balance" })]
    [Describe("Savings Account Balance")]
    SavingsAccountBalance,
    [Terms(new string[] { "current balance", "Current Account Balance" })]
    [Describe("Current Account Balance")]
    CurrentAccountBalance,
    [Terms(new string[] { "creditcard payment", "CreditCard
```

```
              Payment" })]
              [Describe("CreditCard Payment")]
              CreditCardPayment,
              [Terms(new string[] { "delete", "delete an account" })]
              [Describe("Delete an account")]
              DeleteAccount,
        };
```

If you observe in above enum, all the properties are decorated with [Terms(new string[] { "", "" })] and [Describe("")] , The text you mention in the Terms will be used as prompt text to user. The Describe is the text that will defined what is the use of that enum value its similar to help text.

Create account options are the types of accounts the user wants to create. To do this, create an `enum` with the account types:

```
              public enum CreateAccountOptions { SavingsAccount,
              CurrentAccount };
```

Next, add a class called `Customer` and declare it as `Serializable`. This way, the bot will serialize the entire class object and preserve the data for the next step in the FormFlow. The FormFlow will start when a user sends any message. If it is a new conversation, it will prompt the user with options such as **Create Account**, **Savings Account Balance**, and so on, as shown in the following screenshot:

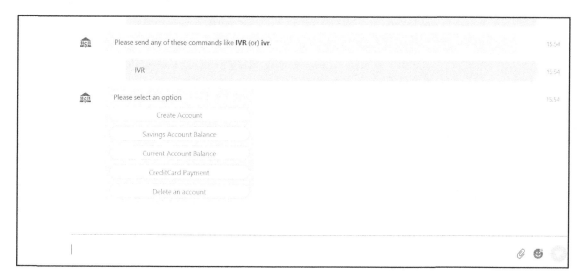

The following is the code for displaying the options shown in the preceding screenshot:

```csharp
[Serializable]
    class Customer
    {
        //Create Account Template
        [Prompt("Please send any of these commands like **IVR** (or) **ivr**.")]
        public string StartingWord;
        public Options? Option;
public CreateAccountOptions? AccountType;

public static IForm<Customer> BuildForm()
        {
            OnCompletionAsyncDelegate<Customer> accountStatus = async (context, state) =>
            {
                await Task.Delay(TimeSpan.FromSeconds(5));
                await context.PostAsync("We are currently processing your account details. We will message you the status.");

            };
            var builder = new FormBuilder<Customer>();
            ActiveDelegate<Customer> isCreate = (customer) => customer.Option == Options.CreateAccount;

            return builder.Field(nameof(Customer.StartingWord),
            validate: async (state, response) =>
                    {
                        var result = new ValidateResult { IsValid = true, Value = response };
                        string str = (response as string);
                        if ("ivr".Equals(str, StringComparison.InvariantCultureIgnoreCase))
                        {
                            result.IsValid = true;
                            return result;
                        }
                        else
                        {
                            result.Feedback = "I'm sorry. I didn't understand you.";
                            result.IsValid = false;
                            return result;
                        }
                    })
```

```
                    .Field(nameof(Customer.Option))
                    .OnCompletion(accountStatus)
                    .Build();
            }
        };
    }
```

Let's say, for example, the user selected the **Create Account** option. The FormFlow will prompt the user for the type of account they want to create, as shown in the following screenshot:

To create the prompt as shown in the preceding screenshot, first we have to define an `enum` with the account type options and declare a public field in the `Customer` class:

```
public enum CreateAccountOptions {
        SavingsAccount,
        CurrentAccount
    };
```

In the `Customer` class, define a public field as follows:

```
public CreateAccountOptions? AccountType;
```

To identify that the user selected the **Create Account** option, we have to create `ActiveDelegate` for each option and save the value as `true` if the user selects that option, or `false` if the user does not select that option. `ActiveDelegate` helps to know the form state and which step is active.

To register `ActiveDelegate`, add the following lines of code:

```
ActiveDelegate<Customer> isCreate = (customer) => customer.Option == Options.CreateAccount;
        ActiveDelegate<Customer> isBalance = (customer) =>
        customer.Option == Options.SavingsAccountBalance;
        ActiveDelegate<Customer> isCurrentBalance = (customer) =>
        customer.Option == Options.CurrentAccountBalance;
        ActiveDelegate<Customer> isCreditCardPayment = (customer)
        => customer.Option == Options.CreditCardPayment;
        ActiveDelegate<Customer> isDelete = (customer) =>
        customer.Option == Options.DeleteAccount;
```

When the user selects an option, then its respective `ActiveDelegate` value is immediately set to `true`--in our scenario, this is when the user selects **Create Account**. Now, the value of the `isCreate` delegate contains `true`. Using this value, we can manage the flow of the form builder.

Now that we know that the user selected `Create Account`, to prompt the type of account we have to append the `AccountType` field to the builder object, as shown here:

```
Field(nameof(Customer.AccountType))
```

We will append the preceding line immediately after the IVR options:

```
return builder.Field(nameof(Customer.StartingWord), validate: async (state,
response) =>
                    {
                        var result = new ValidateResult { IsValid =
                        true, Value = response };
                        string str = (response as string);
                        if ("ivr".Equals(str,
                        StringComparison.InvariantCultureIgnoreCase
                        ))
                        {
                            result.IsValid = true;
                            return result;
                        }
```

```
                    else
                    {
                        result.Feedback = "I'm sorry. I didn't
                        understand you.";
                        result.IsValid = false;
                        return result;
                    }
            })

                .Field(nameof(Customer.Option))
                .Field(nameof(Customer.AccountType))
                .OnCompletion(accountStatus)
                .Build();
```

Next, the user has to provide their details to create an account, for prompting the user for all the required fields, such as name, date of birth, social security number, permanent address, and so on. To do this, we need to define public fields in the `Customer` class.

For this example, we define the following fields:

```
[Prompt("Please enter your {&}")]
        public string FullName;
        [Prompt("Please enter your {&} like "+
            "* CustomerType, DOB, Nationality, Mother's Name,
                            Applicant's Martial Status*")]
        public string PersonalDetails;
        [Prompt("Please enter your {&} like "+
            "* LandMark, District, State, City, PIN, Mobile Number,
                                            Email Address*")]
        public string CorrespondenceAddress;
        [Prompt("Please enter your {&} like " +
            "* LandMark, District, State, City, PIN, Mobile Number,
                                            Email Address*")]
        public string PermanentAddress;
        public string SocialSecurityNumber;
        [Prompt("Please enter your {&} like * Name, Account Number *
                                                ")]
        public string NomineeDetails;
        [Prompt("Please enter the amount like how much do you want to
                                    deposit in your account?")]
        public string SavingsAmount;
        [Prompt("Do you want to create account with the above
                                        details?")]
        public string confirmation;
```

Each field has a `Prompt` annotation. At runtime, the prompt message will be used by the form builder to ask the user for the value they need to enter. For example, when we select **Create Account** and type in **Savings Account**, the next step is to provide our details. However, if we don't know the details we have to enter at that time, the field prompt message will be sent to the user, as shown in the following screenshot:

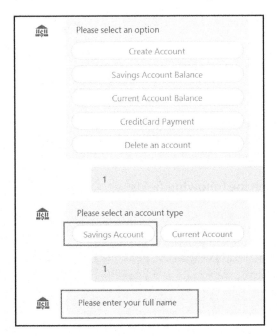

In the preceding screenshot, the prompt text **Please enter your full name** came from the `FullName` field's prompt message. This way we can tell the user the value they need to enter. Similar to `FullName`, we will ask the user to enter all the required details.

To prompt the user as shown in the preceding screenshot, the following code needs to be appended to the builder object:

```
.Field(nameof(Customer.FullName))
            .Field(nameof(Customer.PersonalDetails))
            .Field(nameof(Customer.CorrespondenceAddress))
            .Field(nameof(Customer.PermanentAddress))
            .Field(nameof(Customer.SocialSecurityNumber))
            .Field(nameof(Customer.NomineeDetails))
            .Field(nameof(Customer.SavingsAmount))
```

The FormFlow includes some C# attributes you can add to control the dialog better; here are the attributes:

Attribute	Purpose
`Describe`	Changes how a field or a value is shown in the text.
`Numeric`	Provides limits on the values accepted in a numeric field.
`Optional`	Marks a field as optional, which means that one choice is to not supply a value.
`Pattern`	Defines a regular expression to validate a string field.
`Prompt`	Defines a prompt to use when asking for a field.
`Template`	Defines a template that is used to generate prompts or values in prompts.
`Terms`	Defines the input terms that match a field or value.

After the user has entered all the required fields, we will ask the user for confirmation using the `Message` method, as shown here:

```
            .Message("**These are  your account details: **
{AccountType} {FullName} {PersonalDetails} {CorrespondenceAddress}
{PermanentAddress} {SocialSecurityNumber} {NomineeDetails}
{SavingsAmount}", isCreate)
            .Field(nameof(Customer.confirmation)
```

If the user says yes, we will create an account; otherwise, we will have to ask the user which field they want to modify. Before creating an account, we should validate whether the user has entered the information correctly or not (for example, date of birth). To validate that the user has entered the data, we have the `validate` method, to check the validity of the entered data. If it is valid, we continue the FormFlow; otherwise, we will prompt the user to enter the correct value.

For example, the following code is validates the account creation confirmation:

```
.Message("**These are  your account details: ** {AccountType} {FullName}
{PersonalDetails} {CorrespondenceAddress} {PermanentAddress}
{SocialSecurityNumber} {NomineeDetails} {SavingsAmount}", isCreate)
            .Field(nameof(Customer.confirmation),//),
                validate: async (state, response) =>
                    {
                        var result = new ValidateResult {
                        IsValid = true, Value = response };
                        var userselection = (response as
                        string).Trim();
                        if
                        (userselection.ToString()
                        .ToLower() == "no")
                        {
                            result.Feedback = "I'm sorry. I
                            didn't understand you.
                            Please type **back**, if you can
                            edit your details or type **yes**
                            you can commit your details.";
                            result.IsValid = false;
                        }
                        return result;
                    })
            .OnCompletion(accountStatus)
            .Build();
```

Similarly, we will append the logic for all the other options to the builder, as we did for the account creation.

Now, we are ready with FormFlow. In order to connect your form to the Bot Framework, you need to add it to your controller as follows:

```
First add a method with return type of Idialog<Customer> in your controller
class, in my case it is MessageController.
        internal static IDialog<Customer> MakeRootDialog()
        {
    return Chain.From(() =>
    FormDialog.FromForm(Customer.BuildForm))
        .Do(async (context, order) =>
        {
            try
            {
                await context.PostAsync("Thanks for Choosing
                our Bank!");
            }
```

```
                catch (FormCanceledException<Customer> e)
                {
                    string reply;
                    if (e.InnerException == null)
                    {
                        reply = $"You quit on {e.Last}--maybe you
                            can finish next time!";
                    }
                    else
                    {
                        reply = "Sorry, I've had a short circuit.
                            Please try again.";
                    }
                    await context.PostAsync(reply);
                }
            });
        }
```

Next, in the Post method, modify your code with the following code:

```
        public async Task<Message> Post([FromBody]Message message)
        {
            if (message.Type == "Message")
            {
                return await Conversation.SendAsync(message,
                    MakeRootDialog);
            }
            else
            {
                return HandleSystemMessage(message);
            }
        }
```

The combination of your C# class and connecting it to the Bot Framework is enough to automatically create a conversation.

After adding the preceding lines of code, you are now ready to test your bot with the Bot Framework emulator.

The final flow for account creation will be as follows:

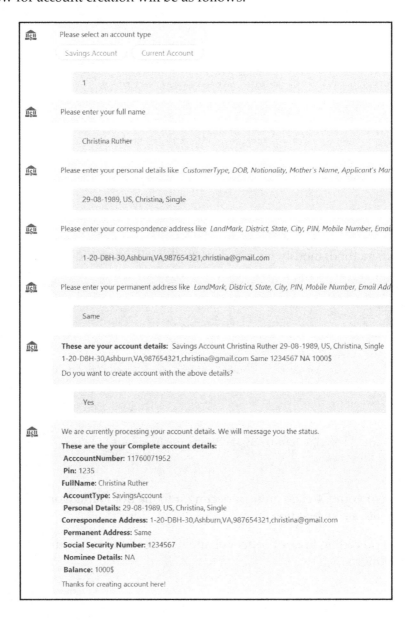

Storing the bot conversation (new account info) data in an Azure SQL database

We are maintaining the state or bot conversation of the user. For this, we will use an Azure SQL database. We save all the transactions that the user performs, such as registering a new user, credit card payments, checking their balance, and so on. These are the steps for storing the bot conversation in the Azure SQL database:

1. In the Azure portal, create a new Azure SQL database. To see how to create a new SQL database in Azure, follow the steps shown at `https://docs.microsoft.com/en-us/azure/sql-database/sql-database-create-databases`.
2. After the successful creation of a database in Azure, you have to create a table in it. For that, you have to open your SQL database in Visual Studio 2015.
3. Next, create a table using the following commands:

```
CREATE TABLE [dbo].[Accountant_Information] (
    [Id]                     NVARCHAR (128)DEFAULT (newid())
        NOT NULL,
    [AccountNumber]          NVARCHAR (MAX)NOT NULL,
            [PinNo]                  INTNOT NULL,
    [AccountType]            NVARCHAR (MAX)NULL,
    [FullName]               NVARCHAR (MAX)NOT NULL,
    [Personal_Information]   NVARCHAR (MAX)NOT NULL,
    [Correspondence_Address] NVARCHAR (MAX)NOT NULL,
    [Permanent_Address]      NVARCHAR (MAX)NOT NULL,
    [SSN]                    NVARCHAR (MAX)NULL,
    [Nominee_Information]    NVARCHAR (MAX)NOT NULL,
            [Saving_Balance]         BIGINTNULL,
            [Current_Balance]        BIGINTNULL,
            [Version]                ROWVERSIONNOT NULL,
            [CreatedAt]              DATETIMEOFFSET (7)
            DEFAULT (sysutcdatetime()) NOT NULL,
            [UpdatedAt]              DATETIMEOFFSET (7) NULL,
            [Deleted]                BITDEFAULT ((0)) NOT
                NULL,
            [Timestamp]              DATETIMEDEFAULT ('1900-
            01-01T00:00:00.000') NOT NULL,
            CONSTRAINT [PK_dbo.Accountant_Information]
                PRIMARY KEY NONCLUSTERED ([Id] ASC)
);
```

4. Now, you have a database and a table. Next, replace the code of the `MakeRootDialog()` method with the following lines of code; these lines contain the logic for storing the entire conversation with this bot:

```
internal static IDialog<Customer> MakeRootDialog()
        {
            return Chain.From(() =>
            FormDialog.FromForm(Customer.BuildForm))
            .Do(async (context, order) =>
                {
                    try
                    {
                        var completed = await order;
                        Random random = new Random();
                        int randomno = random.Next(1025518043,
                        2025518043);
                        string accno = randomno + "2";
                        Random rand = new Random();
                        int randno = rand.Next(0, 9);
                        int accpin = 1234+ randno;

                        await context.PostAsync("These are the
                        your Complete account details:\r \n " +
                        "AcccountNumber:" + accno + "\r \n " +
                        "Pin:" + accpin + "\r \n" + "FullName:" +
                        completed.FullName + "\r \n " +
                        "AccountType:" + completed.AccountType +
                        "\r \n " + "Personal Details:" +
                        completed.PersonalDetails + "\r \n"
                        + "Correspondence Address:" +
                        completed.CorrespondenceAddress +
                        "\r \n " + "Permanent Address:" +
                        completed.PermanentAddress + "\r \n " +
                        "SSN:" + completed.SSN + "\r \n " +
                        "Nominee Details:" +
                        completed.NomineeDetails+"\r \n
                        "+"Balance:"+completed.SavingsAmount);
                        //storing the entire bot conversation
SQLDatabaseService.InsertAccountantInformation
(completed,accno,accpin);
                        await context.PostAsync("Thanks for
                        Choosing SBI!");
                    }
                    catch (FormCanceledException<Customer> e)
                    {
                        string reply;
```

```
                if (e.InnerException == null)
                {
                    reply = $"You quit on {e.Last}--maybe
                    you can finish next time!";
                }
                else
                {
                    reply = "Sorry, I've had a short
                    circuit.
                    Please try again.";
                }
                await context.PostAsync(reply);
            }
        });
    }
```

5. Next, add a new class named SQLDatabaseService. After adding this class to your project, open it and add the following method to insert the account information into the database:

```
internal static void InsertAccountantInformation(Customer
completed, string accno, int accpin)
        {
            try
            {
                SqlConnection connection = null;
                string query = null;
                DateTime datetime = DateTime.Now;
                connection = new SqlConnection("Data
                Source=k8bjlaohq3.database.windows.net;Initial
                Catalog=ivrbot_db;Integrated Security=False;User
                ID=datareadserver;Password=Astrani@2016;Connect
                Timeout=60;Encrypt=False;
                TrustServerCertificate=True;
                ApplicationIntent=ReadWrite;
                MultiSubnetFailover=False");
                connection.Open();
                if (completed.AccountType.ToString() ==
                "SavingsAccount")
                {
                    query = "INSERT INTO [dbo].
                    [Accountant_Information]
                    (AccountNumber,PinNo,FullName,AccountType,
                    Personal_Information,Correspondence_Address,
                    Permanent_Address,SSN,Nominee_Information,
                    Saving_Balance,Timestamp)" +
                            "Values ('" + accno + "','" +
                            accpin + "','" + completed.FullName
```

```
                            + "','" + completed.AccountType +
                            "','" + completed.PersonalDetails +
                            "','" +
                            completed.CorrespondenceAddress +
                            "','" + completed.PermanentAddress
                            + "','" + completed.SSN + "','" +
                            completed.NomineeDetails + "','" +
                            completed.SavingsAmount + "','" +
                            datetime + "')";
                }
                else
                {
                    query = "INSERT INTO [dbo].
                    [Accountant_Information]
                    (AccountNumber,PinNo,FullName,AccountType,
                    Personal_Information,Correspondence_Address,
                    Permanent_Address,SSN,Nominee_Information,
                    Current_Balance,Timestamp)" +
                            "Values ('" + accno + "','" +
                            accpin + "','" +
                            completed.FullName + "','" +
                            completed.AccountType + "','" +
                            completed.PersonalDetails + "','"
                            + completed.CorrespondenceAddress
                            + "','" +
                            completed.PermanentAddress + "','"
                            + completed.SSN + "','" +
                            completed.NomineeDetails + "','" +
                            completed.SavingsAmount + "','" +
                            datetime + "')";
                }

                using (SqlCommand cmd = new SqlCommand(query,
                connection))
                {
                    cmd.ExecuteNonQuery();
                    // connection.Close();
                }
            }
            catch (Exception ex)
            {

            }
        }
```

6. After adding the preceding lines of code, now start your bot application. It will run on your local machine.
7. After successfully launching your application in the browser, you have to test your application in the Bot Framework emulator, as explained in previous chapters.
8. Now, select the **Create Account** option in IVR bot and complete all the preceding steps. After completion of the **Create Account** option, all details will be saved in your database.

Checking your savings account balance using the bot

In this section, I will explain about how to build a FormFlow to check your savings account balance.

To check your balance, we need an account number and PIN. For that, we will add a class called `Balance` with two fields: `AccountNumber` and `PIN`. Next, we will define a public property for the `Balance` class in the `Customer` class, and finally we will append the `Balance` field to the builder object:

```
[Serializable]
class Balance
{
    [Prompt("Please enter your account number")]
    public string AccountNumber;
    [Prompt("Please enter your pin")]
    public string PIN;
};
```

In the `Customer` class, define the `Savings_Balance` property:

```
//Savings Account Balance Template
public Balance Savings_Balance;
```

Append the `Savings_Balance` property to the builder object before the `OnCompletion` method:

```
builder.Field("Savings_Balance.AccountNumber", isBalance,
validate: async (state, response) =>
    {
        var result = new ValidateResult { IsValid = true, Value = response };
```

```csharp
                string accountnumber = (response as
                string);
                int accountnumberlength =
                accountnumber.Length;
                if (accountnumberlength <11||
                accountnumberlength >17)
                {
                    result.Feedback = "Please enter your
                    valid savings account number";
                    result.IsValid = false;
                }

                return result;
})
.Field("Savings_Balance.PIN", isBalance)
.Field(new FieldReflector<Customer>
("Savings_Balance.Availablebalance")
.SetType(null)
.SetActive((state) => state.Option ==
Options.SavingsAccountBalance)
.SetDefine(async (state, field) =>
        {
            if (state.Savings_Balance != null)
            {
                if
                (state.Savings_Balance
                .AccountNumber != null &&
                state.Savings_Balance.PIN !=
                null)
                {
                    string availableBalance =
                    SQLDatabaseService
                    .checkingAccountBalance
                    (state.Savings_Balance
                    .AccountNumber,
                    state.Savings_Balance.PIN);
                    if (availableBalance != null
                    && availableBalance != "")
                    {
                        field.SetPrompt(new
                        PromptAttribute($"Total
                        available savings
                        account balance is
                        ${availableBalance:F2}"
                        ));
                        return true;
                    }
                    else
```

```
                    {
                            return false;
                    }
            }
            else
            {
                    field.SetPrompt(new
                    PromptAttribute($"I'm sorry.
                    I didn't understand you."));
                    return true;
            }
        }
        else
        {
            field.SetPrompt(new
            PromptAttribute($"I'm sorry. I
            didn't understand you."));
            return true;
        }

}))
```

Also, add the following lines of code in the SQLDatabaseService.cs class to get the savings account balance from the database if the account number and pin match what you entered at account creation:

```
internal static string checkingAccountBalance(string accno, string pIN)
    {
        if (accno == null&&pIN==null)
        {
            return null;
        }
        try
        {
            SqlConnection connection = null;
            string query = null;
            connection = new SqlConnection("Data
            Source=k8bjlaohq3.database.windows.net;Initial
            Catalog=ivrbot_db;Integrated Security=False;User
            ID=datareadserver;Password=Astrani@2016;Connect
            Timeout=60;Encrypt=False;TrustServerCertificate=True;
            ApplicationIntent=ReadWrite;
            MultiSubnetFailover=False");
            connection.Open();
            MessagesController.accountnumlist = new
            List<Accountant_Information>();
            Accountant_Information accountantinf = new
            Accountant_Information();
```

```csharp
            string selectquery = "Select Saving_Balance from [dbo].
            [Accountant_Information] where
            AccountNumber="+accno+"AND PinNo="+pIN;// where
            AccountType="+accountType;
            using (SqlCommand cmd = new SqlCommand())
            {
                cmd.CommandText = selectquery;
                cmd.Connection = connection;
                SqlDataReader reader = cmd.ExecuteReader();
                if (reader.HasRows)
                {
                    while (reader.Read())
                    {
                        accountantinf.Balance =
                        reader["Saving_Balance"].ToString();

                    }

                }
                //connection.Close();
            }

            return accountantinf.Balance;
        }
        catch (Exception ex)
        {

        }
        return null;
    }
```

After adding the preceding lines of code, now you are ready to test your bot:

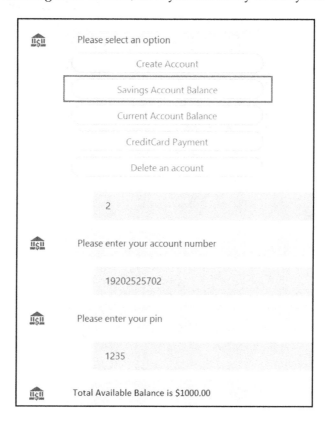

Checking your current account balance using the bot

In this step, I will explain how to build a FormFlow for checking your current account balance. After the savings account balance logic, append the following code for the current account logic:

```
//Current Account Balance Template
        public Currentbalance Current_Balance;

                            .Field("Current_Balance.AccountNumber",
                            isCurrentBalance, validate: async (state,
                            response) =>
                                {
                                    var result = new ValidateResult {
                                    IsValid = true, Value = response };
                                    string accountnumber = (response as
                                    string);
                                    int accountnumberlength =
                                    accountnumber.Length;
                                    if (accountnumberlength < 11 ||
                                    accountnumberlength > 17)
                                        {
                                            result.Feedback = "Please enter
                                            your valid current account
                                            number";
                                            result.IsValid = false;
                                        }
                                 return result;
                             })
                            .Field("Current_Balance.PIN", isCurrentBalance)
                            .Field(new FieldReflector<Customer>
                            ("Current_Balance.CurrentAvailablebalance")
                            .SetType(null)
                            .SetActive((state) => state.Option ==
                            Options.CurrentAccountBalance)
                            .SetDefine(async (state, field) h=>
                            {
                                if (state.Current_Balance != null)
                                {
                                    if (state.Current_Balance.AccountNumber
                                    != null && state.Current_Balance.PIN !=
                                    null)
                                    {
                                        string availableBalance =
                                        SQLDatabaseService
```

```
                            .checkingCurrentAccountBalance
                            (state.Current_Balance.
                            AccountNumber,
                            state.Current_Balance.PIN);
                            if (availableBalance != null &&
                            availableBalance != "")
                            {
                                field.SetPrompt(new
                                PromptAttribute($"Total
                                available current account
                                balance is
                                ${availableBalance:F2}"));
                                return true;
                            }
                            else
                            {
                                return false;
                            }
                        }
                        else
                        {
                            field.SetPrompt(new
                            PromptAttribute($"I'm sorry. I
                            didn't understand you."));
                            return true;
                        }
                    }
                    else
                    {
                        field.SetPrompt(new
                        PromptAttribute($"I'm sorry. I didn't
                        understand you."));
                        return true;
                    }
                }))
```

Also, add the following lines of code in the `SQLDatabaseService.cs` class; They contain the logic for getting the balance of the account whose account number and pin match the input details from the database:

```
internal static string checkingCurrentAccountBalance(string accountNumber,
string pIN)
        {
            if (accountNumber == null && pIN == null)
            {
                return null;
            }
```

```csharp
try
{
    SqlConnection connection = null;
    string query = null;
    connection = new SqlConnection("Data
    Source=k8bjlaohq3.database.windows.net;Initial
    Catalog=ivrbot_db;Integrated Security=False;User
    ID=datareadserver;Password=Astrani@2016;Connect
    Timeout=60;Encrypt=False;
    TrustServerCertificate=True;
    ApplicationIntent=ReadWrite;
    MultiSubnetFailover=False");
    connection.Open();
    MessagesController.accountnumlist = new
    List<Accountant_Information>();
    Accountant_Information accountantinf = new
    Accountant_Information();
    string selectquery = "Select Current_Balance from
    [dbo].[Accountant_Information] where AccountNumber=" +
    accountNumber + "AND PinNo=" + pIN;// where
    AccountType="+accountType;
    using (SqlCommand cmd = new SqlCommand())
    {
        cmd.CommandText = selectquery;
        cmd.Connection = connection;
        SqlDataReader reader = cmd.ExecuteReader();
        if (reader.HasRows)
        {
            while (reader.Read())
            {

                accountantinf.Balance =
                reader["Current_Balance"].ToString();

            }

        }
        //connection.Close();
    }

    return accountantinf.Balance;
}
catch (Exception ex)
{

}
return null;
}
```

After adding the preceding lines of code, now you are ready to test your **Current Account Balance**:

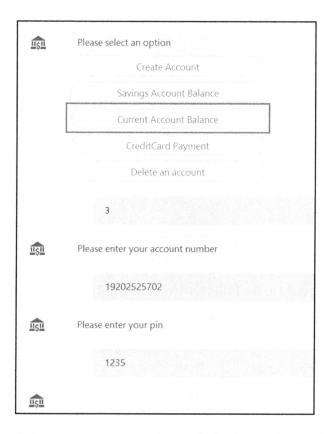

Next, type `quit` to exit the current conversation with this bot and start the next conversation from the initial step.

Paying your credit card bill using the bot

In this section, let's see how to build a FormFlow to pay a credit card bill using the bot. However, here we will not use a database; rather the bot will just contain static information.

Add the `CreditCardPayment` class:

```
[Serializable]
    class CreditCardPayment
    {
        [Prompt("Please enter your creditcard number")]
        public string CreditcardNumber;
        [Prompt("Please enter how much amount do you want to pay")]
        public string Pay;
        public string CreditCardPaymentSuccessMessage;
    };
```

Next, in the `Customer` class, define the following public field/property:

```
public CreditCardPayment CreditCard_Payment;
```

Append the following code to the builder object to perform the credit card payment; add it before `OnCompletion(accountStatus)`:

```
Field("CreditCard_Payment.Pay", isCreditCardPayment)
                .Field(new FieldReflector<Customer>
                ("CreditCard_Payment
                .CreditCardPaymentSuccessMessage")
                .SetType(null)
                .SetActive((state) => state.Option ==
                Options.CreditCardPayment)
                .SetDefine(async (state, field) =>
                {
                    field.SetPrompt(new
                    PromptAttribute($"Successfully paid your
                    credit card payment."+"(Yes)"));
                    return true;
                }))
```

After adding the preceding lines of code, now you are ready to test your bot:

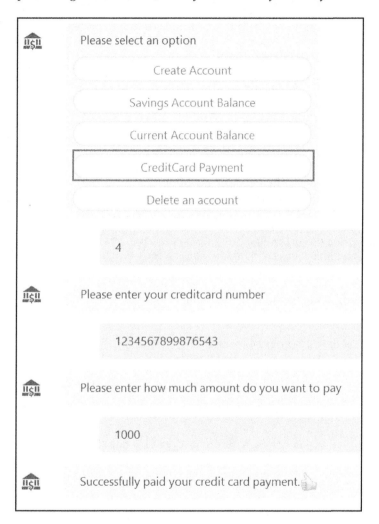

Next, type `quit` to exit the current conversation with this bot and start the next conversation from the initial step.

Deleting an account using the bot

In this step, I will explain how to build a FormFlow to delete an account using this bot.

Add the following class to delete an account:

```
class DeleteAccount
    {
        [Prompt("Are you sure want to delete your account?")]
        public string DeleteConfirmationMessage;
        public string DeleteSuccessMessage;
    };
```

To delete an account, we need the account number. Define a field for the `DeleteAccount` class and one more field for the account number in the `Customer` class, as follows:

```
public DeleteAccount Delete;
        [Template(TemplateUsage.EnumSelectOne, "Please select your {&}
        {||}", ChoiceStyle = ChoiceStyleOptions.PerLine)]
        public string AccountNumber;
```

Append the following code to the `builder` object before `OnCompletion(accountStatus)`:

```
.Field(new FieldReflector<Customer>
        (nameof(Customer.AccountNumber))
            .SetType(null)
            .SetActive((state) => state.Option ==
            Options.DeleteAccount)
            .SetDefine(async (state, field) =>
              {
                if (state.AccountType != null)
                  {
                  MessagesController.accountnumlist
                  = SQLDatabaseService
                  .getAccountNumbers
                  (state.AccountType);

                    if (MessagesController.accountnumlist
                        != null &&
                        MessagesController.accountnumlist
                        .Count() > 0)
                        {
                         foreach (var account in
                         MessagesController.accountnumlist)
                         {
```

```
                    field.AddDescription(account.
                    AccountNumber.ToString(),
                    account.AccountNumber.ToString())


                    .AddTerms(account.AccountNumber.ToString(),
                    account.AccountNumber.ToString(),
                    account.AccountNumber.ToString());

                  }
                return true;
             }
           else
             {
             field.SetPrompt(new PromptAttribute
             ($"I'm sorry. I didn't understand you."));
              return false;
              }
           }
        else
         {
        // field.SetPrompt(new PromptAttribute
             ($"I'm sorry. I didn't understand you."));
             return true;
         }
       }))
    .Field("Delete.DeleteConfirmationMessage",
         isDelete)
    .Field(new FieldReflector<Customer>("Delete")
       .SetType(null)
       .SetActive((state) => state.Option ==
                 Options.DeleteAccount)
       .SetDefine(async (state, field) =>
          {
           if (state.Delete != null)
             {
              if (state.AccountNumber != null &&
                 state.Delete.DeleteConfirmationMessage
                 .ToLower() == "yes")
                   {
                   bool result = SQLDatabaseService.
                   DeleteAccountNumber(state.
                   AccountNumber);
                     if (result == true)
                       {
                        field.SetPrompt(new
                        PromptAttribute($"Successfully
                        deleted your account."));
```

```
                                    return true;
                                }
                                else
                                {
                                    return false;
                                }
                            }
                            else
                            {
                                field.SetPrompt(new
                                    PromptAttribute($"I'm sorry.
                                    I didn't understand you."));
                                return true;
                            }
                        }
                        else
                        {
                            return true;
                        }
                    }))

                .OnCompletionAsync(accountStatus)
                .Build();
        }
    };
}
```

Next, add the following lines of code in the SQLDatabaseService class. These lines contain the logic to delete the selected account from the Azure SQL database:

```
            internal static bool DeleteAccountNumber(string accountNumber)
            {
                bool result = false;
                if (accountNumber == null)
                {
                    return false;
                }
                try
                {
                    SqlConnection connection = null;
                    string query = null;
                    connection = new SqlConnection("Data
                    Source=k8bjlaohq3.database.windows.net;Initial
                    Catalog=ivrbot_db;Integrated Security=False;User
                    ID=datareadserver;Password=Astrani@2016;Connect
                    Timeout=60;Encrypt=False;TrustServerCertificate=True;
                    ApplicationIntent=ReadWrite;MultiSubnetFailover=False"
                    );
```

```
            connection.Open();

            string deletequery = "Delete from [dbo].
            [Accountant_Information] where AccountNumber="
            + accountNumber;
            using (SqlCommand cmd = new SqlCommand())
            {
                cmd.CommandText = deletequery;
                cmd.Connection = connection;
                cmd.ExecuteNonQuery();
                result = true;
                // connection.Close();
                return result;
            }
        }
        catch (Exception ex)
        {

        }
        return result;
    }
```

After adding the preceding lines of code, now you are ready to test your bot:

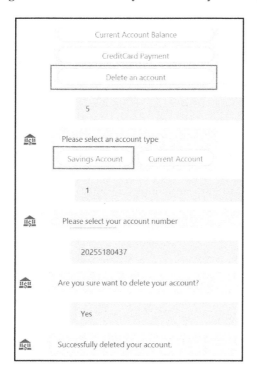

Summary

In this chapter, we have learned about FormFlow. With the help of the FormFlow, we can build bots that depend on guided conversations, such as ordering a sandwich, booking a movie ticket, setting up an appointment with a doctor, and so on. These types of scenario can be built with less effort using FormFlow.

7
Intelligent Bots with Microsoft Bot Framework and Service Fabric

In this chapter, we will learn how **Service Fabric** helps to develop intelligent bots using stateless and stateful microservices.

Azure Service Fabric is an Azure service offered by Microsoft to develop and publish microservice-based applications and perform life cycle management. Developers have the ability to select which architecture they want to use, such as stateless or stateful services. This allows developers to develop an architectural approach where complex applications are involved and composed of small, independently versioned services to scale in the cloud with Azure Service Fabric.

The name **stateless microservices** itself tells that they will not maintain state. Protocol gateways and web proxies do not maintain a mutable state outside a request and its response from the service. The best examples of stateless microservice architecture are Azure Cloud Services worker roles.

Stateful microservices will maintain a mutable state beyond a request and its response. Databases, devices, shopping carts, and queues maintain a mutable state.

The following are the reasons why we need stateful microservices as well as stateless microservices:

- Stateful microservices will help you to build services with high throughput and low latency and also provide failure-tolerant **Online Transaction Processing** (**OLTP**) services. This can be achieved by keeping code and data together on the same machine.
- This also helps to simplify application design. This will remove the need for additional queues and caches, which are required in case of a stateless application. Stateful services naturally have high availability and low latency.

We can make use of microservices to publish our intelligent bots, allow continuous integration and development practices, and also accelerate delivery of new bot features to the application. This also has out-of-the-box support in Visual Studio tooling, as well as command-line support, so developers can quickly and easily build, test, debug, deploy, and update their bot applications on single-box, test, and production deployments.

In previous chapters, we developed and deployed our bot applications in Microsoft Azure App Service. Azure app service is also a great offering by Microsoft, but only when the following scenarios are met:

- Developing large-scale bots that respond to interactions as quickly as possible
- Managing the state of bots that will help us track what the customers said, and potentially use those conversations to learn what our customer's likes and dislikes are
- To apply a granular programming model, which will help us improve our bot without affecting its availability

If you take these scenarios into consideration, the only way to achieve it is with the help of Service Fabric. Service Fabric is a great platform for developing and hosting bots using Microsoft Bot Framework, mainly for the following reasons:

- Service Fabric has an **actor programming model**, which fits nicely into a bot scenario, as potentially each conversation could become an active conversation.
- To store bot state, we can use stateful actors or stateful services for all conversations.
- We don't need to bother about the availability of your bot service; Service Fabric will handle it for us. It also allows us to develop and publish multiple versions of a bot without affecting the previous version and its availability.

If we use stateful microservices, we will accomplish all of these scenarios. However, in this chapter, we mainly focus on getting started with Service Fabric and making the concept simple to understand for beginners. Because of that, we are going with stateless microservices, which will also be a great option to choose for bots.

Getting started using stateless microservices

First, we will learn how to develop a bot and publish/host in Service Fabric using stateless microservices.

Setting up your development environment for Service Fabric

To build and run Azure Service Fabric applications on your development machine, install the runtime, SDK, and tools. It's also necessary to enable execution of the Windows PowerShell scripts that are included in the SDK.

Prerequisites

The following operating system versions are supported for development:

- Windows 7
- Windows 8/Windows 8.1
- Windows Server 2012 R2
- Windows Server 2016
- Windows 10

Installing the SDK and tools

In Visual Studio 2015, Service Fabric tools are installed together with the SDK; if you cannot find the Service Fabric templates or tools, then you can install them with the help of **Web Platform Installer** or go through `http://www.microsoft.com/web/handlers/webpi.ashx?command=getinstallerredirect&appid=MicrosoftAzure-ServiceFabric-VS2015` to download the Service Fabric SDK and tools.

Enabling PowerShell script execution

Service Fabric uses Windows PowerShell scripts to create a local development cluster and to deploy applications from Visual Studio. By default, these scripts are prevented from running by Windows. To enable them, you are required to modify the PowerShell execution policy. Enter the following command after opening PowerShell as an administrator:

```
Set-ExecutionPolicy -ExecutionPolicy Unrestricted -Force -Scope CurrentUser
```

Creating a stateless Service Fabric web API

A Service Fabric application can contain one or more services; every application can have a specific role or specific functionality to deliver what the consumers need. VS2015 will create an application, along with your first service project, if you use the **New Project** wizard. The steps for creating a stateless service fabric web API are as follows:

1. Launch Visual Studio as an administrator.

2. Click on **File** | **New Project** | **Cloud** | **Service Fabric Application**.

Chapter 7

3. Name the application and click on **OK**:

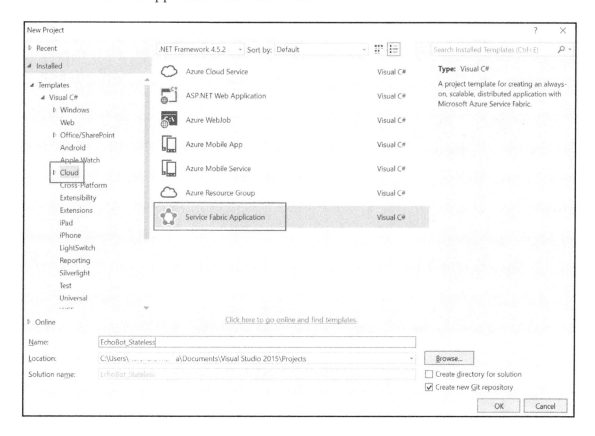

4. On the next page, select **Stateless Web API** as the first service type. Name it and click on **OK**:

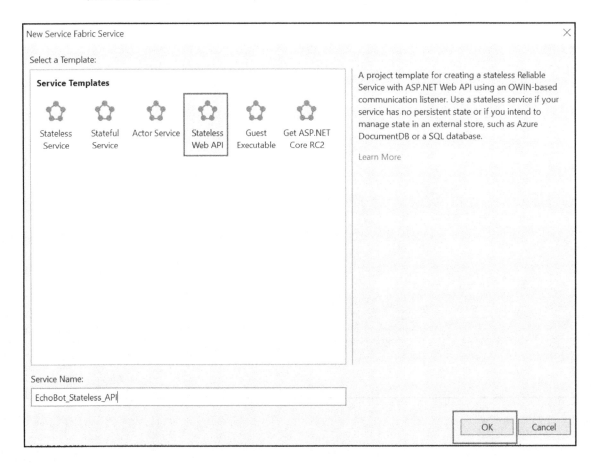

Chapter 7

5. Install the `Microsoft.Bot.Builder NuGet` package. Before installing, change your API project target to **.NET Framework 4.6** under **Target framework**:

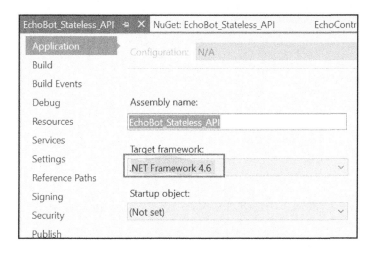

6. Open the **Manage NuGet Packages...** window:

[249]

7. Search for **Microsoft.Bot.Builder**, and install the latest version:

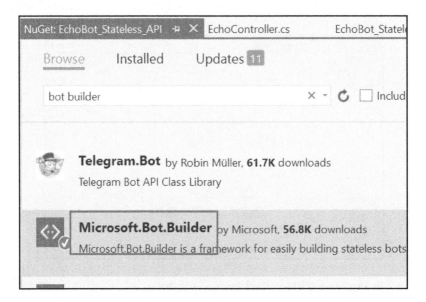

8. Now, modify your API controller. In this section, we are developing an **echo bot**. So, update the code for the echo bot, which will simply reply with an echo of the user's message.
9. The Post method accepts messages from the user as an activity, which contains all conversation information between a user and our bot. Using this, we can see what kind of information the user wants to get from the bot.
10. Update the Post method with the following code, which is similar to the Post method generated by the Bot Application template in previous chapters:

```
[BotAuthentication(MicrosoftAppId ="",MicrosoftAppPassword ="")]
public class EchoController : ApiController
{
public async Task<HttpResponseMessage>
Post([FromBody]Activity message)
```

Here, we defined a sample bot, which will reply to our user with what the user said.

11. Bot Framework provides many features, including how to identify the type of incoming message, and based on that, your bot can respond to the user. To identify that, we have the activity types enum, which will provide information about the conversation.

12. To identify and apply business logic to the message sent by the user, we will write the following code in the `Post` method:

    ```
    if (message.Type.ToLower() == "message")
    {
    }
    ```

13. If the user is sending a message, it means that they are asking the bot something. So, we will receive the messsage, process it, apply some business logic, and reply to the user.
    To reply to the user, we need a `ConnectorClient` object, which provides connector REST API services to forward messages from the bot to the user:

    ```
    if (message.Type.ToLower() == "message
    {
    var connector = new ConnectorClient(new
    Uri(message.ServiceUrl));
    var reply = message.CreateReply($"Service Fabric knows you said
    : {message.Text}");
    await connector.Conversations.ReplyToActivityAsync(reply);
    }
    else
    {
    HandleSystemMessage(message);
    }
    ```

14. The following is the code for handling activity types other than the Message type Activity:

    ```
    private Activity HandleSystemMessage(Activity message)
    {
    if (message.Type == "Ping")
    {
    //Message reply = message.CreateReplyMessage();
    //reply.Type = "Ping";
    //return reply;
    }
    else if (message.Type == "DeleteUserData")
    {
    // Implement user deletion here
    // If we handle user deletion, return a real message
    }
    else if (message.Type == "BotAddedToConversation")
    {
    }
    else if (message.Type == "BotRemovedFromConversation")
    {
    ```

```
}
else if (message.Type == "UserAddedToConversation")
{
}
else if (message.Type == "UserRemovedFromConversation")
{
}
else if (message.Type == "EndOfConversation")
{
}
return null;
}
```

We can reply to the user from the bot based on the Activity done by the user with the help of the preceding code.

15. The `Post` method accepts an input as an Activity type, which will hold all the information related to the conversation between the bot and the user. The `Activity` class is very important and is responsible for all chats/conversations between the bot and user; the bot knows from which user it got the message because of the activity object. It holds complete information about the user, message information, previous conversations, and more.
16. When a user sends a message to the bot, the `Post` method receives that message along with all other information and saves it as an activity object. The following is the information our activity object will have at the time of the `Post` request.
17. Here is the complete code example:

```
public async Task<HttpResponseMessage>
Post([FromBody]Activity message)
{
if (message.Type.ToLower() == "message")
{
var connector = new ConnectorClient(new Uri(message.ServiceUrl));
var reply = message.CreateReply($"Service Fabric knows you said : {message.Text}");
await connector.Conversations.ReplyToActivityAsync(reply);
}
else
{
HandleSystemMessage(message);
}
return new
HttpResponseMessage(System.Net.HttpStatusCode.Accepted);
}
private Activity HandleSystemMessage(Activity message)
{
```

```
            if (message.Type == "Ping")
            {
            //Message reply = message.CreateReplyMessage();
            //reply.Type = "Ping";
            //return reply;
            }
            else if (message.Type == "DeleteUserData")
            {
            // Implement user deletion here
            // If we handle user deletion, return a real message
            }
            else if (message.Type == "BotAddedToConversation")
            {
            }
            else if (message.Type == "BotRemovedFromConversation")
            {
            }
            else if (message.Type == "UserAddedToConversation")
            {
            }
            else if (message.Type == "UserRemovedFromConversation")
            {
            }
            else if (message.Type == "EndOfConversation")
            {
            }
            return null;
            }
```

18. The `Post` method receives this in JSON format from the user as an Activity. It contains the Activity Type, Service URL (which is a bot published URL), Channel ID (Facebook, Slack, Skype, and so on), from whom we received message from the sender, conversation information, and text means message typed by user; if it has any attachments, it will be under attachments section. Based on this information, the bot will respond to the user.

19. Before debugging your application, make sure that no other application on your PC is using the port that is going to be used by Service Fabric stateless microservice, since the port numbers are automatically assigned by Visual Studio at the time of project creation. You can modify it if any other application is already using it in your dev machine. The following step explains how to change/modify it.

Intelligent Bots with Microsoft Bot Framework and Service Fabric

20. You can check which port your microservice is configured on. Follow these steps to check which port is being used and how to change the URL if you want:
    1. Right-click on your Service Fabric project and select **Properties**, as shown in the following screenshot:

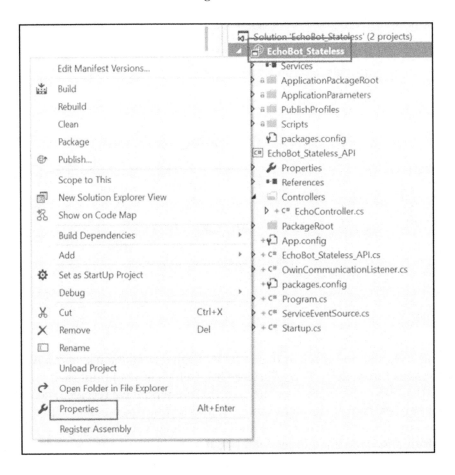

Chapter 7

2. After choosing **Properties**, the next window will open, as shown in the following screenshot:

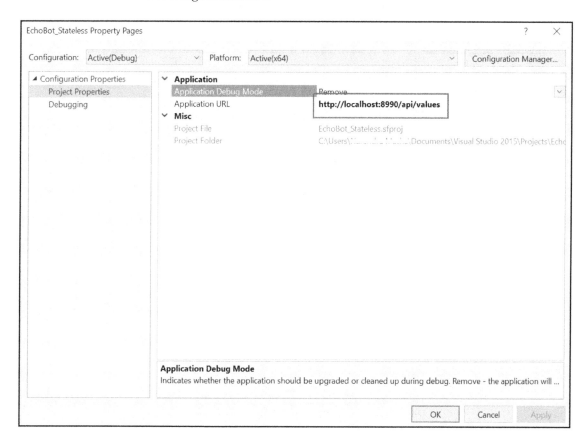

3. Just check the **Application URL**, choose the edit option from the drop-down list, and then modify your URL if you want as shown in the following screenshot:

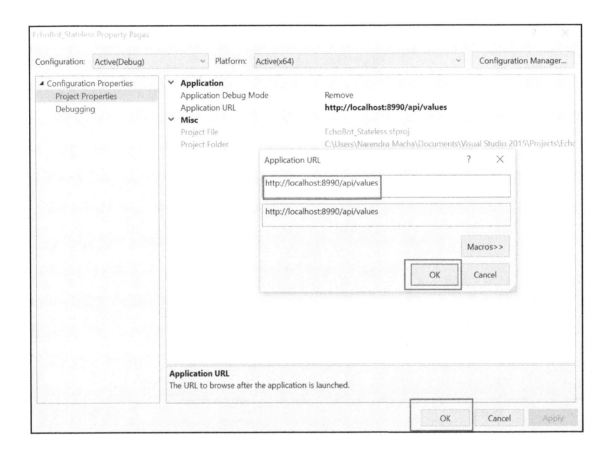

Chapter 7

21. Next, you have to build your project without any errors, and then click on the **Start** button to start debugging your project, as follows:

[257]

22. After clicking on the **Start** button, your application will be deployed to the local cluster, as follows:

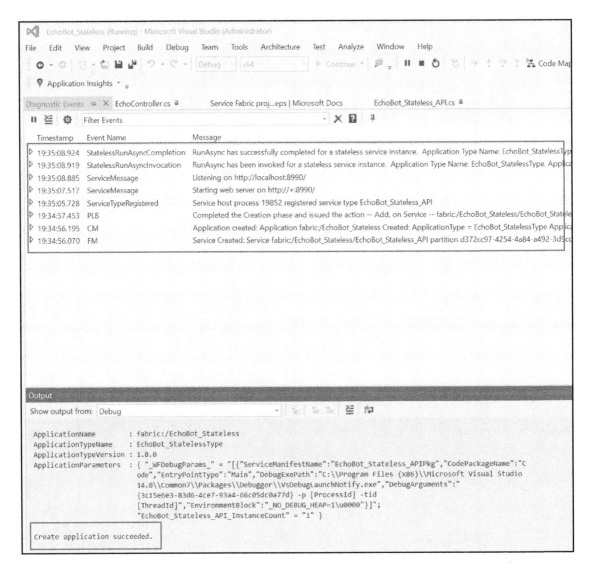

Chapter 7

23. After successfully deploying your application to the local cluster (which is automatically installed as part of the Service Fabric SDK), open your **Service Fabric Explorer** by clicking on **Manage Local Cluster**. You can find this inside settings, as shown in the following image:

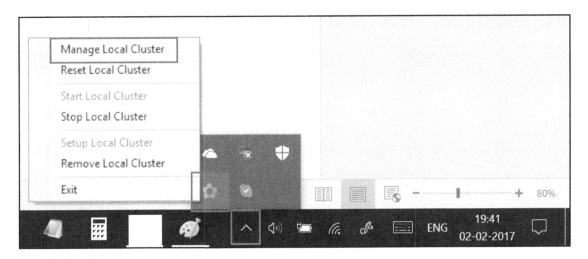

24. After selecting the **Manage Local Cluster** option, the following window will open:

[259]

25. Now, Open the bot emulator. Then, you just have to start the emulator and change the URL to `http://localhost:8990/api/echo`, which is where we are publishing the stateless web API:

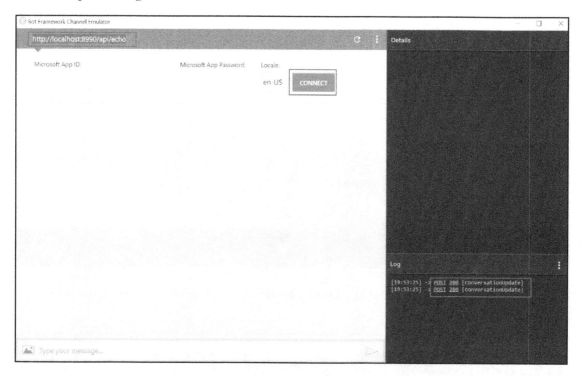

26. Type your message and then the bot should politely repeat what you said, as shown here:

Chapter 7

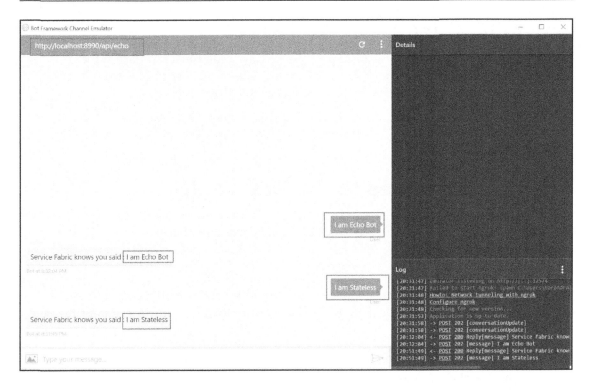

We have now developed, built, and tested on the local Service Fabric cluster, but if you want to access it in Skype or Slack through Bot Framework, you must publish the Service Fabric cluster in Azure. Next, we will see how to publish the Service Fabric project in Azure.

Publishing a Service Fabric project in Azure

It is important that we need to create a secure cluster in Azure. For that, we need to set up a **Key Vault** to manage keys and certificates. For more information on the Azure Key Vault and certificates, follow this
link, `https://docs.microsoft.com/en-us/azure/key-vault/key-vault-get-started`

Create Key Vault

Create a **Key Vault** in the new resource group. The Key Vault must be enabled for deployment to allow the Service Fabric resource provider to get certificates from it and install on cluster nodes. The following is the PowerShell script:

```
New-AzureRmKeyVault -VaultName 'myvault' -ResourceGroupName
'mycluster-keyvault' -Location 'East US' -EnabledForDeployment
```

Adding certificates to the Key Vault

This certificate is required to secure a cluster and prevent unauthorized access to it. To make this process easier, a PowerShell module is available on GitHub (https://github.com/kishoreismac/Service-Fabric/tree/master/Scripts/ServiceFabricRPHelpers).

The `ServiceFabricRPHelpers.psm1` module provides helper methods for adding certificates to the Key Vault for use in the Service Fabric cluster. Follow these steps to use the module:

1. Go to the module directory.
2. Import the module:

   ```
   Import-Module .\ServiceFabricRPHelpers.psm1
   ```

3. The following screenshot explains the preceding code:

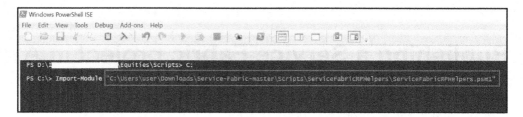

4. The command name is as follows:
   `Invoke-AddCertToKeyVault`

   The following is the syntax:

   ```
   Invoke-AddCertToKeyVault -SubscriptionId {Enter your Subscription
   ID} -ResourceGroupName BotFabric -Location "East US" -VaultName
   Bot-key-vault -CertificateName botscert -Password "password" -
   CreateSelfSignedCertificate -OutputPath "C:\Certs" -DnsName
   https://{yourclustername}.centralus.cloudapp.azure.com:8080
   ```

5. The DNS URL will be the URL of your cluster. Before using it, check whether the URL is available to you. The following is the example I generated using PowerShell:

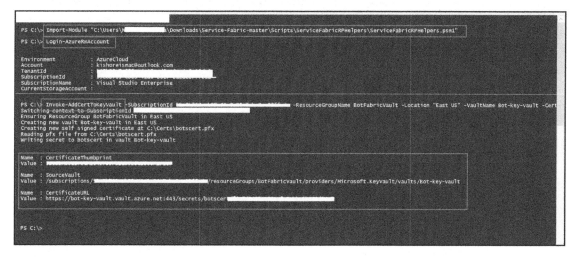

6. Copy the `CertificateThumbprint`, `SourceVault`, and `CertificateURL`.

Creating a cluster in the Azure portal

Follow these steps to create the cluster in the Azure portal:

1. Sign in to the `Azure portal`.
2. Click on **New**, then search for **Service Fabric Cluster** under **Everything**.
3. Select **Service Fabric Cluster:**

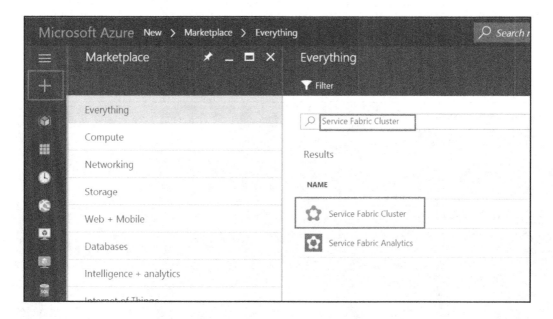

4. It navigates to the **Service Fabric Cluster** blade like shown in the following screenshot; click on **Create:**

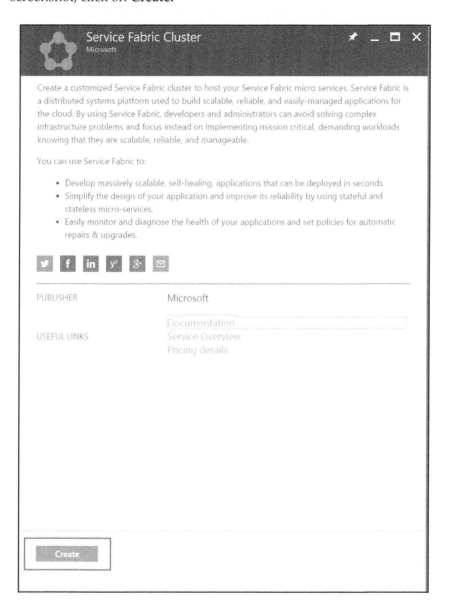

5. The following four steps are shown in the **Create Service Fabric cluster** window:

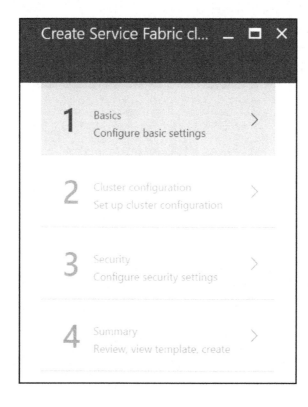

Chapter 7

6. You are required to provide the basic details of your cluster in the **Basics** tab:

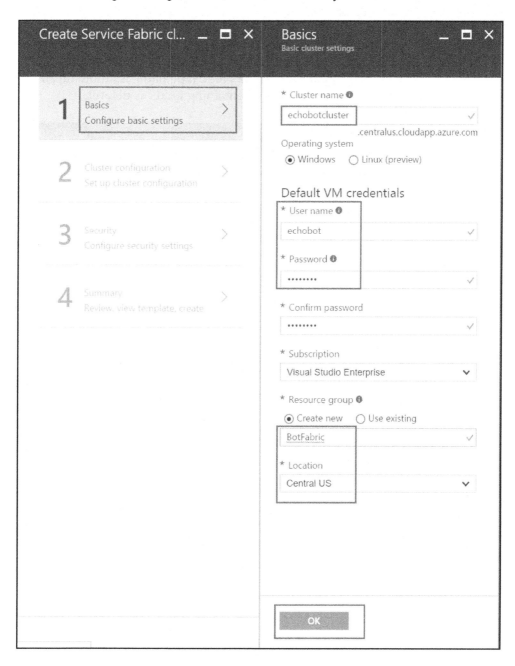

7. In **Cluster Configuration**, configure your cluster nodes. Node types define the VM sizes, the number of VMs, and properties. The cluster can have more than one node type, but it is necessary that the primary node type (the first one that was defined in the portal) must have at least five VMs, as this is the node type where the Service Fabric system services are placed. Placement properties, because a default placement property of Node type name is automatically added. Enter all required fields and leave the remaining fields as default:

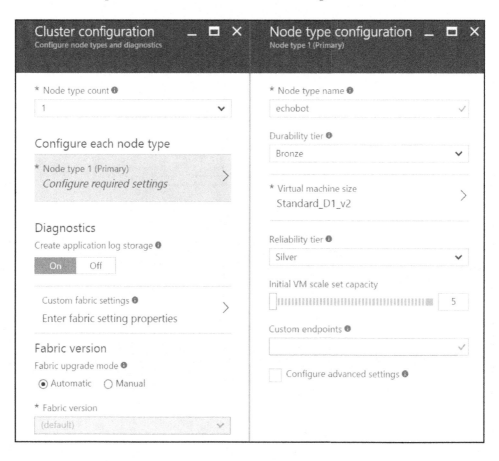

Chapter 7

8. In the **Security** tab, you must select **Secure** and enter the details that you copied in the Key Vault creation step:

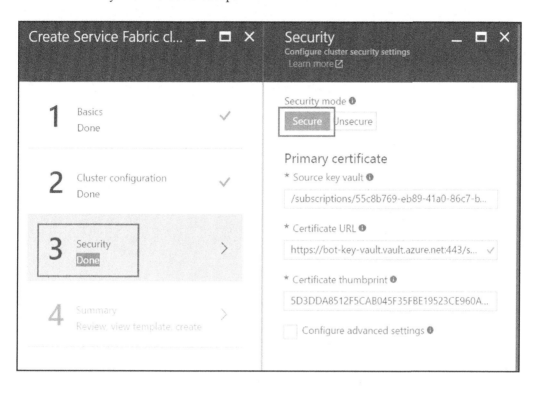

9. The final step is **Summary**; once validation is successful, you can click on the **Create** option on the **Summary** window:

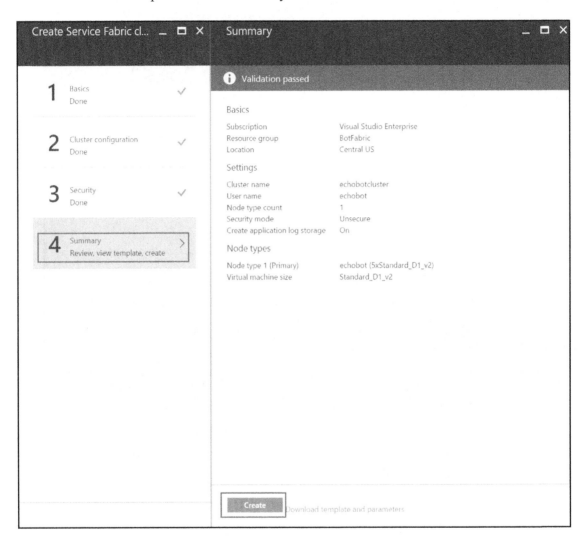

10. It takes several minutes to deploy a cluster; after the successful creation of the cluster, verify it by opening it.
11. Click on **More services**:

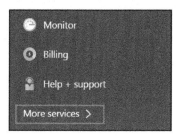

12. Select **Service Fabric clusters**:

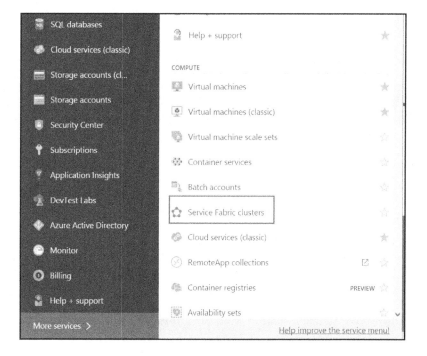

13. You can now see your list of clusters; click on your recently created cluster:

14. Now, click on **Explorer** to open **Service Fabric Explorer**:

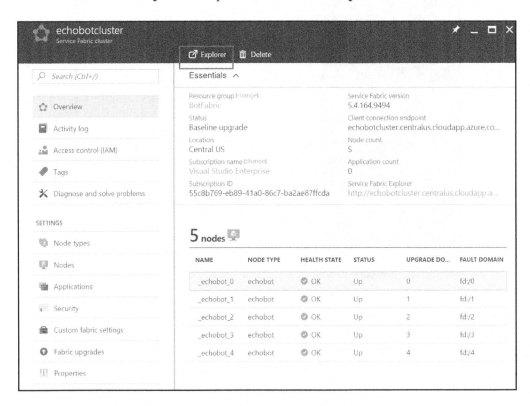

Chapter 7

15. In **Service Fabric Explorer**, you can see details of the services, health logs, and more.

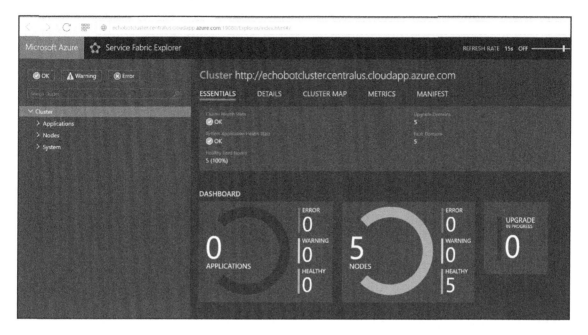

16. Now, go back to Visual Studio, where our echo bot stateless service project is being developed. Right-click on the Service Fabric project and click on **Publish**.

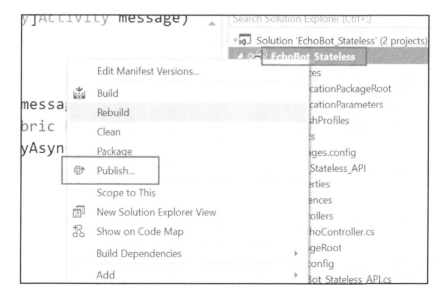

[273]

17. In the **Publish Service Fabric Application** window, select your Azure account and select the cluster endpoint, then click on **Publish**.

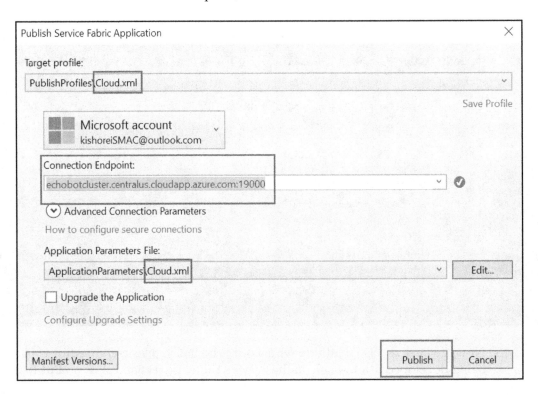

18. Once it has been published, go to Azure echobot cluster Service Fabric explorer; you will see the recently published cluster and its services, as shown in the following screenshot:

Chapter 7

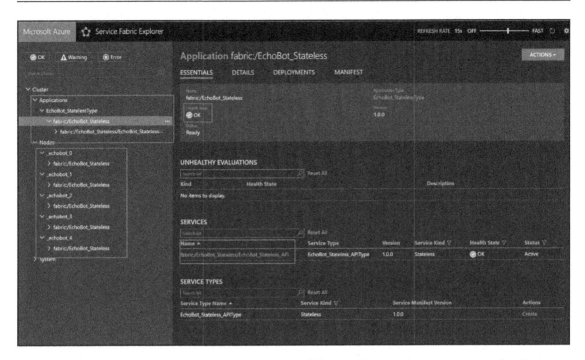

19. Now, copy the client endpoint that will be used as the bot message endpoint:

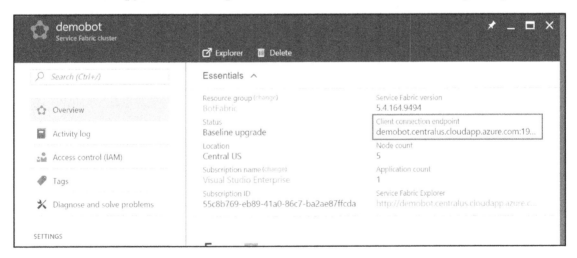

20. Now, register a new bot in `dev.botframework.com` (refer to `Chapter 9`, *Publishing a Bot to Skype, Slack, Facebook, and the GroupMe Channel* the *Registering your Bot with Microsoft Bot Framework* section), enter the message endpoint as your Service Fabric endpoint, and append `/api/echo` to it in the bot's settings, as shown in the following screenshot:

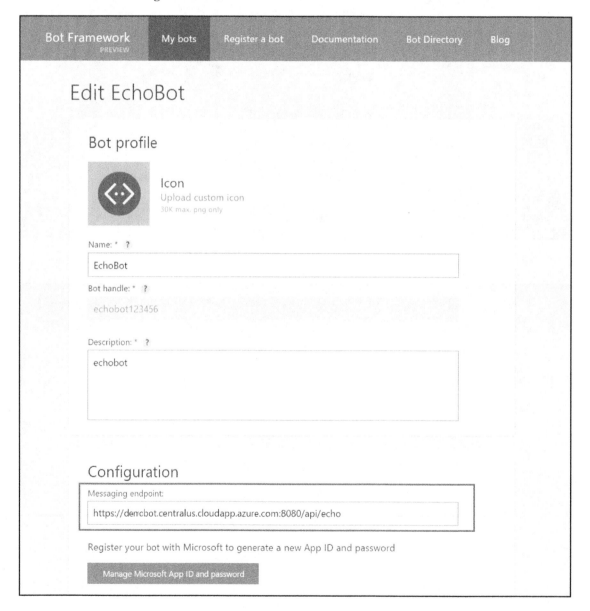

21. The port number 8080 mentioned in the endpoint will be the same as mentioned in the stateless API microservice project, under `ServiceManifest.xml`:

```xml
</CodePackage>
<!-- Config package is the contents of the Config directoy under PackageRoot that
    independently-updateable and versioned set of custom configuration settings
<ConfigPackage Name="Config" Version="1.0.0" />

<Resources>
  <Endpoints>
    <!-- This endpoint is used by the communication listener to obtain the port o
        listen. Please note that if your service is partitioned, this port is sh
        replicas of different partitions that are placed in your code. -->
    <Endpoint Protocol="http" Name="ServiceEndpoint" Type="Input" Port="8080" />
  </Endpoints>
</Resources>
</ServiceManifest>
```

22. Now, copy the `MicrosoftAppId` and `MicrosoftAppPassword` of the bot and update them in the `EchoController` class, as shown in the following screenshot:

```csharp
namespace EchoBot_Stateless_API.Controllers
{
    [BotAuthentication(MicrosoftAppId = "e...",
        MicrosoftAppPassword = "...")]
    public class EchoController : ApiController
    {
        // GET api/values
```

23. Now, add your bot to Skype and Slack; refer to Chapter 9, *Publishing a Bot to Skype, Slack, Facebook, and the GroupMe Channel* the *Configuring channels* section.

[277]

Summary

In this chapter, we introduced Service Fabric and stateless and stateful microservices, and how these help in the development of bots using Microsoft Bot Framework. Also, we saw how to set up a development environment, the prerequisites for Service Fabric, and the tools needed for programming. This chapter is based on helping developers quickly and easily build, test, debug, deploy, and update their bot applications for single-box, test, and production deployments. It also shows how Service Fabric helps our bots to scale and be managed easily with a Service Fabric cluster.

In the coming chapters, we will see how bots can help us with the **Internet of Things** (**IoT**).

8
Developing Intelligent Facial Expression Identification Bot for IoT Using Azure and Power BI

In previous chapters, we have gone through the concepts of Bot Framework and Cognitive Services, such as LUIS, the linguistic service, and so on that are involved in developing and publishing bot applications. In this chapter, we will mainly focus on integrating IoT, the bot, and Power BI and see how can we leverage the power of bots and Cognitive Services in IoT. Here, we will develop an IoT application that will capture photos from a USB camera connected to the Raspberry Pi, then process it using the Face API and Emotion API of Cognitive Services to identify facial expressions. Once it completes the processing and identifies the face and emotional expression, the IoT application then sends it to the Facial Expression and Identification bot and also to Power BI to show reports.

Before getting started

I assume that you have some knowledge of the following topics. If you don't go through the following topics and links:

1. Bot Framework.
2. Raspberry Pi: In this chapter, we will not cover how to configure the Raspberry Pi, so check out the following link on how to set up the device for development: https://developer.microsoft.com/en-us/windows/iot/getstarted
3. Windows 10 IoT Core: In this chapter, we will use Windows 10 IoT Core as our operating system on the Raspberry Pi. For how to install set it up on the Raspberry Pi, check out the following link: https://developer.microsoft.com/en-us/windows/iot/getstarted
4. UWP app development: The project we are developing for the Raspberry Pi is a UWP app, so you must have some basic knowledge of UWP app development: https://docs.microsoft.com/en-in/windows/uwp/get-started/whats-a-uwp
5. Microsoft Azure IoT Hub: We need Microsoft Azure IoT Hub to easily and securely connect your IoT devices (Raspberry Pi2). Use device-to-cloud telemetry data to understand the state of your devices and assets, and be ready to take action when a device needs your attention: https://docs.microsoft.com/en-us/azure/iot-hub
6. Storage account, and blobs: As part of facial analysis, we will save captured pictures in Azure blob storage: https://docs.microsoft.com/en-in/azure/storage/storage-dotnet-how-to-use-blobs
7. Stream analytics: The stream analytics job will take IoT Hub telemetry data and send it to Power BI to show reports: https://docs.microsoft.com/en-us/azure/stream-analytics
8. Power BI: It will generate reports, charts, and analysis of the facial analysis data: https://powerbi.microsoft.com/en-us/learning

Configuring Raspberry Pi and sensors

In this project, we will use the Raspberry Pi 2 and Adafruit kit components to use a PIR (Pyroelectric/Passive Infrared Sensor) motion sensor to detect the motion of an object, which triggers a USB webcam to snap a photo and send it to the bot.

Prerequisites

Before getting started with the project, let's take a look at the hardware and software requirements.

Hardware

The following list details are the hardware required for the project:

- Raspberry Pi2 Model B
- Breadboard
- Logitech USB camera (this component is not there in Adafruit kit)
- PIR motion sensor
- LED
- Resistor
- Adafruit female to male jumper wires (only five wires needed)

Software

Now, let's take a look at the software required for the project:

- Windows 10 PC
- Visual Studio 2015 Community Edition or Enterprise Edition
- Azure subscription
- Azure App Service (API App)
- Azure IoT Hub

Now that we are equipped with all the hardware and software required for this project, let's get started with configuring the Raspberry Pi and sensors.

Setting up sensors

Before setting up the sensors, you need to know about the Raspberry Pi's GPIO pins. In the following diagram, you can see the pins and their specifications. In later sections, we will mention these names as part of the development process.

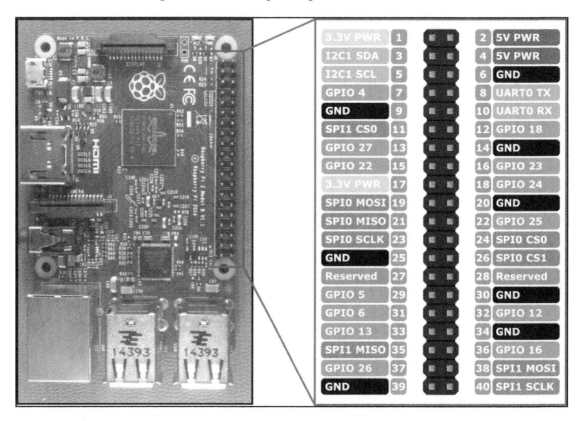

Take a look at the circuit diagram for our project, drawn using the Fritzing application, which is freely available to enthusiasts. For more information, check out `http://fritzing.org/home/`:

Chapter 8

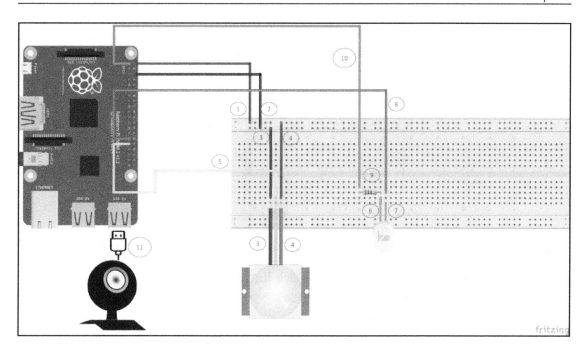

Now that we are familiar with the circuit diagram, let's take look at the following steps to understand it:

1. **Providing a 5V power supply to the breadboard**: In the first step, you have to provide a 5V power supply to the breadboard from the Raspberry Pi. For that, take a female to male jumper wire, connect the female end to the Raspberry Pi 5V pin, which is next to the positive line on the breadboard, as shown in the following diagram:

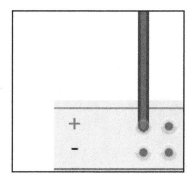

2. **Connect Ground to breadboard**: In this step, you have to connect Ground to the breadboard. For that, take a female to male jumper wire, connect the female end to the Raspberry Pi ground pin, which is the sixth GND pin shown in the preceding GPIO pin reference diagram. Now, connect the male end to the negative line on the breadboard, as shown in the following diagram:

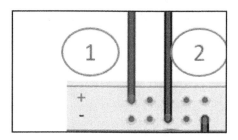

3. **Now Connect Ground/Negative/Black line of PIR sensor**: The breadboard PIR sensor has three pins--GND, OUT, and 5V; connect the GND pin to the breadboard, as shown in the following diagram:

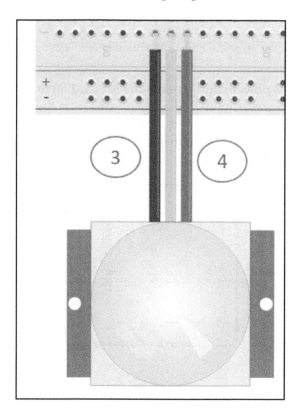

Now, take the male to male jumper wire and connect one end to the PIR sensor's GND pin, and the other end to the breadboard ground, as shown in the following figure:

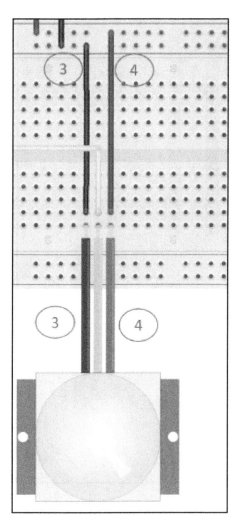

4. Similarly, as in the preceding step, now connect the 5V power supply/red line from the PIR sensor to the breadboard:

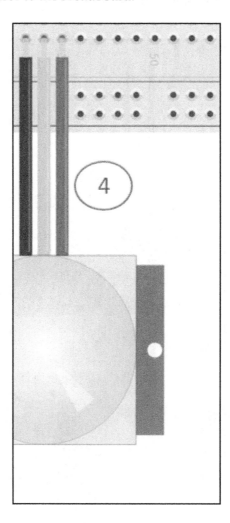

Now, take a male to male jumper wire and connect one end to the PIR sensor power supply pin, and the other end to the breadboard 5V power supply, as shown in the following figure:

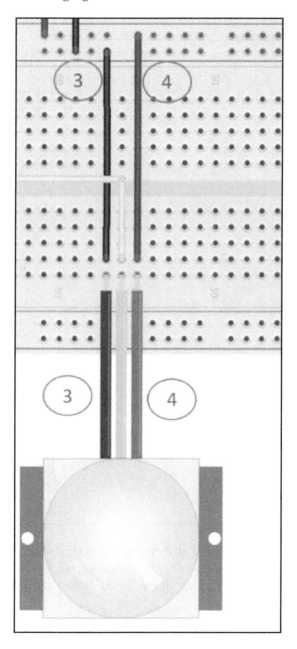

5. **Connect the OUT pin of the PIR sensor to the breadboard, and the other end to the Raspberry Pi's GPIO6 which is pin 31**: Now, connect the OUT pin of the PIR sensor to the breadboard as shown in the preceding step. From breadboard, take a male to female jumper wire and connect it to the Raspberry Pi:

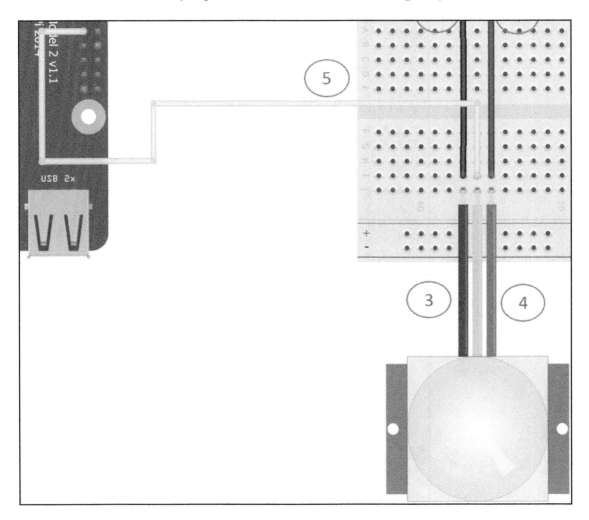

6. **In step 6 and 7, take an LED and connect it to the breadboard**: Now, connect the LED to the breadboard; remember that the long edge is the anode (+) and the short edge is the cathode (-), as shown in the following diagram:

Chapter 8

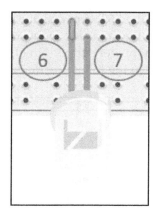

 You should not the place anode and cathode points in the same vertical hole on the breadboard. They can be in the same horizontal hole but not in the same vertical hole.

7. **Now connect the cathode point of the LED to GPIO pin 5 which is pin 29 on the Raspberry Pi**: Take a look at the eighth step in the following diagram-- the purple line that connects the LED cathode to the Raspberry Pi GPIO pin 5.

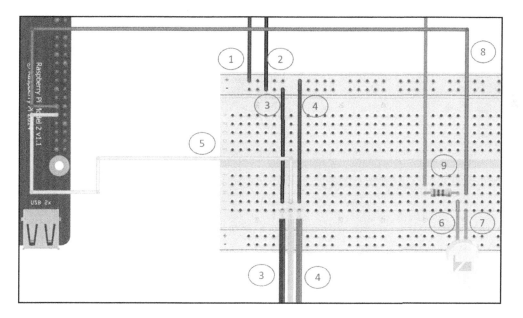

[289]

8. **In this steps we connect the 560-ohm resistor to the breadboard**: Take a 560-ohm resistor and connect the gold side to the anode side of LED and the green side of the resistor to 3.3V power supply pin of the Raspberry Pi; refer to the orange line marked as 10 in the following diagram:

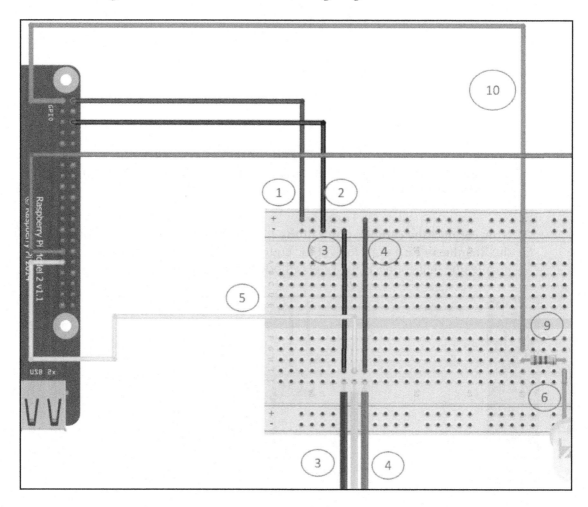

9. **In this step we connect the camera to the Raspberry Pi**: Now, connect the camera to the Raspberry Pi using the USB/on beardboard; in this project, we used the USB camera as shown in the following diagram:

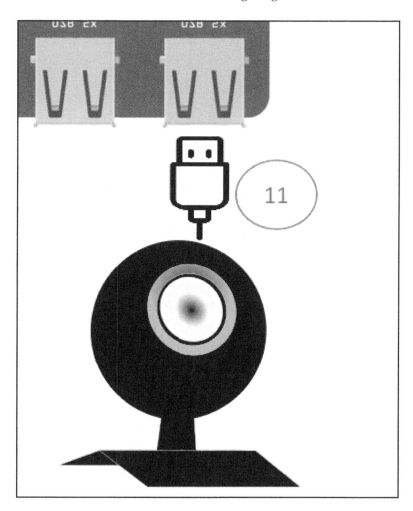

Schematic diagram

Now that we have configured the sensors, let's take a look at the schematic diagram of our project:

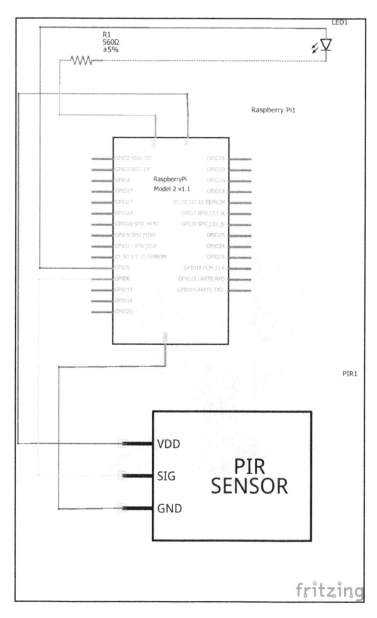

So far, you have configured the IoT device (the Raspberry Pi2). The next step is to register your Raspberry Pi2 with Azure IoT Hub. This enables your IoT device to send sensor data to your Azure IoT Hub; from there, we can redirect it to Power BI.

Device identity and registry with IoT Hub

The main purpose of device identity registration is to allow access to the device-facing endpoints. For each device, it creates resources in Azure IoT Hub, which enables device-to-cloud messages and also cloud-to-device messages, if needed.

You can do this in different ways. Here, I will explain a technique using Device Explorer.

Using Device Explorer

You can use this tool to manage devices connected to your IoT Hub. For example, you can register a device with your IoT hub, monitor messages from your devices, and send messages to your devices. Device Explorer runs on your local machine and connects to your IoT hub in Azure. Following are the steps for using Device Explorer:

1. Download and install **Device Explorer** from `https://github.com/Azure/azure-iot-sdks/releases`.

2. Assuming that you already have IoT Hub in Azure--if not, check out the getting started link mentioned at the start of this chapter--you need an IoT Hub connection string, to get it, log in to your Azure Portal, open your IoT Hub, and under **Shared access policies** | **Iothubowner**, copy the **Connection string-- primary key**.

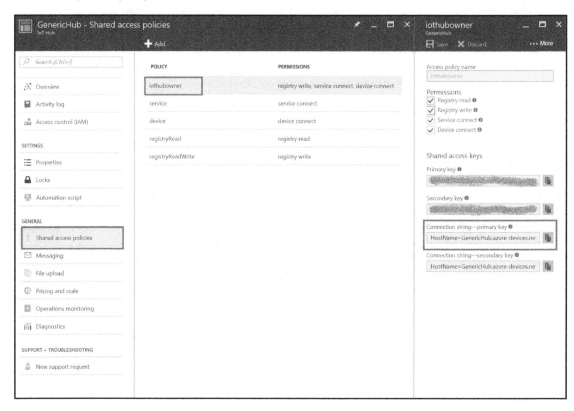

Chapter 8

3. Open **Device Explorer**, which you installed in step 1, enter your IoT Hub connection string, and click on **Update**.

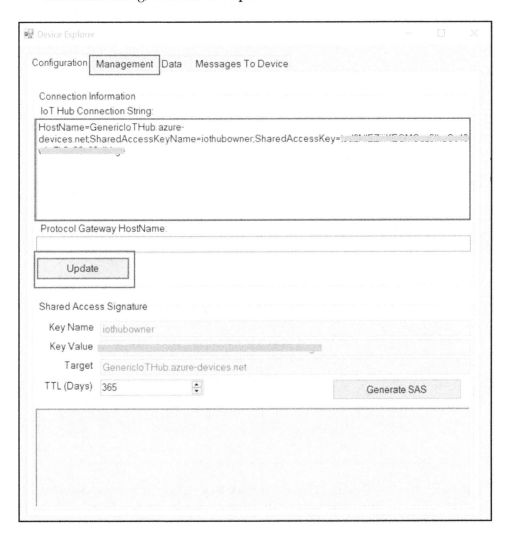

4. Now, go to the **Management** tab and click on the **Create** button to create a device.

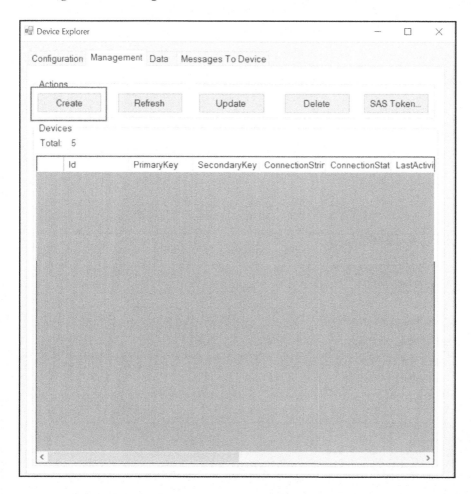

5. Finally, save the **Device ID** and **Primary Key** values in another database or a safe place; these will be used to send data from your Raspberry Pi to IoT hub. This way, we can register your Raspberry Pi2 with IoT hub to send data.

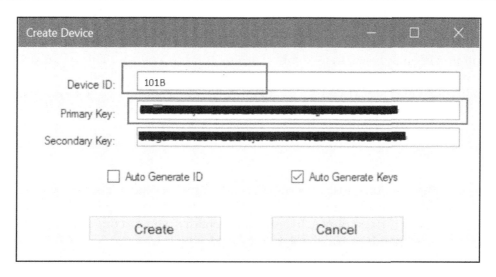

Next, let's develop the facial identification bot, for which we will implement face and emotion analysis code. This bot will receive images from the IoT device and then process them using the Face and Emotion APIs to identify the facial expressions in them. Before jumping into the code, let's take a look at what the Face API and Emotion API are.

Face API

The **Face API** will detect human faces; tag them as people; save people into groups based on similarity between images, such as images of the same person; and also identify the previously tagged people in images. The Face API can do face detection, identification, verification, similar face search, and face grouping. The Face API takes an image as an input, processes it to detect one or more human faces in that image, and returns face rectangles for all the faces in the image. It also returns face attributes, which contain features. The face features are age, gender, pose, smile, and facial hair, along with 27 landmarks for each face in the image. These predictions are based on the application of machine learning algorithms to facial features. For more information, refer to https://www.microsoft.com/cognitive-services/en-us/face-api/documentation/overview.

Emotion API

The **Emotion API** analyzes faces to identify the emotions of a person. This API takes facial expression from an image as input and returns feelings/expressions for that face. If a user has already called the Face API on a particular image, they can submit the face rectangle from that image as an optional input. The emotions detected by the Emotion API are anger, contempt, disgust, fear, happiness, neutral, sadness, and surprise. For more information, refer to https://www.microsoft.com/cognitive-services/en-us/emotion-api/documentation.

Both the Face and Emotion APIs can also detect face attributes and emotions from a video. For a video, the Emotion API will detect the facial expressions of people in the video and return a summary of their emotions. In real-time scenarios, you can use these APIs to find out how a crowd responds to your speech or content.

Sign Up Microsoft Cognitive Services

These two APIs are part of the services offered in **Microsoft Cognitive Services** provided by Microsoft. It is currently free; to use these APIs, you first need to sign up for Microsoft Cognitive Services. Follow the sign-up process explained in Chapter 4, *Natural Speech and Intent Processing Bot Using Microsoft Cognitive Services* in the *Signing up for Microsoft Cognitive Services* section.

Once you complete the signup process, perform the following steps to get Face and Emotion API keys:

1. On the free trails page, navigate down to the Emotion API section and copy **Key 1** to a safe place; we will need it in later steps.

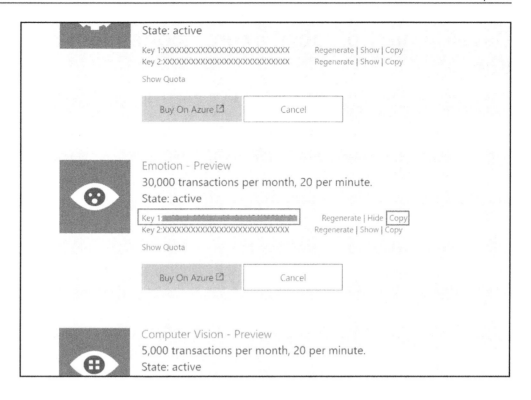

2. Similarly, copy the Face API **key 1** to a safe place.

Development of facial expressions identification bot

Now, we are ready to build a bot application. Go to Visual Studio and create a new bot project using the Bot Application template, as follows:

1. Open Visual Studio, click on **New** | **Project**, and select **Visual C#** from the left-hand side template category. Then, in the templates section, you will see the **Bot Application** template.

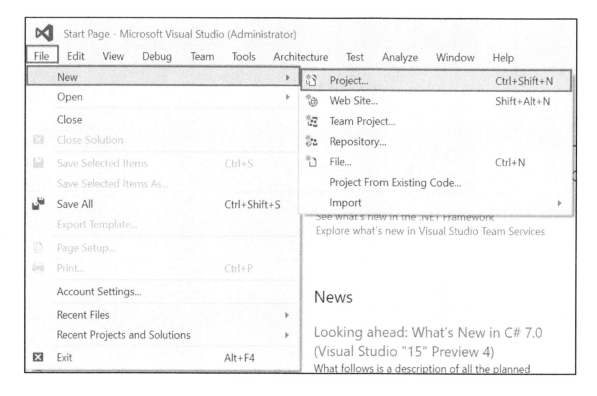

Chapter 8

2. Select the **Bot Application** template, name the project, and then click on **OK**.

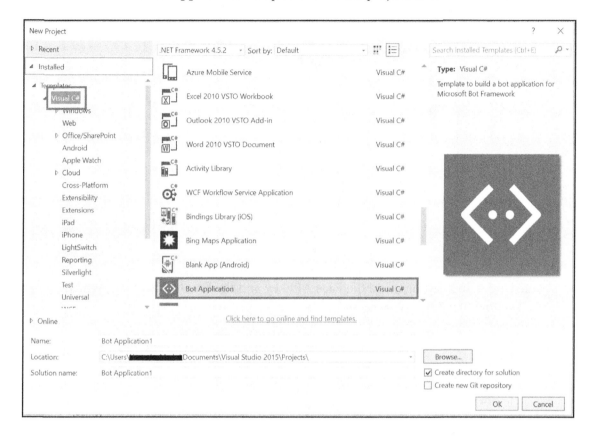

[301]

3. After the successful creation of your project, go to solution explorer and open the `Web.config` file, as shown in the following screenshot:

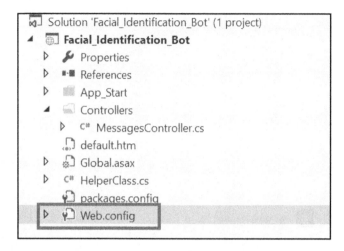

4. Under app Settings, add the Face API key and the Emotion API key, which you copied in earlier steps, as follows:

```
<configuration>
  <appSettings>
    <!-- update these with your BotId, Microsoft App Id and your Microso
    <add key="BotId" value="" />
    <add key="MicrosoftAppId" value="" />
    <add key="MicrosoftAppPassword" value="" />
    <add key="FaceKey" value="                                    "/>
    <add key="EmotionKey" value="                                   "/>
  </appSettings>
```

5. Next, you have to add the references to the Face API and the Emotion API to the project. For that, go to *NuGet Package Manager*, search for **Microsoft.ProjectOxford**, and install the Face and Emotion packages, as follows:

Chapter 8

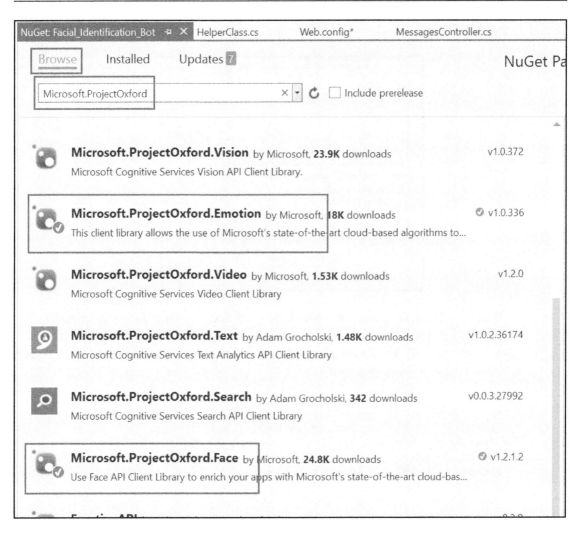

6. Now, add a new class named `HelperClass.cs` to the project, then import the following references:

```
using Microsoft.ProjectOxford.Face.Contract;
using Microsoft.ProjectOxford.Face;
using Microsoft.ProjectOxford.Emotion;
using System.Configuration;
```

The following screenshot explains the preceding code:

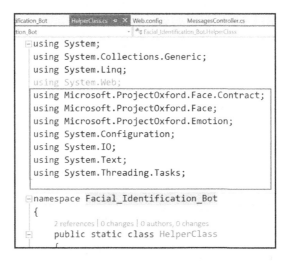

7. Next, to call the Face and Emotion APIs, we have two `ServiceClient` classes called `FaceServiceClient` and `EmotionServiceClient`. Initialize both Face and Emotion API keys, and also add some other variables at the class level, which will be used in following steps:

```
public static FaceServiceClient faceClient = new
FaceServiceClient(ConfigurationManager.AppSettings
["FaceKey"].ToString());
public static EmotionServiceClient emotionClient = new
EmotionServiceClient(ConfigurationManager.AppSettings
["EmotionKey"].ToString());
public static Face face = null;
public static Microsoft.ProjectOxford.Face.Contract.Face
FaceclientFace = null;
```

The following screenshot explains the preceding code:

```
2 references | 0 changes | 0 authors, 0 changes
public static class HelperClass
{
    public static FaceServiceClient faceClient =
        new FaceServiceClient(ConfigurationManager.AppSettings["FaceKey"].ToStr
    public static EmotionServiceClient emotionClient =
        new EmotionServiceClient(ConfigurationManager.AppSettings["EmotionKey"]
    public static Face face = null;
    public static Microsoft.ProjectOxford.Face.Contract.Face
        FaceclientFace = null;
```

8. Now, write code to perform facial analysis on an image received from a user. To do that, define a method called `faceAPIAnalysis` in `HelperClass`, which takes an image in stream format as input.
9. We will pass that stream to the Face API client to analyze the facial attributes. The `FaceServiceClient` class has the `DetectAsync` method, which will take the image stream and whatever attributes you want to track as input:

```
Microsoft.ProjectOxford.Face.Contract.Face[]
                    faceDetectionResult  = await
                    faceClient.DetectAsync(
                      attachemntData,
                      true, true, new FaceAttributeType[]
                      {
                          FaceAttributeType.Age,
                          FaceAttributeType.FacialHair,
                          FaceAttributeType.Gender,
                          FaceAttributeType.HeadPose,
                          FaceAttributeType.Smile,
                          FaceAttributeType.Glasses
                      });
```

10. The `DetectAsync` method returns the attributes for the face identified in the given image stream. From the face detection results, you will get all the attribute values shown in the following code:

```
var firstResult = faceDetectionResult.FirstOrDefault();
if (firstResult != null)
    {
      var attributes = firstResult.FaceAttributes;
      var beard1 = LabelFromConfidenceValue(
      "beard", attributes.FacialHair.Beard);
```

```
var moustache = LabelFromConfidenceValue(
"moustache", attributes.FacialHair.Moustache);
var sideburns = LabelFromConfidenceValue(
"sideburns", attributes.FacialHair.Sideburns);
var smile = LabelFromConfidenceValue(
"smile", attributes.Smile);
return "Age: "+ attributes.Age + " \r \n "+
"Gender: " + attributes.Gender + " \r \n " +
"HeadPose: " + attributes.HeadPose + " \r \n "
+beard1+ " \r \n " + moustache + " \r \n " +
sideburns+ " \r \n " + smile+ " \r \n "
+ attributes.Glasses;
}
```

Let's code to know the emotions

Now, we will write code to find out the emotions of faces in the image that we received as input. We will perform the following steps to do so:

1. We will define another method called `emotionAPIAnalysis` in `HelperClass.cs`, which takes an image in stream format as input, similar to the `faceAPIAnalysis` method. We will pass that stream to the Emotion API to analyze the facial expressions. The `EmotionServiceClient` class has the `RecognizeAsync` method, which will take an image stream as its input. The following is the code to send the stream to the Emotion API:

    ```
    public static async Task<string> emotionAPIAnalysis(Stream
    attachemntData)
    {
    string emotionList = "";
    var emotionresults = await
    emotionClient.RecognizeAsync(attachemntData);
    }
    ```

2. The `RecognizeAsync` method returns all the emotions found in the face identified in the given image stream. Parse the resulting emotions and save them in a string using the `StringBuilder` class. The following code is used to parse the results of the facial expression analysis:

    ```
    var legend = new StringBuilder();
    foreach (var person in emotionresults)
    {
    var emotionScores = person.Scores.ToRankedList();
    var labelledScores =
    ```

```
emotionScores
.OrderByDescending(entry => entry.Value)
.Select(
entry => new KeyValuePair<string, string>(
entry.Key,
LabelFromConfidenceValue(entry.Key, entry.Value)));
var listOfScores = string.Join(
" \r \n ",
labelledScores.Select(entry => entry.Value));
legend.AppendLine(listOfScores);
emotionList = legend.ToString();
}
if (emotionList != "")
return emotionList;
else
return "Unable to process the given image";
```

3. The emotion results will return all emotions detected with a confidence level. For example, if the face is a smiling face, then the confidence that the face displays happiness will be greater than 0.5; if the face doesn't show anger, then the anger confidence value will be less than 0.3, and there will be a confidence value for all other emotions. To understand these values, we created a `helper` method, which will return the emotion if the confidence value is greater than 0.5; otherwise, no emotion will be returned. This method takes the *emotion type* and *confidence* value as its input. The following is the `helper` method code:

```
static string LabelFromConfidenceValue(string label, double confidence){
var returnLabel = label;
if (confidence < 0.3)
{
returnLabel = $"No {label}";
}
return (returnLabel);
}
```

4. Add the following class to hold the face attribute details returned by the Face API in `HelperClass`:

```
public class Face
{
public FaceAttributes FaceAttributes { get; set; }
public Guid FaceId { get; set; }
public FaceLandmarks FaceLandmarks { get; set; }
public FaceRectangle FaceRectangle { get; set; }
}
```

Registering your Bot in Bot Framework

Next, you need to register your bot with Bot Framework so that you can integrate your bot with channels such as Slack, Skype, Facebook, and many more. In Chapter 9, *Publishing a Bot to Skype, Slack, Facebook, and the GroupMe Channel,* section *Registering your Bot with Microsoft Bot Framework,* we explained how to register your bot with `dev.botframework`, and refer to it to find out how to register your bot with Bot Framework. Following are the steps to register a bot:

1. Once you are done registering your bot, copy the *Microsoft App ID* and *Password*, which you generated when you registered your bot. You can also get these values from your existing bot--edit settings page under **Configuration** section--as shown in the following screenshot:

2. Now, go to bot project and open the `web.config` file. Under appSettings, update the `MicrosoftAppID`, `MicrosoftAppPassword`, and the `BotId`. The `BotId` is nothing but b*ot handle* name of your bot:

```
<configuration>
  <appSettings>
    <!-- update these with your BotId, Microsoft App Id and your Microsoft App
    <add key="BotId" value="FacialIdentificationBot" />
    <add key="MicrosoftAppId" value="" />
    <add key="MicrosoftAppPassword" value="" />
    <add key="FaceKey" value=""/>
    <add key="EmotionKey" value=""/>
  </appSettings>
```

3. Next, go to the `MessageController.cs` file, `Post` method. We need to update the `Post` method to receive and support attachments/images from the user. Your bot should accept an image from the user and send it to the Face and Emotion APIs. Basically, the bot receives the image as an attachment in `Activity object`. Here, we have a problem, because we cannot directly access the attachment's data. Since we received the attachment as a URL instead of direct image/data, which is stored securely somewhere by Bot Framework, the bot needs to send a get request with the help of the URL to get the real content in the attachment. This will be secure because only your bot can request the attachment/image, so in the HTTP get request you need to send the *Microsoft App Id* and *Password* as authentication headers. This way only your bot can request the real content from Bot Framework.

4. First, you need to check whether the user sent the attachment/image, with the help of the following code:

   ```
   var attachment = activity.Attachments?.FirstOrDefault();
   ```

5. In the attachment, you will find a content URL property in which the user-uploaded image is stored. You have to check whether `ContentUrl` is empty or not:

   ```
   if (attachment?.ContentUrl != null)
               {
   }
   ```

6. If content URL is not empty, then we need to request a token based on credentials--Microsoft App Id and Password--which will be available under the `ConnectorClient` object. The code will be as follows:

   ```
   var attachment = activity.Attachments?.FirstOrDefault();
   if (attachment?.ContentUrl != null)
   {
   using (var connectorClient = new ConnectorClient(new
   Uri(activity.ServiceUrl)))
   {
   var token = await (connectorClient.Credentials as
   MicrosoftAppCredentials).GetTokenAsync();
   }
   }
   ```

7. Once we get the token, we pass the token in the Authentication header as a bearer in a `HttpClient` request. The following code explains the Authentication token:

```
var token = await (connectorClient.Credentials as
MicrosoftAppCredentials).GetTokenAsync();
                var uri = new Uri(attachment.ContentUrl);
                using (var httpClient = new HttpClient())
                {
                    if (uri.Host.EndsWith("skype.com") &&
                    uri.Scheme == Uri.UriSchemeHttps)
                    {
httpClient.DefaultRequestHeaders.Authorization = new
AuthenticationHeaderValue("Bearer", token);

httpClient.DefaultRequestHeaders.Accept.Add(new
MediaTypeWithQualityHeaderValue("application/octet-stream"));
                    }
                    else
                    {
httpClient.DefaultRequestHeaders.Accept.Add(new
MediaTypeWithQualityHeaderValue(attachment.ContentType));
                    }
                }
```

8. Now, do a get request using `GetStreamAsync`, then pass the stream to the `FaceAPIAnalysis` and `EmotionAPIAnalysis` helper methods to detect facial expressions and attributes, as follows:

```
var emotions= await HelperClass.emotionAPIAnalysis(await
httpClient.GetStreamAsync(uri));
                var faceAttributes = await
HelperClass.faceAPIAnalysis(await
httpClient.GetStreamAsync(uri));
```

9. Finally, reply to the user with the details, of the face analysis and emotion analysis as follows:

```
                // return our reply to the user
                Activity reply = activity.CreateReply($"**Face
                Analytics of given Image are** \r \n
                {faceAttributes} \r \n \r \n **Emotion
                Analytics of given image are** \r \n
                {emotions}");
                await
connectorClient.Conversations
.ReplyToActivityAsync(reply);
```

Publish and test your bot

Now, publish the bot application to Azure. Refer to `Chapter 9`, *PPublishing a Bot to Skype, Slack, Facebook, and the GroupMe Channel*, in the *Publishing your bot application to Microsoft Azure web app* section.

After publishing successfully, update the endpoint URL of your bot, which is registered in the `dev.botframework`.

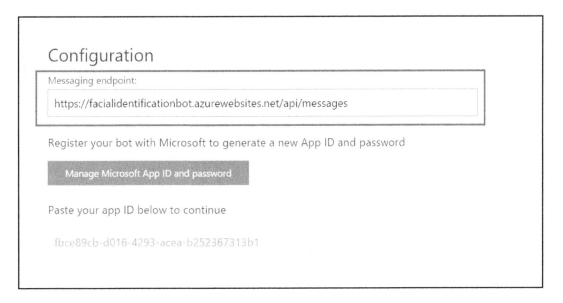

You can test it by adding it to Skype using the **Add to skype** option.

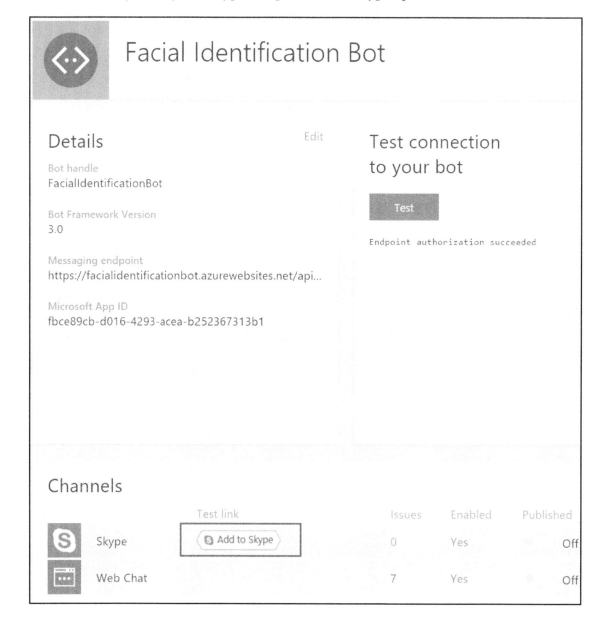

After successfully adding to your Skype, send an image to the bot and see the results of the Face API and Emotion API directly in Skype, as shown in the following screenshot:

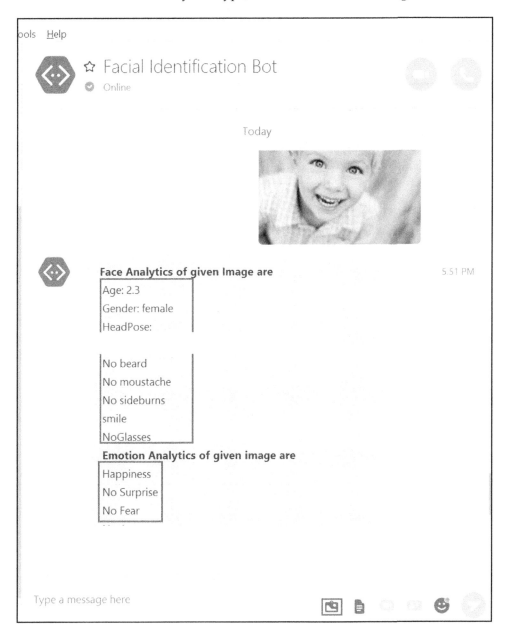

Configure Direct Line Channel

To call the bot from the IoT application, we need to configure Direct Line channel. Let's perform the following steps to do that:

1. Go to `dev.botframework.com`, click on the **My Bots** section, and select your bot:

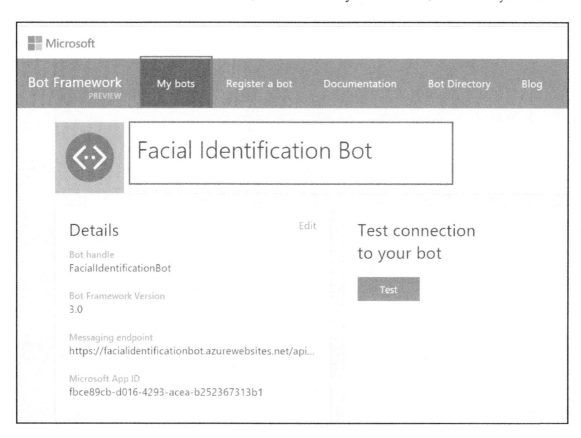

Chapter 8

2. Under the **Channels** section, click on the **Add** option of the **Direct Line** channel. It opens a configuration page:

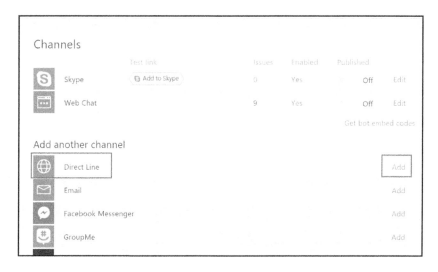

3. On the Direct Line configuration page, click on the **Add New Site** option and add a name:

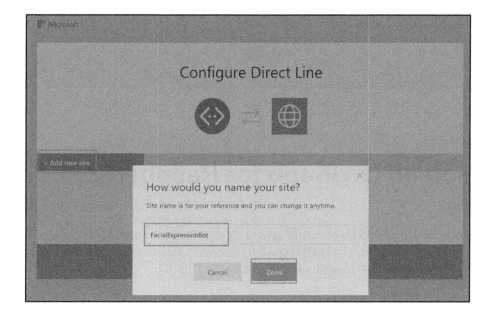

4. Next, copy the primary secret key we will use in later steps, as shown in the following figure, and finally click on **I am done configuring Direct Line**:

Next, you need to develop a **Universal Windows Platform** (**UWP**) app for Raspberry Pi2.

Develop an UWP app for Raspberry Pi device

A UWP app is responsible for collecting sensor data, which means it captures a photo of a person and sends it to the bot, and the bot will process it and send back the results to the Raspberry Pi2. The processed results will be sent to IoT Hub.

Chapter 8

Create an UWP App project

Now, let's take a look at the steps we need to follow to create the UWP app:

1. Open Visual Studio and create a new project by selecting Universal app as **Universal | Blank App** template, as follows:

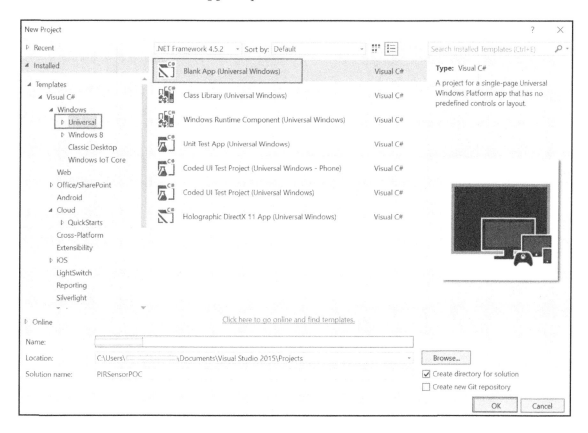

2. After the successful creation of the project, right-click on the **Project** and select the **Add Reference** option from the menu.

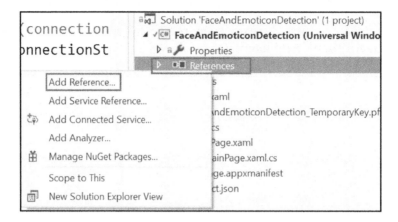

3. Next, from Reference Manager windows select the **Extensions** category under Universal Windows and then select Windows IoT Extensions for the UWP.

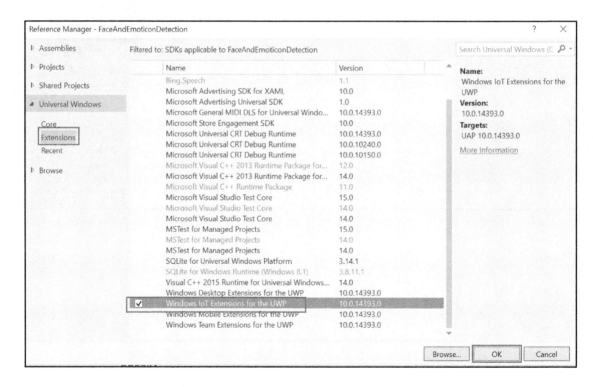

Chapter 8

4. Select the appropriate version of IoT Extensions; here I am using the `10.0.14393.0` version and my Raspberry Pi2 also has the same version of the Windows 10 IoT Core OS.

How to detect the motion of the object using PIR Sensor and How to define the LED states

To detect the motion of an object, an important sensor is PIR. For that, first you need to define a variable for the PIR sensor by setting the respective pin number into it. You need to define a variable for the LED sensor and set it to its respective Pi number, as explained in the step 1 in the following list. By using these pin numbers, we will identify whether the PIR sensor detected an object or not; based on the PIR sensor value, you will turn the LED light on/off.

1. Open the `MainPage.xaml.cs` file and declare the following properties at the top of the class, as follows:

   ```
   //Status LED variables
     private const int LED_PIN = 5;
     private GpioPin PinLED;

   //PIR Motion Detector variables
     private const int PIR_PIN = 16;
     private GpioPin PinPIR;
   ```

2. Next, add the following lines of code in the `MainPage.xaml.cs` file constructor, to call the `InitializeGPIO()`, `InitilizeWebcam()` method and the `LightLED()` method:

   ```
   //camera initilization
     InitilizeWebcam();

     InitializeGPIO();

     //Turn the Status LED on
     LightLED(true);

     // At this point, the application waits for motion to be detected by
     // the PIR sensor, which then calls the PinPIR_ValueChanged()
     function
   ```

[319]

3. Add the following lines of code in the `MainPage.xaml.cs` file, which gets the current `GpioController` and sets the **drive mode** of the GPIO pin:

```
private void InitializeGPIO()
    {
        try
        {
            //Obtain a reference to the GPIO Controller
            var gpio = GpioController.GetDefault();

            // Show an error if there is no GPIO controller
            if (gpio == null)
            {
                PinLED = null;
                Debug.WriteLine("No GPIO controller found on
                this device.");
                return;
            }

            //Open the GPIO port for LED
            PinLED = gpio.OpenPin(LED_PIN);

            //set the mode as Output (we are WRITING a signal to
            this port)
            PinLED.SetDriveMode(GpioPinDriveMode.Output);

            //Open the GPIO port for PIR motion sensor
            PinPIR = gpio.OpenPin(PIR_PIN);

            //PIR motion sensor - Ignore changes in value of
            less than 50ms
            PinPIR.DebounceTimeout = new TimeSpan(0, 0, 0, 0,
            50);

            //set the mode as Input (we are READING a signal
            from this port)
            PinPIR.SetDriveMode(GpioPinDriveMode.Input);

            //wire the ValueChanged event to the
            PinPIR_ValueChanged() function
            //when this value changes (motion is detected), the
            function is called
            PinPIR.ValueChanged += PinPIR_ValueChanged;
        }
        catch (Exception ex)
        {
            Debug.WriteLine(ex.Message);
        }
```

                }

Here, I have the explained the preceding code line by line:

- First, we use `GpioController.GetDefault()` to get the GPIO controller.
- If the device does not have a GPIO controller, this function will return `null` and display the error message in the output window of your Visual Studio 2015 when you're running the project in debug mode.
- Then, we attempt to open the pin by calling `GpioController.OpenPin()` with the `LED_PIN` value.
- We also set the pin to run in output mode (we are *writing* a signal to this port) using the `GpioPin.SetDriveMode()` function.
- Next, we attempt to open the pin by calling `GpioController.OpenPin()` with the `PIR_PIN` value.
- We also set the `DebounceTimeout` for the PIR motion sensor to ignore changes in value of less than 50 ms--the meaning of this `DebounceTimeout` is "don't report events that happen within 50 milliseconds of each other". Try running the app with this line removed, or with the setting at 100-500ms, and see what different behaviors you get from your PIR sensor.
- We also set the pin to run in input mode (we are *reading* a signal from this port) using the `GpioPin.SetDriveMode()` function.
- This line is the most important, as it ties the **Typed Event Handler** of the GPIO pin 16's value changed event to the function `PinPIR_ValueChanged()....;` this means that the app will continually poll pin 16 of the Raspberry Pi's GPIO port, and when a signal is detected (motion was detected), the `PinPIR.ValueChanged += PinPIR_ValueChanged` function is called.
- Next, add the following lines of code in the `MainPage.xaml.cs` file:

```
private async void PinPIR_ValueChanged(GpioPin sender, 
GpioPinValueChangedEventArgs args)
    {
        //simple guard to prevent it from triggering this 
        function again before it's compelted the first time - 
        one photo at a time please
        if (IsInPictureCaptureMode)
            return;
        else
            IsInPictureCaptureMode = true;

        // turn off the LED because we're about to take a
```

```csharp
                picture and send to Bot
                LightLED(false);
                try
                {

                    StorageFile picture = await TakePicture();

                    if (picture != null)
                        UploadPictureToBot();
                }
                catch (Exception ex)
                {
                    Debug.WriteLine(ex.Message);
                }
                finally
                {
                    //reset the "IsInPictureMode" singleton guard so
                    the next
                    //PIR movement can come into this method and take
                    a picture.
                    IsInPictureCaptureMode = false;

                    //Turn the LED Status Light on - we're ready for
                    another picture
                    LightLED(true);
                }

                return;
        }

    private void LightLED(bool show = true)
        {
            if (PinLED == null)
                return;

            if (show)
            {
                PinLED.Write(GpioPinValue.Low);
            }
            else
            {
                PinLED.Write(GpioPinValue.High);
            }
        }
```

Chapter 8

4. Here, I have the explained the preceding code line by line available inside the `PinPIR_ValueChanged` event:
    - The `PinPIR_ValueChanged` event will be called only when GPIO pin 16 (the PIR signal) changes; this means that it will be called only when the PIR sensor detects object movement.
    - In that event, you will see the variable as `IsInPictureCaptureMode`; the reason I am using this variable is that by using it, we can prevent this function from being triggered a second time before its logic is completed.
    - What logic completed means that it takes some time to snap a picture and send it to bot.
    - After setting a `true` value for the `IsInPictureCaptureMode` variable, I will call method as `LightLED()` with the value `false`; the meaning of this line is that the LED will be turned off until we send the picture to the bot, That's why in this event I will call the `TakePicure()` method and the `UploadPicturetoBot()` method. Using these two methods, we can take a photo when the PIR sensor detects object motion. After completion, the photo will be sent to the bot.

Initializing camera on detection of motion

There's very little C# code required to get the photo-taking functionality we need. There's an `InitializeWebcam()` function that configures the .NET `MediaCapture` object we'll use to take the picture. We also register a callback function with the `MediaCapture`'s failed event. This callback event will get called if there's any sort of error in the picture-taking process.

Add the following lines of code in the `MainPage.xaml.cs` file, in which you have to write the code for how to initialize the webcam, and after initializing the webcam, how to make it take a photo of the object detected by the PIR sensor:

```
#region Webcam code
    /// <summary>
    /// Initializes the USB Webcam
    /// </summary>
    /// <param name="sender"></param>
    /// <param name="e"></param>
    private async void InitilizeWebcam(object sender = null,
    RoutedEventArgs e = null)
    {
        try
```

```csharp
        {
            //initialize the WebCam via MediaCapture object
            MediaCap = new MediaCapture();
            await MediaCap.InitializeAsync();

            // Set callbacks for any possible failure in TakePicture()
            logic
            MediaCap.Failed += new
            MediaCaptureFailedEventHandler(MediaCapture_Failed);
        }
        catch (Exception ex)
        {
            Debug.WriteLine(ex.Message);
        }

        return;
    }

    /// <summary>
    /// Takes a picture from the webcam
    /// </summary>
    /// <returns>StorageFile of image</returns>

    string path = "";
    public async Task<StorageFile> TakePicture()
    {
        try
        {
            //gets a reference to the file we're about to write a
            picture into
            StorageFile photoFile = await
            KnownFolders.PicturesLibrary.CreateFileAsync(
            "RaspPiSecurityPic.jpg",
             CreationCollisionOption.GenerateUniqueName);
            path = photoFile.Path;
            //use the MediaCapture object to stream captured photo to a
            file
            ImageEncodingProperties imageProperties =
            ImageEncodingProperties.CreateJpeg();
            await
MediaCap.CapturePhotoToStorageFileAsync(imageProperties,
photoFile);
            return photoFile;
        }
        catch (Exception ex)
        {
            Debug.WriteLine(ex.Message);
            return null;
```

Chapter 8

```
        }
    }
```

Handle call back event as `MediaCapture's Failed` if in case there is any exception occuring during the time of taking photo of the detected object by PIR sensor:

```
/// <summary>
/// Callback function for any failures in MediaCapture operations
/// </summary>
/// <param name="currentCaptureObject"></param>
/// <param name="currentFailure"></param>
private void MediaCapture_Failed(MediaCapture currentCaptureObject,
MediaCaptureFailedEventArgs currentFailure)
{
    Debug.WriteLine(currentFailure.Message);
}
#endregion
```

How to send picture file to Facial Expression Bot and receive reply from it

Sending a picture to the bot means calling your facial expression bot from the IoT application through the Direct Line channel. To do that, first add a `Microsoft.Bot.Connector.DirectLine` reference to your UWP project.

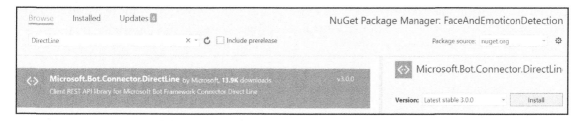

Next, add a method called `InitializeBotConversation` and call this method from the `OnNavigatedTo` method of `MainPage.cs`. In this method, we will initialize the bot conversation using the Direct Line channel's secret key:

```
async Task InitializeBotConversations()
    {
        //Initialize Direct Client with secret obtained in the Bot
        Portal:
        _directLineClient = new
```

[325]

```
                DirectLineClient("SecretKey_From_Bot_DrectLine_Channel");
                //Initialize new converstation:
                _directLineAConv = await
                _directLineAConv.Conversations.NewConversationAsync();
                //Wait for the responses from bot:
                ReadMessagesAsync(_directLineClient,
                _directLineAConv.ConversationId);

        }
```

In the preceding `InitializeBotConversations` method, we also called the `ReadMessagesAsync` method; this method will always try to read bot replies. If any reply is received from the bot, it will send it to IoT Hub:

```
    private async Task ReadBotMessagesAsync(DirectLineClient _client, string
    conversationId)
            {
                // You can optionally set watermark -this is last message
                id seen by bot
                //It is for paging:
                string watermark = null;
                while (true)
                {
                   //Get all messages returned by bot:
                   var messages = await
                   _directLineClient.Conversations
                   .GetMessagesAsync(conversationId, watermark);
                   watermark = messages?.Watermark;
```

Get messages from your bot - `FromProperty`--should match your Bot handle; you can find it in `dev.botframework.com`, under your Bot settings; here, the Bot handle name is `FacialIdentificationBot`:

```
    var messagesFromBotText = from x in messages.Messages
    where x.FromProperty == "FacialIdentificationBot"
    select x;
    //Iterate through all messages:
    foreach (Message message in messagesFromBotText)
    {
```

We will save all messages in a collection related to a conversation. The following condition checks whether we have already received that bot messages or not. If a new message is received, then we will save it to the collection and also send that message to IoT Hub.

```
                if (!_messagesFromBot.Contains(message))
                {
                _messagesFromBot.Add(message);
```

Chapter 8

```
            SendBotMessageToIoTHub(message);
        }
    }
                    }
}
```

In the `SendBotMessageToIoTHub` method, we will initialize the `IoTHub` client to send messages to Azure. Before that, we need to add references for `Microsoft.Azure.Devices.Client`:

```
public async Task SendMessageAsync(Message message)
        {
            var deviceClient =
            DeviceClient.CreateFromConnectionString
            ("Replace_Connection_String_From_Device_Registration_Step")
            ;
            var stringContent = JsonConvert.SerializeObject(message);
            var jsonStringInBytes = new
            Microsoft.Azure.Devices.Client.Message
            (Encoding.ASCII.GetBytes(stringContent));
            Debug.WriteLine("Message: " + stringContent);
            await deviceClient.SendEventAsync(jsonStringInBytes);

        }
```

Send Picture to Bot

Now, add the `UploadPictureToBot` method. In this method, first we will upload a picture to our storage account and get the blob URL from it. Then, we will send the blob URL to Direct Line client in bot message attachments.

To work with Azure Storage Account, you need to add a `WindowsAzure.Storage` reference to your project:

```
async Task UploadPictureToBot (StorageFile photoFile)
        {
// Parse the connection string and return a reference to the storage
account.
CloudStorageAccount storageAccount =
CloudStorageAccount.Parse("DefaultEndpointsProtocol=https;AccountName=***
REPLACE_WITH_YOUR_STORAGE_ACCOUNT_NAME***;AccountKey=***REPLACE_WITH_YOUR_S
TORAGE_ACCOUNT_KEY****");
// Create the blob client.
            CloudBlobClient blobClient =
            storageAccount.CreateCloudBlobClient();
```

```
                // Retrieve a reference to a container.
                CloudBlobContainer container =
                blobClient.GetContainerReference("mycontainer");
                // Retrieve reference to a blob named "myblob".
                CloudBlockBlob blockBlob =
                container.GetBlockBlobReference("myblob");

                // Create or overwrite the "myblob" blob with contents
                from a local file.
                using (var fileStream = await
                photoFile.OpenStreamForReadAsync())
                {
                    await blockBlob.UploadFromStreamAsync(fileStream);
                }

    //Add blob URL in bot message as attachment as shown

    Message userMessage = new Message
                {
                    FromProperty = App.username,
                    Text = txtdsplyTxtBx.Text
                };
                userMessage.Attachments.Add(new Attachment() {
                ContentType = "blob", Url = blockBlob.Uri });
                await
                _directLineClient.Conversations.PostMessageAsync
                (_directLineClientConv.ConversationId, userMessage);
}
```

Now, we are ready to deploy and test the code with the Raspberry Pi; to do so, take a look at the following section.

Deploy Code in to Raspberry Pi

Now that we are done with the code for our project, let's look at the following steps to deploy code to the Raspberry Pi:

1. First, connect your Raspberry Pi to your developer machine using a LAN cable, or connect to your Wi-Fi router in the same network.
2. Download and install the *Windows 10 IoT Core Dashboard tool* from `http://go.microsoft.com/fwlink/?LinkID=708576`.

3. Open it: after a few seconds it will show your Raspberry Pi device on the **My Devices** page shown in the following screenshot. Then, copy the IP address.

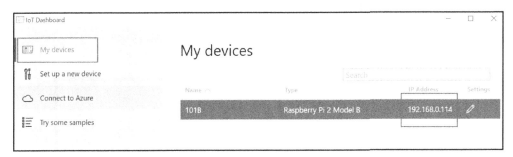

Before deploying the code, make sure that the registered device ID in Device Registry with IoT Hub step and your Raspberry Pi device name is the same. For example, in device registry step 1 given device Id as 101B and my Raspberry Pi device name 101B, both are same. So, we can identify and manage easily from IoT hub.

4. Open the Raspberry Pi UWP app solution in Visual Studio, and set the architecture in the toolbar dropdown to **ARM**.

5. Next, in the Visual Studio toolbar, click on the Local Machine dropdown and select **Remote Machine**, as shown in the following screenshot.

6. At this point, Visual Studio will present the **Remote Connections** dialog. You can enter the name of your device here (in this example, I used 101B). Otherwise, use the IP address of your Windows IoT Core device. After entering the device name/IP, select Universal for Windows Authentication; then if Visual Studio detected it automatically, you can select it directly, as shown in the following screenshot:

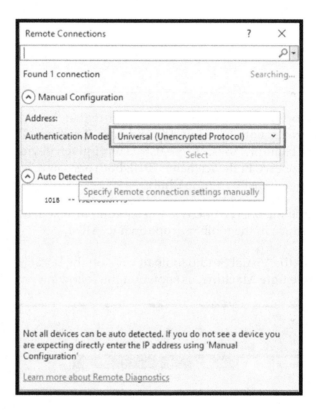

7. You can verify or modify these values by navigating to the project **Properties** (select **Properties** in Solution Explorer) and choosing the **Debug** tab on the left-hand side:

8. When everything is set up, press *F5* from Visual Studio to deploy the code.

After successfully deploying the project to your IoT device, the first thing that we have to is that by default LED will be turned on. Now to test this, just move in front of the PIR motion sensor. First it detects your movement and takes a photo. Next, it uploads the photo to your Azure storage account, and finally it sends the blob URL to your bot. Once it sends the message to the bot, the bot will start processing and analyzing the picture to identify the facial expressions in it, and returns the results to IoT Device. In the last step, the IoT device will send these results to IoT Hub.

Next, we will see how we can show facial analytics data in Power BI.

Show facial analytics data in Power BI

Power BI is a service that helps you to visualize your data in reports, charts, and interactive insights. It also has a set of software services, apps, and connectors, which all work together to help you turn your data into logical, consistent, and visually immersive. Power BI lets you easily connect to your data sources, visualize what you want, and also share with anyone. In the following steps, we will just give you a brief idea of how you can use Power BI in a real-time scenario, such as an IoT environment, where you will collect enormous amounts of data from your devices and want to see your data visually to take decisions. In this chapter, you will see how to show facial analytics data in Power BI.

Set up Azure Stream Analytics to send IoT Hub data to Power BI

Let's follow these steps to set up Azure Stream analytics:

1. Create a **Stream Analytics Job** in azure, and log in to your Azure portal. Select **New** and search for **Stream Analytics job**.

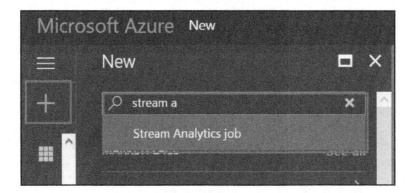

2. Select, create, and enter **Job name**, and select **Region** and **Resource group**.

Chapter 8

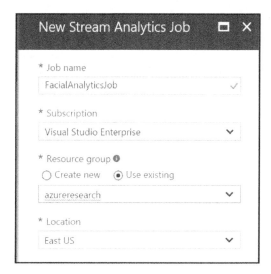

3. Open the newly created stream analytics, and click on **Inputs**.

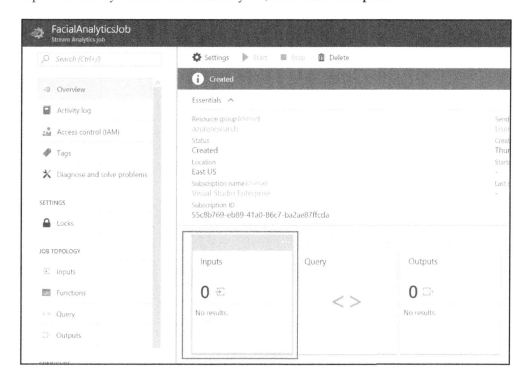

[333]

4. Select the **Add** option. In the **Add an Input Popup** window, select **Data Stream** as the **input**, select **IoT Hub** as the data stream input type, and enter the Input stream alias name, which will be used in later steps, select **Subscription**, choose the IoT Hub that we are using in this project, and select **iothubowner** as the shared access policy name, set Event serialization format to JSON and **Encoding** to **UTF-8**; then click on **Create**.

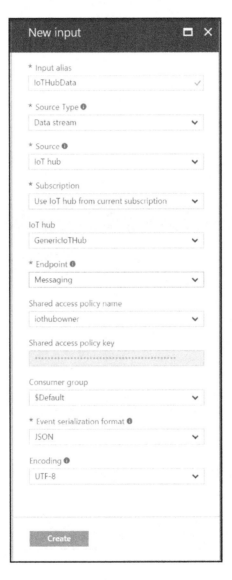

5. Now, add an output for the stream analytics job so that we can process the data coming from the input stream and send it to the list of supported outputs.

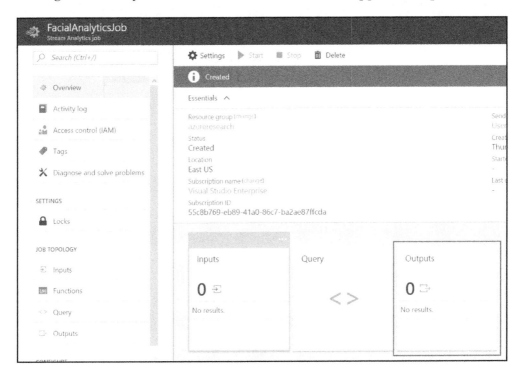

Here, we are using Power BI as an output to the stream analytics job.

6. To use Power BI, you need to authorize Stream Analytics to access your organizational Microsoft Power BI subscription to create a live dashboard. If you are not yet registered, you can register a free account using your organization's e-mail ID through the **Sign up** now link on the page.

7. After the successful authorization of your Power BI account, it will ask you to enter Output alias name, a friendly name to reference in output queries. Provide a dataset name that it is desired for a Power BI output to use, a table name which is under dataset of the Power BI output from stream analytics jobs *(you can only have one table in a dataset)*, and finally a workspace, which is for enabling data sharing with other Power BI users, writing data to group workspaces. You can select group workspaces inside your Power BI account, or choose **My Workspace** if you don't want to write to a group workspace.

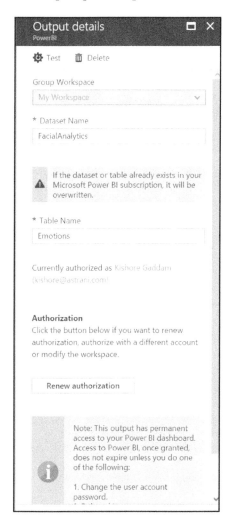

8. Now, go to the Query tab and write a query to filter the data coming from the IoT Hub input stream and give it to Power BI.

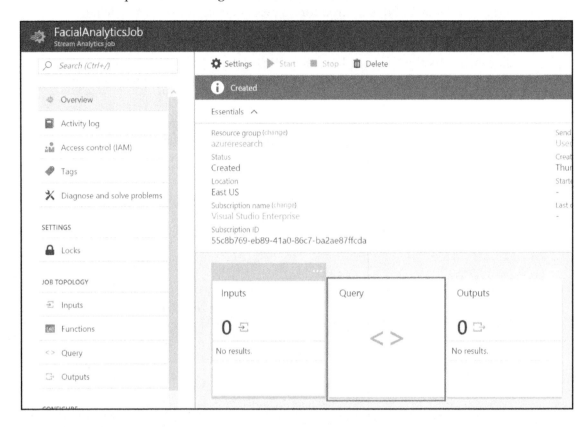

9. The following is the query I used to filter the data coming from IoT Hub:

```
SELECT
    *
INTO
    [PowerBI]
FROM
    [IoTHubData] TIMESTAMP by Time
```

Chapter 8

We can filter the data by selecting the required columns and with useful information, such as average of the values:

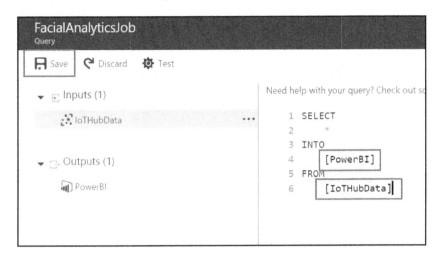

10. Now, click on the **Start** icon in the overview:

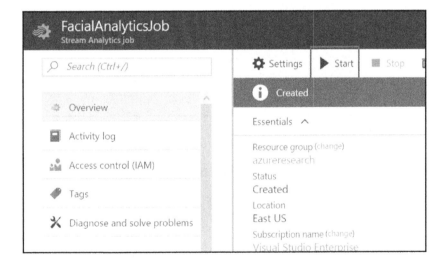

If stream analytics fails to run, then go to the Diagnostic Logs of your stream analytics job for more information on why it failed.

Set up Power BI

After successful starting a Stream Analytics job, sign in to Power BI and check for the newly created dataset in the **Datasets** section; click on **Streaming datasets** and start creating charts based on the data that you received.

Let's see how to create a chart for the data we received from the IoT device:

1. Click on the **Create Report** option under the **ACTIONS** tab.

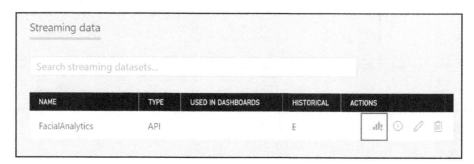

2. Drag and drop, or select, the fields you want to show on a table chart.

3. First, select a **Table** chart, which is located under the **Visualization** tab.

4. The following is a chart that displays all the results sent by the IoT device to IoT Hub:

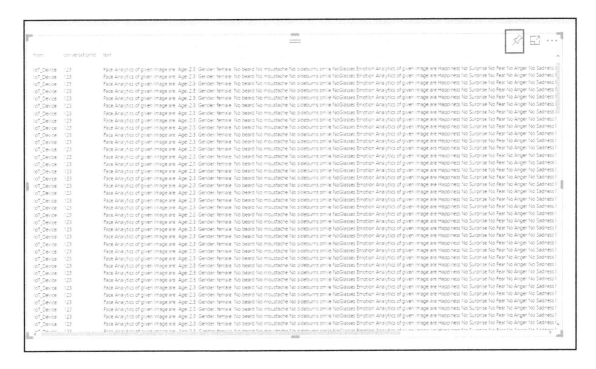

5. Click on the **pin** symbol on the top right of the chart to add it to the dashboard, as shown in the preceding screenshot. Save it before pinning it to the dashboard.

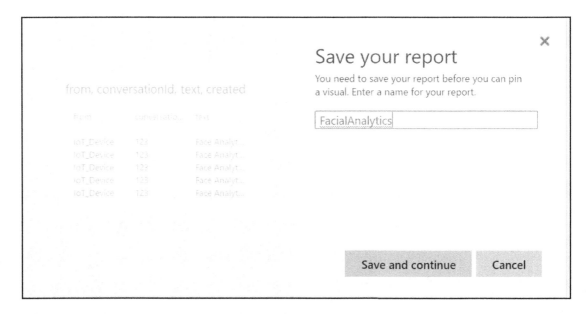

6. Select the dashboard where you want to pin it. If you don't have the dashboard, select **New dashboard**; otherwise, select **Existing dashboard**.

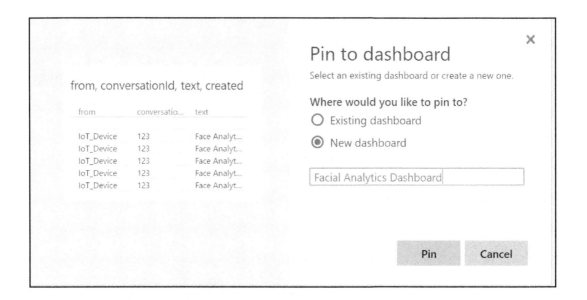

7. The newly created report and dashboards will be added to the left-hand menu. From the left-hand menu, you can navigate to the report or dashboard directly.

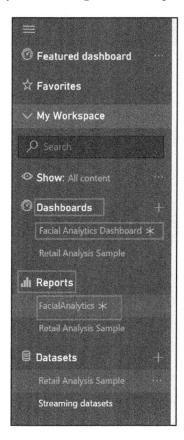

Developing Intelligent Facial Expression Identification Bot for IoT Using Azure and Power BI

The following is a screenshot showing, how the report looks in the dashboard:

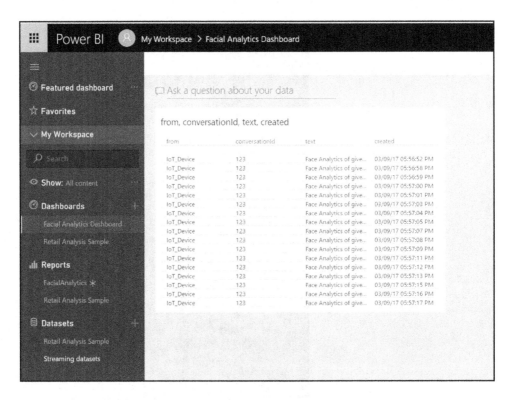

Report and chart creation depends on what data you are sending to Power BI. Before sending data, make sure you are formatting it and filtering the unwanted data with the help of the Stream analytics query editor.

Summary

In this chapter, you have learned the following:

- **IoT Hub**: Azure IoT Hub is a fully managed service that helps us to enables reliable and secure bidirectional communications between millions of IoT devices
- **Stream Analytics**: It is a fully managed event-processing engine in the cloud
- **Power BI**: With the help of Power BI, you can analyze and visualize your important data and it always work with real-time data
- **Storage Account**: It provides one place to store all your data
- **Cognitive Services**: The Face API will detect human faces and tag them as people, also do face detection, identification, verification, similar face search, and face grouping
- **Emotion API**: It analyzes faces to identify the emotions of a person is feeling and also detects facial expressions in an image

In the next chapter, you will learn about registering bots with Bot framework, and also how to publish bots to Slack, Skype, GroupMe, and Facebook channels.

9
Publishing a Bot to Skype, Slack, Facebook, and the GroupMe Channel

In this chapter, we will use the **Microsoft Bot Connector**, which is a part of the **Microsoft Bot Framework**, as a way to create a single backend and then publish it to a bunch of different platforms called **Channels** as quickly as possible. The goal is to have the user input natural language and your bot to perfectly understand and execute the action your user wants.

At the confluence of the rise in messaging applications, advances in text and language processing, and mobile form factors, bots are emerging as a key area of innovation and excitement. Bots (or conversation agents) are rapidly becoming an integral part of your digital experience--they are a vital way for people to interact with a service or application, as is a website or a mobile experience. Developers writing bots all face the same problems--bots require basic I/O, they must have language and dialog skills, and they must connect to people--preferably in any conversation experience and language a person chooses. This book focuses on how to solve these problems using the Microsoft Bot Framework, a set of tools and services to easily build bots and add them to any application.

Publishing bots to various channels

Let's look at publishing bots to various channels in the following image:

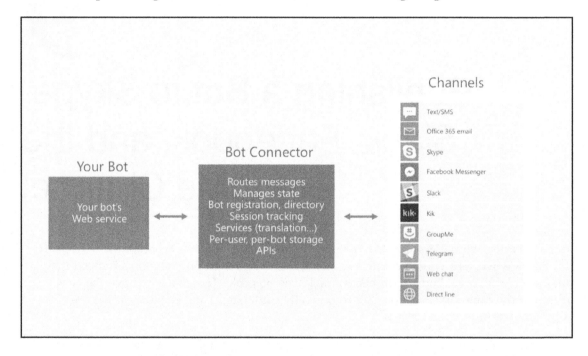

Figure1: How a single bot can be published to various channels through the bot connector

In order to publish your bot to the available directories, you need to do the following three things:

1. Publish your bot application to **Microsoft Azure** web app.

2. Connect your bot to at least one channel that appears in the Bot Framework.

3. Select **Publish** in the bot dashboard.

Publishing your bot application to Microsoft Azure web app

We use Microsoft Azure to host the bot application. To publish your bot application, you will need a **Microsoft Azure subscription**. You can get a free trial from `https://azure.microsoft.com/en-us/`.

In the preceding chapter, we created a bot, and now we are ready to publish the bot. By default, the bot should be published as a **Microsoft Azure App Service**. When publishing, keep track of the URL you chose because we'll need it when we have to register the Bot Framework endpoint, which is nothing but your bot messages, API URL. There are a few extra steps that you have to do the first time you publish, but you only have to do them once. Let's take a look at those steps:

1. In Visual Studio, right-click on the **Project** in Solution Explorer and select **Publish...**, or alternately navigate to **Build** | **Publish;** it displays the following dialog:

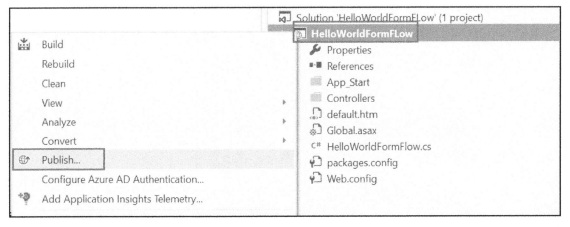

Figure 2: Screenshot showing step 1

2. On the **Publish Web** wizard, select **Microsoft Azure App Service** as the publish target type:

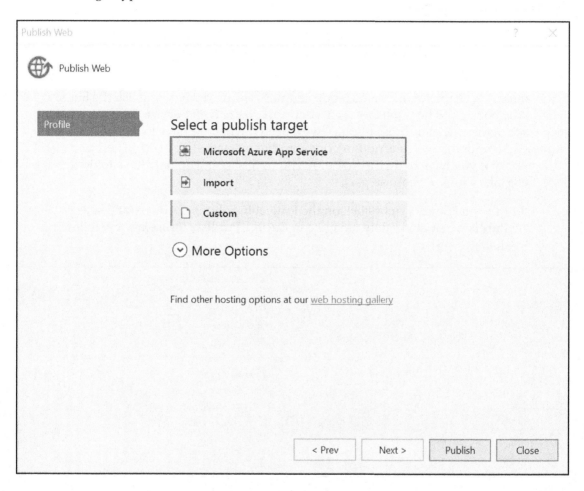

Figure 3: Screenshot showing step 2

Chapter 9

3. The next step in the Azure App Service publishing process is to create your app service. Click on **New...** at the right side of the dialog to create the app service:

Figure 4: Screenshot showing step 3

[353]

4. The **Create App Service** dialog will be displayed. Fill in the details as appropriate. Ensure that you choose **Web App** from the **Change Type** drop-down on the top right instead of **API App** (which is the default):

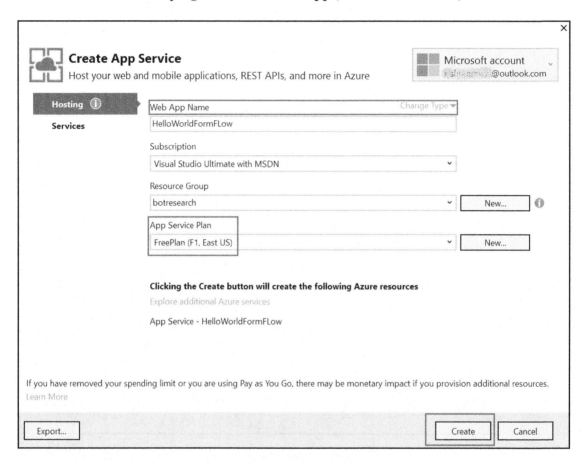

Figure 5: Screenshot showing step 4

5. Once you have entered all the required information, click on the **Create** button; it will create a web app for our bot and take you back to the **Publish Web** wizard.

Chapter 9

6. Now that you've returned to the **Publish Web** wizard, copy the **Destination URL** to the clipboard; you'll need it in a few moments. Click on **Validate Connection** to ensure that the configuration is good, and if all goes well, click on **Next**:

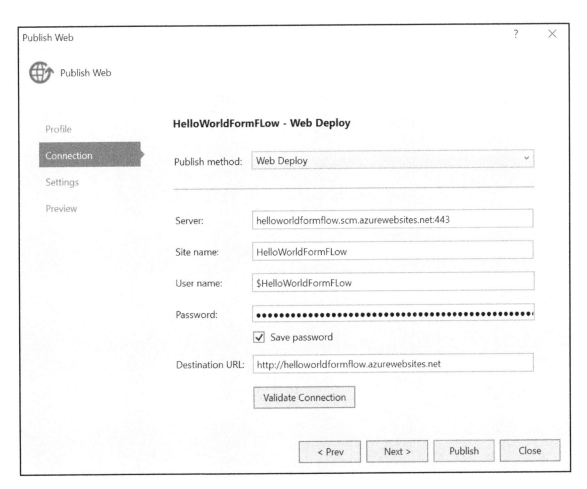

Figure 6: Screenshot showing step 6

7. By default, your bot will be published in a **Release configuration**. If you want to **debug** your bot, change **Configuration** to **Debug**. Regardless, from here you'll click on **Publish**, and your bot will be published to Azure:

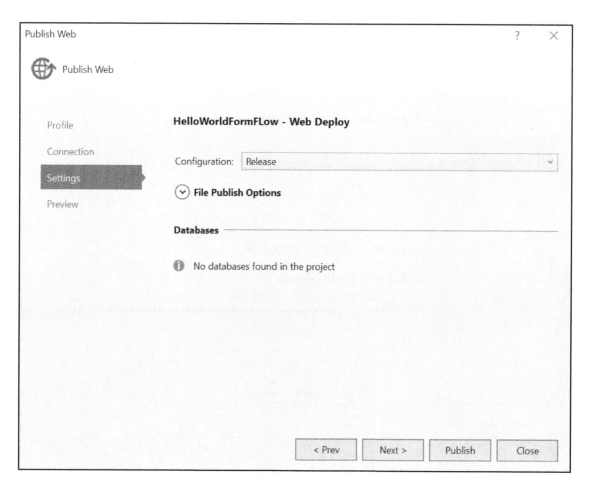

Figure 7: Screenshot showing step 7

8. You will see a number of messages displayed in the Visual Studio 2015 output window. Once publishing is complete, you will also see the web page for your bot application displayed in your browser (the browser will launch and render your bot application start page, as shown in the following screenshot):

Figure 8: Screenshot showing step 8

Registering your bot with Microsoft Bot Framework

Registering your bot tells the connector how to call your bot's web service. Note that the Microsoft App ID and Microsoft App Password are generated when your bot is registered with the Microsoft Bot Framework Connector; the App ID and AppSecret are used to authenticate the conversation and allows the developer to configure their bot with the channels they'd like to be visible on. Let's look at the following steps to register your bot:

1. Go to the Microsoft Bot Framework portal at `https://www.botframework.com` and sign in with your Microsoft account.
2. Register an agent.

3. Click on the **Register a bot** button and fill out the **Bot Profile** form. You have to enter the name of your bot handle, which means a unique name that will be used in the bot connection, and then enter a description:

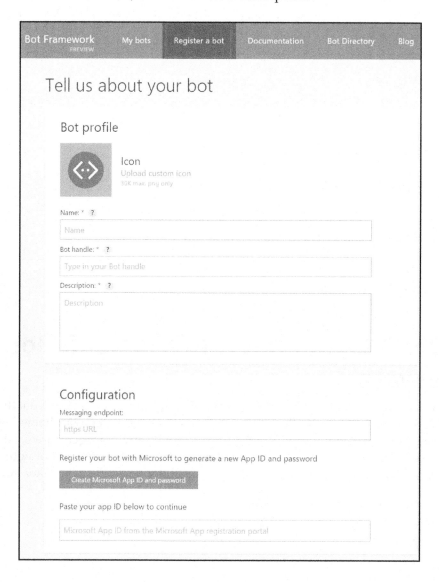

Configuration

Under the **Configuration** section, enter your published bot service endpoint that you copied during the Azure deployment step in **Messaging endpoint**, and don't forget that when using the bot application template, you'll need to extend the URL you pasted in which the path to the endpoint at /api/messages. You should also prefix your URL with HTTPS instead of HTTP; Azure will take care of providing HTTPS support on your bot:

Configuration

Messaging endpoint ?

https://helloworldformflow.azurewebsites.net/api/messages

The following are the steps to configure Microsoft Bot Framework:

1. Enter your Microsoft App ID, if you haven't created one already, then click on the **Create Microsoft App ID and password** button on the bottom of the **Configuration** section:

Configuration

Messaging endpoint ?

https://helloworldformflow.azurewebsites.net/api/messages

* Microsoft App ID ?

Microsoft App ID from the Microsoft App registration portal

Create Microsoft App ID and password

2. It will navigate to the Microsoft app creation page, as shown in the following screenshot, with your **App name** and **App ID**. Copy the **App ID** in a safe place as we need it in later steps. After that, click on **Generate a password to continue**:

3. Once you click on the generate button, the password will be generated. Copy the password to a safe place; we will need it in later steps. Finally, click on **Finish** and go back to the bot registration page:

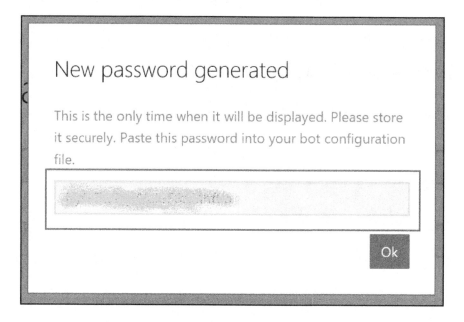

4. Now, in the bot registration page, the **Microsoft App ID** will be automatically added into it. If not, then manually paste the **Microsoft App ID** that you copied in the preceding step:

5. Enter all remaining mandatory fields, and finally accept the privacy agreement at the bottom of the page, and then click on **Register**:

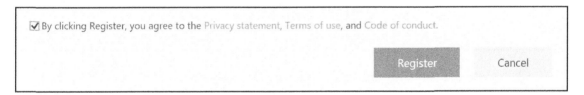

6. On clicking **Register**, you will receive a popup saying **Bot created**:

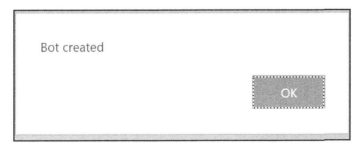

7. Once you have successfully registered your bot, Microsoft Bot Framework will automatically configure **Skype** and **Web chat** by default; you can check it under **Channels**:

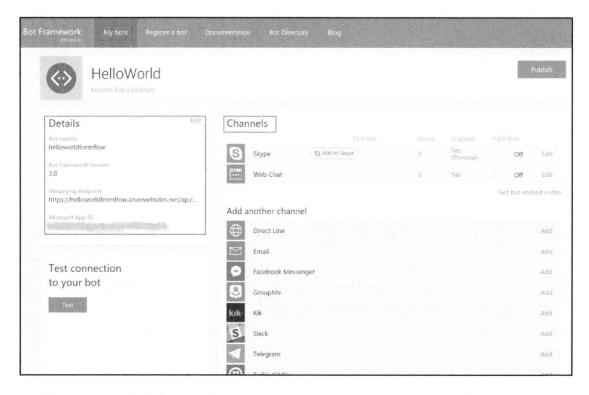

8. Now that the bot is registered, you need to update the keys in the `web.config` file in your bot service project:

9. Change the following keys in the `web.config` file to match the ones generated when you saved your registration, and you're ready to build:

```xml
<appSettings>
  <!-- update these with your BotId, Microsoft App Id and your Microsoft App Password-->
  <add key="BotId" value="YourBotId" />
  <add key="MicrosoftAppId" value="" />
  <add key="MicrosoftAppPassword" value="" />
</appSettings>
```

10. `BotId` is nothing but the bot handle name. Copy the **Microsoft App ID** and **Microsoft App Password** from the preceding steps and paste it here:

```xml
<configuration>
  <appSettings>
    <!-- update these with your BotId, Microsoft App Id and your Microsoft App Password-->
    <add key="BotId" value="helloworldformflow" />
    <add key="MicrosoftAppId" value="b356043c-werf-3edc-3456-c1a54cb22595" />
    <add key="MicrosoftAppPassword" value="qwerrtrty56567rgfgt" />
  </appSettings>
```

11. Update your `web.config` file, and republish your bot to Azure.

Testing the connection to your bot

To test the connection to your bot, follow these steps:

1. Back in the developer dashboard for your bot, there's a test chat window that you can use to interact with your bot without further configuration and verify that the Bot Framework can communicate with your bot's web service:

2. Note that the first request after your bot starts up can take 20-30 seconds, as Azure starts up the web service for the first time. Subsequent requests will be quicker:

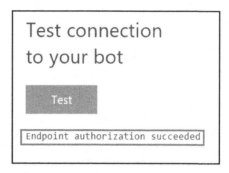

Configuring channels

Channels are a mechanism of connecting the bot with the various communication platforms and making the channels available on those platforms.

Now that you have a bot up and running, you'll want to configure it for one or more channels that your users are using. Configuring channels is a combination of Microsoft Bot Framework workflow and conversation service workflow, and it is unique for each channel you wish to configure:

- On the right-hand side of the dashboard, you can see all the channels you can connect with your bot

- You can connect your bot to the services that I mentioned before, such as **SMS**, **Telegram**, **Slack**, and so on

Channels				
	Test link	Status	Published	
Web Chat		Disabled	Off	Edit
				Get bot embed codes

Add another channel

	Direct Line	Add
	Email	Add
	Facebook Messenger	Add
	GroupMe	Add
	Kik	Add
	Skype	Add
	Slack	Add
	SMS	Add
	Telegram	Add

Configuring your bot with Slack

In this example, we will show you how to configure your bot to Slack. All channels in Microsoft Bot Framework require you to bring your own account model, so you can sign up each of these services on your own. You take your username and password for them and give them to the Bot Framework, which stores them in encrypted format, but it allows us to communicate on behalf of your bot. What this means is that if you already have an account for your bots, you can just bring it in, and you don't have to register a new one. Later on, if you want to take control of that account again, it's yours and you just have to deal with authorizing from the Bot Framework developer portal. Let's get the process started:

1. You just have to click on the **Add** button of the Slack channel, and the Bot Framework gives us all of the steps to add bot to Slack, as shown in the following screenshot:

How to

∨ Log in to Slack and create a Slack Application for your bot

∨ Create application and set redirect URI

∨ Create a Slack Bot

∨ Add Interactive Messages (optional)

∨ Configure Interactive Messages (optional)

∨ Gather your Credentials

∨ Submit your Credentials

☑ Enable this bot on Slack

Chapter 9

2. First, click on **Log in to Slack and create a Slack Application for your bot**:

3. When you click on the link mentioned in the preceding screenshot, it navigates to the Slack application creation page. If you are not signed in, then it will ask you to sign in using your Slack account, as shown in the following screenshot:

Your Apps

You'll need to sign in to your Slack account to create an application.

4. Enter your Slack team name, click on **Continue**, and then enter your Slack credentials to login to your Slack account:

5. After successfully signing in, click on `https://api.slack.com/applications/view` again; now you will see **Your Apps** page in your Slack account. Click on the **Create App** button to create a new app:

Your Apps

Welcome! Apps you've created will appear here (both public apps listed in the App Directory and private apps only your team uses).

Need ideas for what to build? Our Ideaboard features requests and suggestions directly from Slack users.

Create App

Chapter 9

6. The next step is **Create Application and set redirect URI**; when you click on **Create App** on Slack, you will get a similar kind of form; enter all the information about your bot:

Publishing a Bot to Skype, Slack, Facebook, and the GroupMe Channel

7. Copy the redirect URI from the preceding step to the Slack app creation **Redirect URI(s)** field:

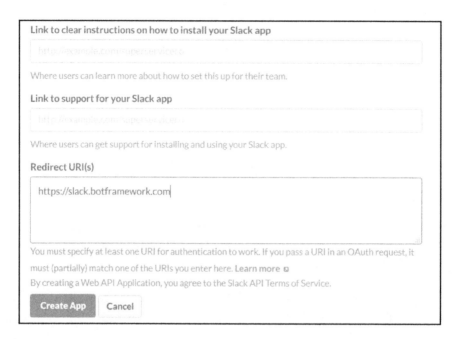

8. Now, click on the **Create App** button at the bottom of the Slack window:

[370]

Chapter 9

9. Next, create a Slack bot:

10. Click on the **Bot Users** option from the left-hand side menu, then click on the **Add a Bot User** button:

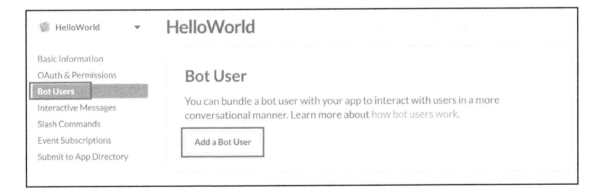

Publishing a Bot to Skype, Slack, Facebook, and the GroupMe Channel

11. On the **Bot User** page, enter the default username for the bot and click on the **Add bot user** button:

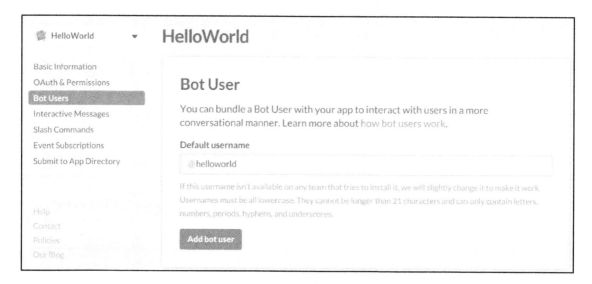

12. Next, add and configure **Interactive Messages** (optional):

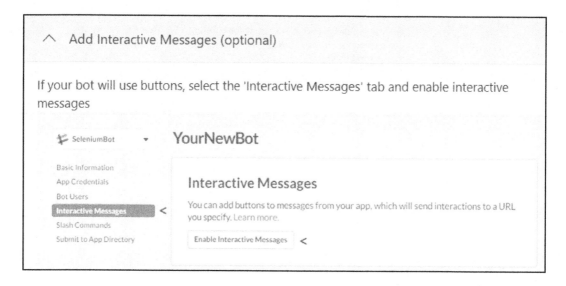

[372]

13. Now, let's configure **Interactive Messages**:

14. Select the **Interactive Messages** option from the left-hand side menu, and click on the **Enable Interactive Messages** button:

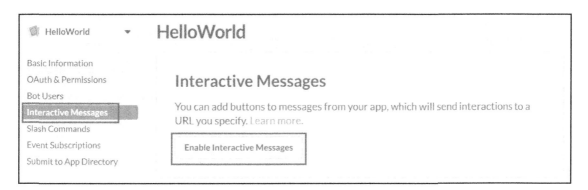

15. Now, paste the **Redirect URI** to the **Request URL** box that we copied earlier and click on **Enable Interactive Messages**:

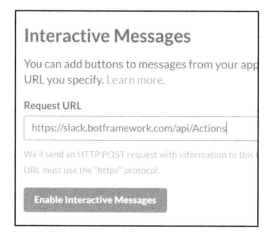

16. Click on **Save changes**:

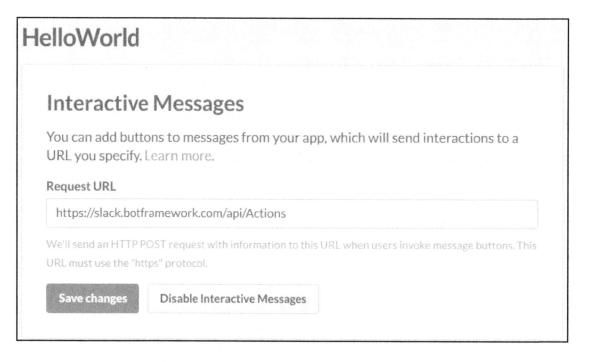

Chapter 9

17. The next step is to fill up your credentials in **Gather your Credentials**:

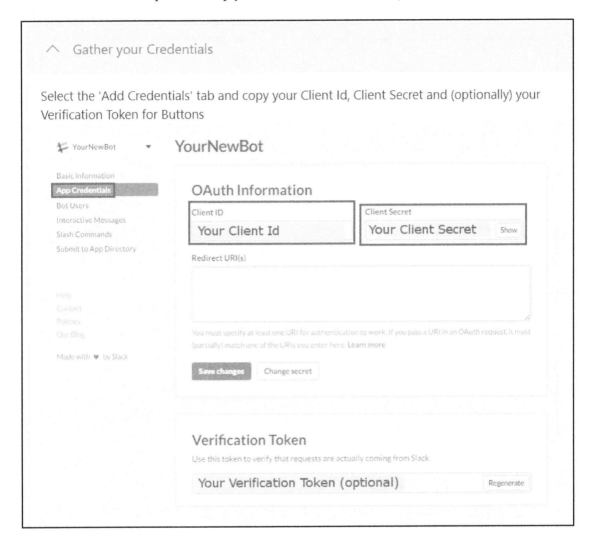

18. Select the **App Credentials** option from the left-hand side menu and copy the **Client ID** and **Client Secret** from the **OAuth Information** dialog box:

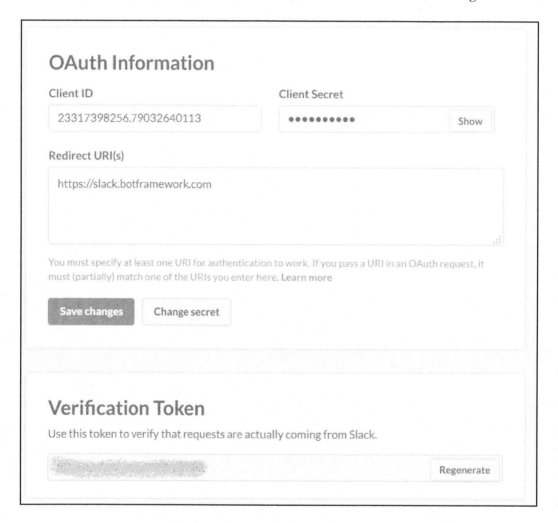

19. Next, submit your credentials and paste the respective values, which you copied in the preceding step.
20. Click on the **Submit Slack Credentials** button. Now, in the background, the Bot Framework is submitting our application credentials to Slack:

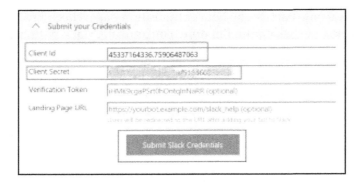

21. It will ask you to authorize access of the HelloWorld bot to your Slack team; click on **Authorize**:

22. Now, come back to the bot configuration page; check **Enable this bot on Slack** and click on the **I'm done configuring Slack** button:

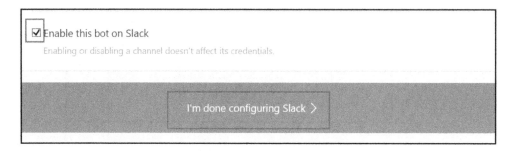

23. Slack bot has been added to your list of channels now:

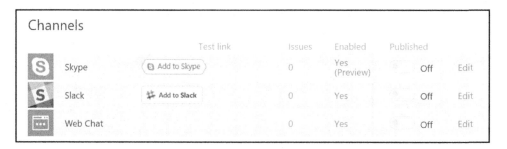

Configuring your bot with Skype

As part of Bot Framework version 3, the bot is already configured with Skype, but we just need to add it to the account by clicking on the **Add to Skype** option on the channel list:

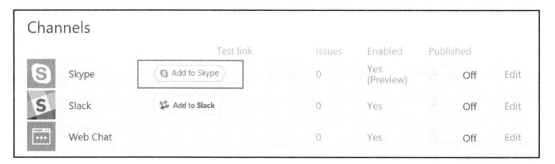

Chapter 9

Configure your bot with Skype by following these steps:

1. Click on the **Add to Contacts** button:

2. **Sign in** to your Skype account to add it as a contact to your Skype. Make sure that you have logged in to your Skype account on your PC as well:

3. Now, it will prompt you to open Skype on your desktop to add it to Skype. Once you are done adding it to Skype, then you can start talking with the **HelloWorld** bot:

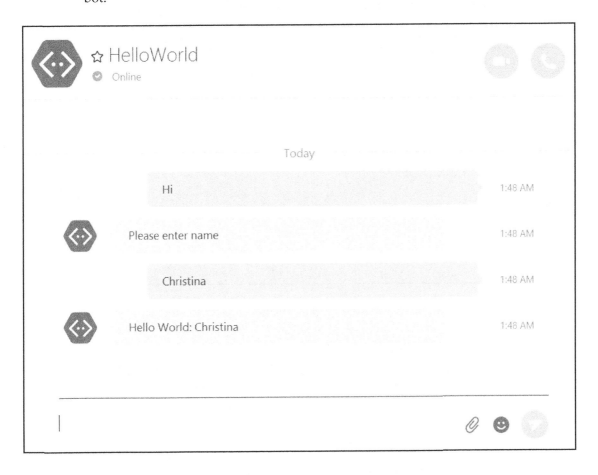

Configuring your bot with Facebook Messenger

Click on the **Add** button of the **Facebook Messenger** channel, and the Bot Framework will give us all of the steps required to add the bot to Facebook:

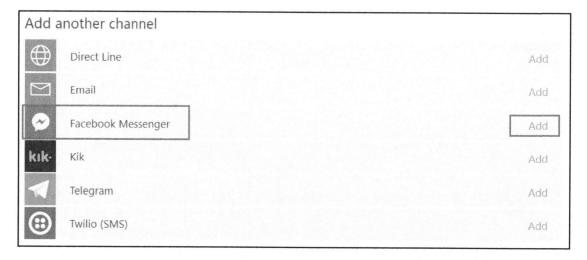

Configure your bot with Facebook Messenger by following these steps:

1. First, click on **Getting Started**:

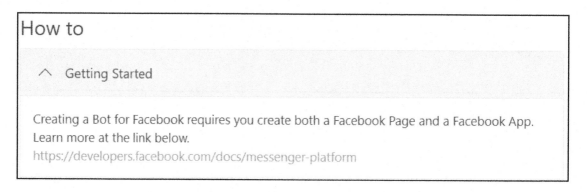

Chapter 9

2. Click on the link mentioned in the previous screenshot and the Facebook for developers page will open:

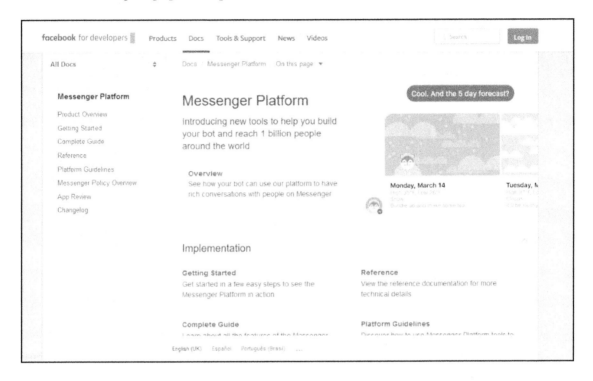

3. Next, create a Facebook page for your bot. Your bot is accessed through a Facebook page. Go to this link and create a page or go to an existing page at `https://www.facebook.com/bookmarks/pages`:

4. After successfully logging in, click on the **Create Page** button under the **Pages** section, as shown in the following screenshot:

5. Alternatively, you can click on **Create** Page under the drop-down menu next to Privacy shortcuts:

6. On **Create a Page**, select any one of the options as to which type your bot is, such as business, organization or entertainment, or app. Enter the name of your page and click on **Create**:

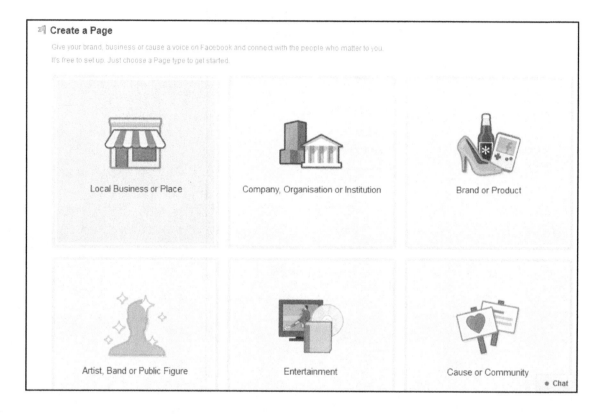

7. Now, add the details of the page/bot and save the information, then click on **Next** and complete all the required steps:

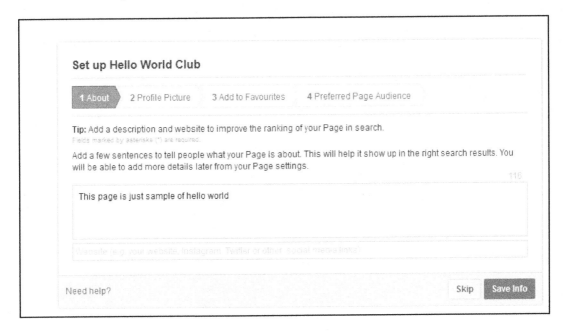

8. Once you have successfully created a page, then save the **Facebook Page ID** for later purposes. The **Facebook Page ID** can be found in your Facebook page's **About** section:

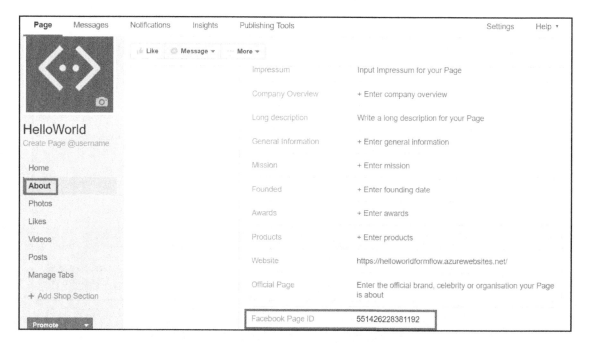

9. Next, create the Facebook app for your bot. Your bot will also need a Facebook app; click on the following mentioned link to create a new app:

The Facebook UI may be different depending on what version you're looking at: `https://developers.facebook.com/quickstarts/?platform=web`

Chapter 9

10. Enter **Display Name**, **Contact Email**, and select the Category of your bot:

[389]

11. Click on **Create App ID**.

12. After successful creation of the Facebook app, click on the **Dashboard** option from the left-hand side menu and copy the **App ID** and **App Secret** to a safer place, which will be used in later steps:

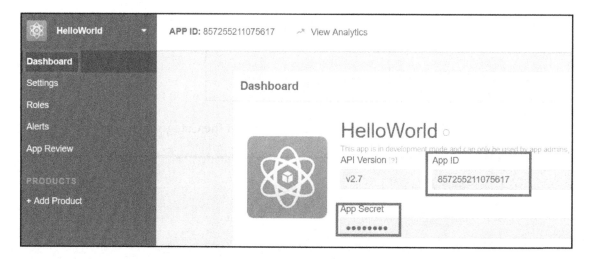

13. Next, enable messenger. Now, select the **Add Product** option from the left-hand side menu on the Facebook app page. Then, click on the **Get Started** button of the **Messenger** section:

Chapter 9

14. Click on the **Get Started** button again on the **Messenger Platform** page:

15. Under the **Token Generation** section of the product page, select the page from the drop down to which you want to generate the token:

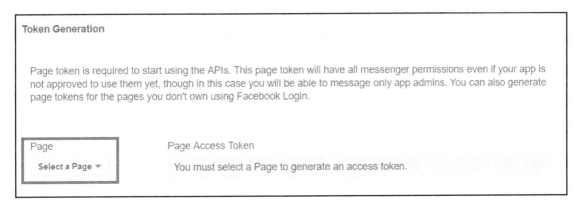

[391]

16. Select HelloWorld as the page. Now, you will get a prompt for allowing permissions to read your profile; click on **OK**:

17. If you don't want to give any specific permission, then you can select the **Choose what you allow** option, otherwise click on **OK**:

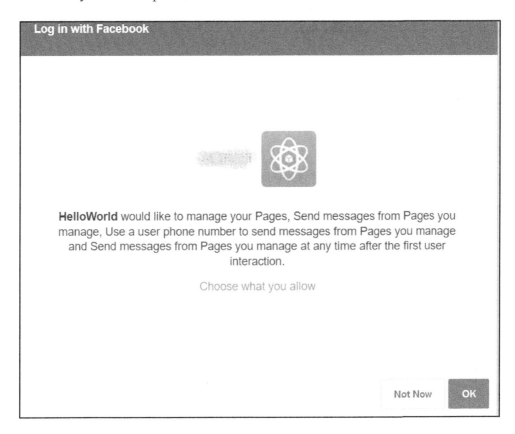

18. Copy the **Page Access Token** to a safer place; we need it in later steps:

Token Generation

Page token is required to start using the APIs. This page token will have all messenger permissions even if your app is not approved to use them yet, though in this case you will be able to message only app admins. You can also generate page tokens for the pages you don't own using Facebook Login.

Page	Page Access Token
HelloWorld ▼	EAAMLq0hWiCEBAEvWDiuK4m8pUIBT8mwEd7KxtoPZABox164tsgrrBPTg1RiD4JsG

19. Set up and configure **webhooks**. Enable the webhook to forward messaging events sent by Facebook Messenger. Click on the **Setup Webhooks** option on the same page under the **Webhooks** section:

20. Configure the webhook in the same way as mentioned on the configure Facebook Messenger page; under **Configure webhook callback URL and verify the token** and paste it into your Facebook webhook configure step:

[394]

21. Enter the **Callback URL** and the **Verify** token from the Facebook Messenger configure page. Then, select **message_deliveries**, **messages**, **messaging_optins**, and **messaging_postbacks** under **Subscription fields** to set the correct permissions. Then, click on **Verify and Save**:

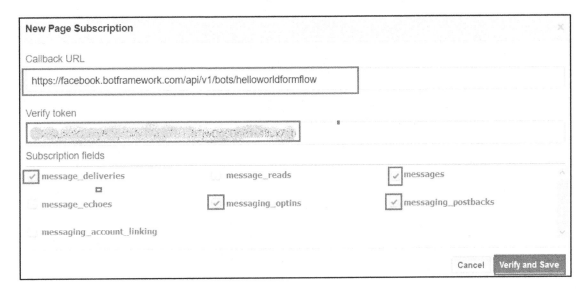

22. Enter your credentials. This is the final step to configure your bot to Facebook Messenger. Here, you have to enter your previously saved **Facebook Page Id**, **Facebook App Id**, **Facebook App Secret**, and **Page Access Token**:

23. After entering your details, click on the **Submit/Resubmit** button. After successful validation, you will receive the following message:

> Credentials have been validated.

24. Finally, check the **Enable this bot on Facebook Messenger** option, and click on the **I'm done configuring Facebook Messenger** button:

> ☑ Enable this bot on Facebook Messenger
> Enabling or disabling a channel doesn't affect its credentials.
>
> I'm done configuring Facebook Messenger >

25. Now, you can communicate with your bot through **Facebook Messenger** as well:

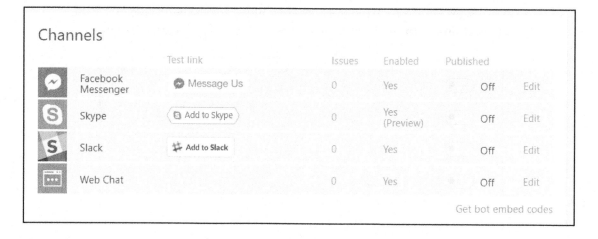

Chapter 9

26. To chat with your bot from Facebook Messenger, click on the **Message Us** button in the channels list:

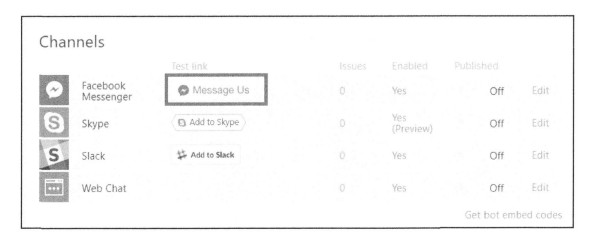

27. It will navigate to the Facebook Messenger web app:

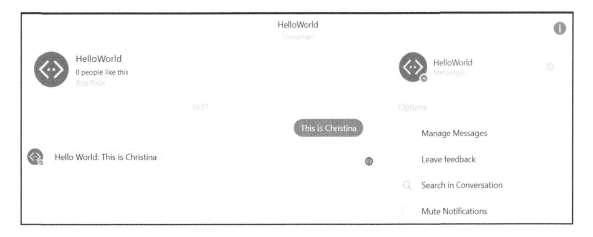

Configuring your bot with GroupMe

For configuring GroupMe, click on the **GroupMe** channel **Add** button. Bot Framework gives us all of the steps to add a bot to GroupMe:

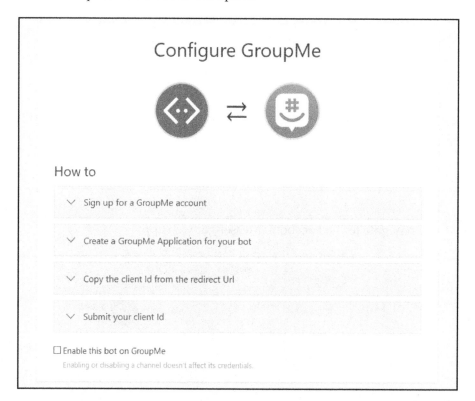

Configure your bot with GroupMe by following these steps:

1. Now, **Sign up for a GroupMe account**. Expand **Sign up for a GroupMe account**, and then go at `https://web.groupme.com/signup` to sign up:

2. If you already have an account, then click on **Log in** on the top-right side of the page. Otherwise, enter your mail ID and then click on the **Continue** button to sign up.

3. Next, create a GroupMe application for your bot. To create a GroupMe application to your bot, you have to follow `https://dev.groupme.com/applications/new`. Here, you have to provide the logging details, then it will redirect you to create the application for your bot page:

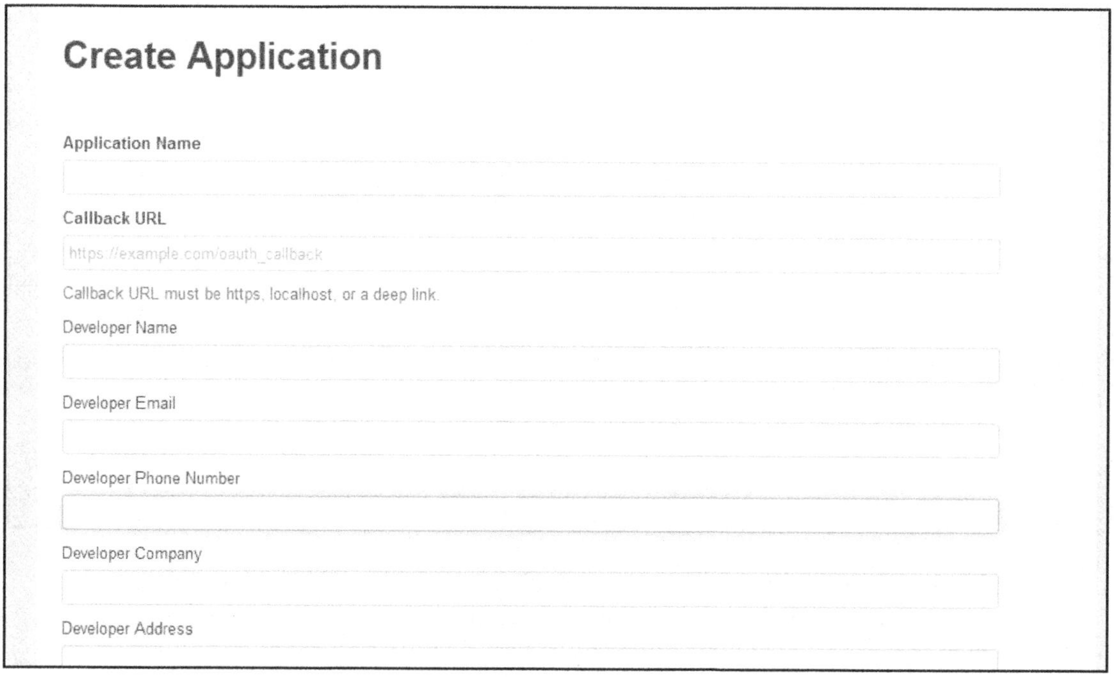

Create Application

Application Name

Callback URL

https://example.com/oauth_callback

Callback URL must be https, localhost, or a deep link.

Developer Name

Developer Email

Developer Phone Number

Developer Company

Developer Address

4. Enter all the required details. For the call back URL, go back to the bot's configure GroupMe page under create a GroupMe application for your bot; you will find the callback URL. Copy and paste it in the GroupMe application creation callback URL box.

5. Click on the **Save** button. It redirects to the GroupMe app details page; it looks similar to the following screenshot:

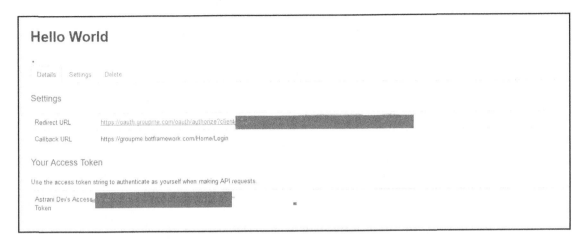

6. Next, copy the client ID from your redirect URL. Copy the client ID from the previous step; you will find it at the end of **Redirect URL**:

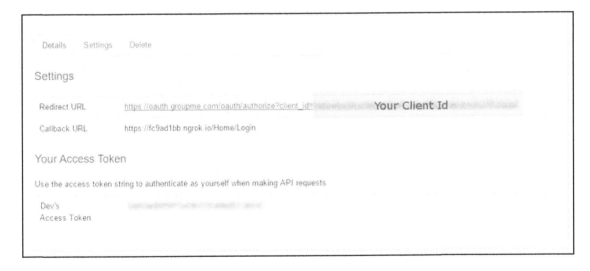

7. Submit your client ID. Here, you have to enter your client ID, which you copied from the previous step. Then, click on the **Submit GroupMe Credentials** button:

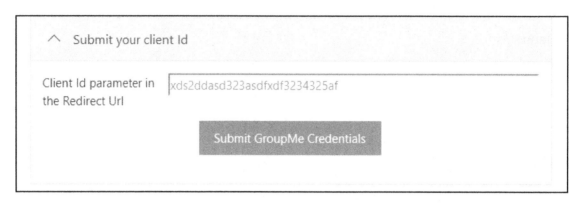

8. Now, click on **I'm done configuring GroupMe;** before that, check the **Enable this bot on GroupMe** box:

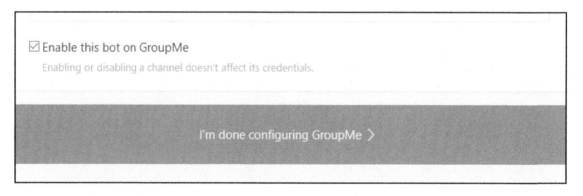

9. Bot Framework has added GroupMe on your configured channels list:

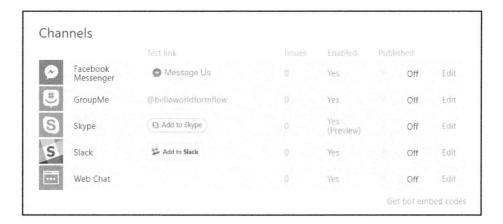

10. Now, you can chat with your bot from GroupMe. To test it, click on the `@yourbotname` button in the channels list. It will navigate to the GroupMe web app, where you can start chatting with your bot, as shown in the following screenshot:

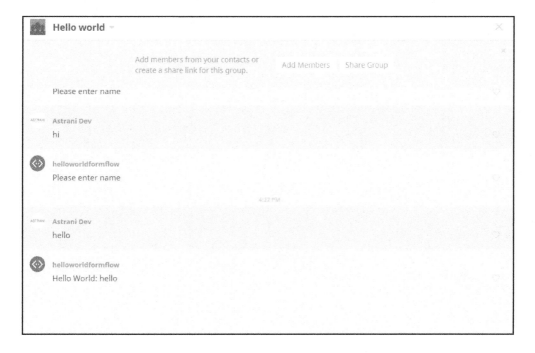

Summary

In this chapter, we have learned the following:

- **Registering a bot**: Once registered, we use the dashboard to test the bot to ensure that it is talking to the connector service and/or use the web chat control, and an auto-configured channel, to experience what users will experience when conversing with the bot
- **Connecting to channels**: Connect the bot to the conversation channels such as Skype, Slack, and/or Facebook Messenger using the channel configuration page
- **Testing bot**: Test the bot's connection to the Bot Framework and try it out using the web chat control
- **Publishing bot**: We get to publish the bot
- **Measuring bot**: We get to learn how to link the bot to Azure Application Insights analytics directly from the bot dashboard in the Bot Framework website
- **Managing a bot**: Once registered and connected to channels, we can manage the bot via the bot's dashboard in the Bot Framework Developer Portal

Index

A

Actor programming model 244
API key 193
ASP.NET Web API component 13
Azure blob storage
  reference 280
Azure Key Vault
  URL 261
Azure Service Fabric 243
Azure SQL database
  bot conversation data, storing 223, 227
  URL 223
Azure Stream Analytics
  setup, for sending IoT Hub data to Power BI 335, 339
Azure
  cluster, creating 264, 271, 274, 277
  Service Fabric project, publishing 261
  URL, for subscription 15

B

Bot Application template, default files
  AssemblyInfo.cs file 37, 38
  Default.htm file 44
  Global.asax file 45
  MessageController.cs file 42, 43
  Microsoft Bot Builder 39
  Microsoft Bot Connector 40
  Packages.config file 45
  References 39
  Web.config file 45
  WebApiConfig.cs file 40
Bot Application template
  URL 15
Bot Builder SDK 34
Bot Connector 13, 14, 34
Bot Directory 14, 34
Bot Framework Connector SDK .NET
  setting up 15, 16, 17
Bot Framework emulator
  bot application, deploying 49, 50
  bot application, executing 49, 50
  URL 50
Bot Framework
  bot, registering 308, 311
bot
  configuring, Slack used 366, 368, 370, 372, 373, 376
  configuring, with Facebook Manager 384, 386, 388, 391, 392, 395, 397
  configuring, with GroupMe 398, 400, 402, 403
  configuring, with Skype 378
  connection, testing 363, 364
  pictures, sending 327
  publishing 311
  publishing, to Microsoft Azure web app 351, 353, 355, 357
  publishing, to various channels 350
  registering, in Bot Framework 308, 311
  registering, with Microsoft Bot Framework 357
  testing 311
buttons 20

C

C# class
  creating, for LUIS response 171
C# SDK
  used, for building conversation bots 35, 36, 37
calls
  handling 28
cards
  about 20
  carousel card 23

hero card 20
receipt card 26
sign in card 25
thumbnail card 22
using 93
carousel card
  actions 24
  actions, properties 24
  buttons 24
  images 24
  images, properties 24
Channels 349
channels
  about 13
  configuring 364
Cloud/Internet of Things (IoT) 9
constituency parsing tree 108, 142
Conversation as a Platform (CaaP) 12, 31
Conversation as a Service (CaaS) 10, 11, 12
conversation bots
  building, with C# SDK 35, 36, 37
  creating 34
  developing 33, 34
  dialogs, using 54, 58
  evolution 32
  FormFlow, using 58, 60, 63, 64
  Post method 46, 48
  use cases 32
conversation concept 209
Cortana Intelligence Services 95, 96
custom APIs
  used, for developing Nearby bot 191, 193, 196, 198, 203, 206

D

Dependency Inversion Principle 57
development environment
  Bot Framework Connector SDK .NET, setting up 15, 16, 17
  prerequisites 15
  setting up 14
Device Explorer
  URL 293
  using 293, 296
device identity registry

  with IoT Hub 293
Direct Line Channel
  configuring 314, 315

E

Emotion API
  about 298
  reference 298
Employee Enroll
  creating, LUIS prompt dialogs used 157, 163
  publishing 169, 171
  service, training 165, 168
  training 169, 171
emulator
  URL 16
Entities 73

F

Face API
  about 297
  reference 297
Facebook Messenger
  used, for configuring bot 382, 388, 391
Facebook UI
  reference 388
Facebook
  URL 384
  used, for configuring bot 394, 397
Facial Expression Bot
  picture file, sending 325
  reply, receiving 325
Facial Identification bot 297
FormFlow
  about 209
  using, in conversation bots 58, 60, 63, 64
Fritzing
  reference 282

G

Google Places API
  reference 193
GroupMe
  reference 399
  sed, for configuring bot 401, 402
  used, for configuring bot 398, 400

groups
  creating 27

H

hero card
  about 20
  layout 21
high-level architectural diagram 210

I

Intent 73
Interactive Voice Response (IVR) bot
  about 209
  account, creating 212, 222
  coding 211
  conversation data, storing in Azure SQL
    database 223, 227
  used, for checking current account balance 232, 235
  used, for deleting account 238
  used, for paying credit card bill 236, 237
  used, to check savings account balance 227, 231
Internet of Things (IoT) 31

J

JSON Class Generator
  reference 198
JSON
  reference 171

K

Key Vault
  about 261
  certificates, adding 262
  creating 262
killer technology 9

L

Language Understanding Intelligent Service (LUIS) 12
  about 66, 126, 148
  calling, from natural speech and intent processing bot 153

calling, from WeatherBot 89
company, identifying 110, 112, 144, 147
features 66
name, identifying 110, 112, 144, 147
place, identifying 110, 112, 144, 147
URL 70
using 67, 73
LED states
  defining 319, 323
Linguistic Analysis API 99
LUIS prompt dialogs
  used, for Employee Enroll 157, 163
LUIS response
  C# class, creating 171

M

messages
  basic format 18
  pictures, sending 19
  rich text, using 18
  sending 17
  Skype emoticons, sending 19
  videos, sending 19
  welcome messages, sending 19
Microsoft Azure 350
Microsoft Azure IoT Hub
  reference 280
Microsoft Azure subscription
  reference 351
Microsoft Azure web app
  bots, publishing to 351, 353, 354, 357
Microsoft Bot Builder SDK 13
Microsoft Bot Builder
  features 39
Microsoft Bot Connector 349
Microsoft Bot Framework 349
  about 12
  bot, registering 357
  configuration section 359, 360, 362, 363
  reference 357
Microsoft Cognitive Services
  about 66, 126
  Analyzers Results, obtaining 144
  bot application, building 130, 133, 136, 139
  code, for detecting face emotions 306

facial expressions identification bot, developing 300, 303, 305
signing up 129, 298
URL 67, 96, 126
used, for natural speech and intent processing bot 98, 100, 104, 108
Microsoft Project Oxford 126
motion detection
  camera, initializing 323, 325

N

Natural Language Understanding (NLU)
  about 66
natural speech and intent processing bot
  LUIS, calling 153
  training, with utterances 148, 153
  with Microsoft Cognitive Services 95, 98, 100, 104, 108
Nearby Bot application
  QueryLUIS method, updating 190
  creating 173, 176, 180, 183
  designing 184
  Get/SetProperty methods 185
  Post method, updating 187
  state client, creating 185
Nearby bot
  developing, custom APIs used 192, 194, 197, 202, 206

O

object motion
  detecting, PIR Sensor used 319, 323

P

parts-of-speech (POS) tags 108, 140
Post method, conversation bots
  about 46, 48
  BotID 49
  Microsoft App ID 49
  MicrosoftAppPassword 49
Power BI
  facial analytics data, displaying 332
  IoT Hub data sending, by Azure Stream Analytics setup 332
  reference 280

setting up 340, 345
PowerShell module
  URL 262
prerequisites, Raspberry Pi
  about 281
  hardware 281
  software 281

R

Raspberry Pi and sensors configuration
  prerequisites 281
Raspberry Pi
  code, deploying 328, 331
  configuring 280
  UWP, developing 316
receipt card
  about 26
  properties 26
Rich Text Messaging 95

S

sensors
  configuring 280
  schematic diagram 292
  setting up 284, 289
Service Fabric Explorer 259
Service Fabric
  about 243
  development environment, setting up 245
  PowerShell script execution, enabling 246
  prerequisites 245
  project, publishing to Azure 261
  reference 246
  SDK, installing 246
  tools, installing 246
sign in card
  properties 25
Skype
  used, for configuring bot 378, 380, 381
Slack
  used, for configuring bot 366, 368, 369, 370, 373, 374, 376, 378
stateful microservices 243
stateless microservices
  about 243

Service Fabric, development environment setting up 245
stateless service fabric web API, creating 246, 250, 254, 261
using 245
stream analytics
  reference 280
suite of intelligent APIs 126

T

thumbnail card 93
thumbnail
  properties 22
tokens 107, 139
Transaction Processing (OLTP) services 244

U

Universal Windows Platform (UWP) 316
utterances
  about 78
  examples 149
  used, for training natural speech and intent processing bot 148, 153
  used, for training WeatherBot 78
UWP app
  creating 317, 319
  developing, for Raspberry Pi device 316
  development, reference 280

V

Visual Studio 2015
  URL 15

W

Weather Underground
  URL 91
  using 91
WeatherBot
  app, creating 73, 77
  cards, using 93
  code, developing 81, 85, 87, 89
  Language Understanding Intelligence Service (LUIS), calling 89, 116, 123
  LUIS app, testing 80
  training 113, 116
  training, with utterances 78, 80
  Weather API, calling 91
Web Platform Installer 246
WebHook 28
Windows 10 IoT
  reference 280

Made in the USA
Las Vegas, NV
13 April 2024